When You're Ready

When You're Ready

A Love Story

Kareem Rosser

Simon Element

New York   Amsterdam/Antwerp   London
Toronto   Sydney   New Delhi

**SIMON
ELEMENT**

An Imprint of Simon & Schuster, LLC
1230 Avenue of the Americas
New York, NY 10020

First Simon Element hardcover edition February 2025

SIMON ELEMENT is a trademark of Simon & Schuster, LLC

For information about special discounts for bulk purchases, please contact Simon
& Schuster Special Sales at 1-866-506-1949 or business@simonandschuster.com.

The Simon & Schuster Speakers Bureau can bring authors to your live event. For
more information or to book an event, contact the Simon & Schuster Speakers
Bureau at 1-866-248-3049 or visit our website at www.simonspeakers.com.

Interior design by Laura Levatino

Manufactured in the United States of America

10 9 8 7 6 5 4 3 2 1

Library of Congress Cataloging-in-Publication Data has been applied for.

ISBN 978-1-6680-3073-8
ISBN 978-1-6680-3075-2 (ebook)

To Lee Lee Jones

and all other traumatic brain injury survivors

Disclaimer

THIS IS A WORK OF CREATIVE NONFICTION. The events and timelines in this book are based upon real-life experiences but have sometimes been adjusted or compressed in deference to the larger story. The characters in this book are based upon real people, but many names and identifying features have been changed. All conversations are meant to capture the spirit and feeling of what was said but should not be considered exact.

When You're Ready

Prologue

EVERY DAY, FOR FOUR YEARS, I watched the clock at work, waiting for the minute it hit 5:00 p.m. It didn't matter if I was in the middle of a call. It didn't matter if everyone else was staying late. I didn't care if there was a big project due. Five o'clock rolled around, and it was time to snap my laptop shut, grab my coat, and walk out the door.

Every day, for four years, I made an hour-long drive each way. First it was to the hospital in Newark, Delaware, then to the rehab center in Malvern, Pennsylvania, and, finally, to her home out in the Pennsylvania countryside. During those sixty minutes in the car, I'd call my mother. Or one of my brothers. Sometimes I'd ring a friend who I had shamefully neglected and hope that an hour-long car-conversation could make up for months of missed dinners and parties and unreturned texts.

The drive there was all about distraction. Putting myself in the right frame of mind. Maintaining my control: *Keep yourself busy. Don't think too much. Don't dwell. Stay upbeat. You cannot carry your grief into the room with you. Lee Lee needs you to be strong.*

THE FIRST TIME I MADE THAT DRIVE to Newark, Delaware, it was three days before Christmas. I had been at work, but I wasn't working. I was alone in the office and shopping online for a last-minute Christmas gift for my girlfriend, Cordelia "Lee Lee" Jones.

I was deep in love, dreaming about our first real holiday together. I was thinking about how, someday—once we had kids—we would need to give equal holiday time to both her family and mine.

Or maybe we'll make our own traditions.

I imagined the pristine white farmhouse we would live in. Our barns and fences draped in snow. The horses gathered around the feeding troughs in the fields, nosing into the hay, their breath crystallizing into plumes of icy fog in the winter air.

My phone rang, busting me out of my daydream.

There had been an accident.

Lee Lee was hurt. Bad.

I needed to come right away.

AT THE HOSPITAL, IN THE BEGINNING, I'd always sit on her right side. The right side of her face and head looked like the Lee Lee Jones I knew. My girlfriend. My best friend. My love. Her long brown hair was intact on that side. Her right eye was closed, her lashes were so long that they practically grazed the top of her cheek. That side of her face looked almost peaceful. If I just looked at the right side of her face, I could pretend she was merely sleeping.

The left side was draped with a towel. The nurses had laid the towel over that side of her head to try to hide the fact that doctors had removed half of her skull. But it didn't really hide anything. I could still see the sunken spot where the bone was missing. I could see that half of her hair was gone. I could see the blood that soaked through the bandages—all the way through—leaving a constant bright red splotch on the white terry-cloth fabric.

I would talk to Lee Lee. Bargain with her. Tell her that if she made it through, if she stayed alive, I would never walk away. I would be there, by her side, no matter what.

Or I'd sing to Lee Lee. She and I both had terrible singing voices, but we never cared. We'd belt out songs in the car, trying to harmonize, cracking ourselves up with our off-key wailing. Teasing each other about who was worse.

Just before the accident, we had the Weeknd's *Starboy* on repeat. We listened to it over and over, singing along until we knew all the lyrics by heart.

When we were alone in the ICU, I'd quietly sing her favorite song off the album, "Die for You," stretching my voice into a wavering falsetto.

I desperately wanted to hold Lee Lee. To crawl into bed with her, to push aside all the tubes and machines and PICC lines, and wedge my body against hers. Bury my face in her neck. Let her warm, familiar scent replace the frigid, sterile air of the ICU.

Instead, I'd gently wiggle two of my fingers into the clenched fist of her right hand.

Before the accident, Lee Lee and I loved to walk around with our arms around each other. We were constantly hugging and kissing on each other. If we sat, we were always close enough for some part of our bodies to touch. My arm warm against hers. Her thigh squeezed up next to mine. But we almost never held hands. Because no matter what the temperature was, within a couple of minutes of tangling our fingers together and pressing palm to palm, we'd start to sweat, and then we'd start to giggle. We were both naturally afflicted with *palmar hyperhidrosis*—clammy hands—and we quickly learned to avoid the slippery, squelchy result.

At the hospital, I imagined how, someday—after everything was better—I would tell Lee Lee about the way I had held her hand.

How I didn't care at all anymore about the film of perspiration that still grew slick between our skins. How it was the only way I could hold her. I would imagine how I would tell her that I waited and waited for her to squeeze my fingers. To show me she was still there. To show me that she still recognized who I was and that she understood what I so desperately wanted from her.

AT THE REHAB CENTER, I'd sit by the bed and talk to Lee Lee. Telling her about my day. Telling her about a new song I'd heard. Sometimes I'd tell her the same story twice, hoping that the second time around might elicit some sort of new response. Sometimes I'd help the nurses turn her from side to side to avoid bedsores. I'd try not to dwell on the flash of anger in Lee Lee's eyes as we rolled her over. The expression on her face that made me think that she was absolutely, achingly aware of all she had lost.

Sometimes I'd run out of things to say, so I'd take her hand and we'd just sit. Lee Lee had so much support, so many people who loved her, the best medical care that money could buy—and yet, her body was healing so slowly. She was still in such obvious pain. And there was nothing I could do. Nothing anyone could do, really. It was entirely out of my control. And so, sometimes, instead of talking to Lee Lee, I found myself talking to God. Which felt a little odd and unnatural, because I was not a religious man, but it also felt entirely necessary.

Please, I would chant in my head as I held her hand. *Please, just a small miracle.*

I suppose some people might call it denial, or magical thinking, but, for a while, my makeshift prayers felt like my last and only option.

ONCE LEE LEE WAS BACK HOME on her farm, I was certain her healing would accelerate. I was sure that being home with her horses and dogs and family—being surrounded by all her familiar things— would change everything.

But, of course, as I would learn over and over, my being certain about something hardly qualified as a guarantee.

We'd sit in her room. Sometimes Lee Lee would be in bed. Sometimes in her wheelchair. I'd turn on the TV, and we'd watch shows that we had enjoyed together before the accident. *Shameless.* *Grey's Anatomy.*

I'd laugh loudly at the funny parts. Loud enough for both of us. Loud enough to cover her silence.

AT THE HOSPITAL, THE REHAB, Lee Lee's home, I always stayed with her for at least an hour. Longer if I could. Talking to her. Singing to her. Helping her eat. Hoping to hear her laugh.

Holding her hand.

Then I'd kiss her goodbye, get back in my car, and drive another hour, crying the entire way home.

EVERY DAY, FOR FOUR YEARS. This was my life: work and Lee Lee. There was nothing else. Nobody else who mattered. It was all I wanted. It was all I felt I deserved. It was all I could allow.

"But what would happen if you left just twenty minutes early?" asked my psychiatrist, Ellen.

My response was instant. "I couldn't do that."

Her gaze was steady. "But what would happen if you did?"

All the promises I'd made to Lee Lee started to swim around inside my head.

I promise that I will never leave.

"I can't do that," I said.

I promise that I will never stop loving you.

"Okay, then," Ellen said. "What about fifteen minutes early?"

I promise that I will always be here, no matter what.

"No," I said.

I promise to be yours forever.

Ellen picked up her teacup and then put it back down without taking a drink. She met my eyes. "You are twenty-six years old, Kareem. It's very likely that you have a long life ahead of you. Is this it? Is this what you want the rest of your life to be?"

I promise that what is between us will never end.

I looked away from her. I swallowed, trying to push down the burning lump of tears in my throat. "No," I finally whispered. "No."

"Ten minutes, then," she said. "Just ten minutes."

I LEFT WORK AT 5:00 P.M. SHARP. I called my younger brother, Gerb, from my car. We talked about football. We talked about a girl he was dating. We didn't talk about Lee Lee.

I parked outside Lee Lee's farmhouse. I said hello to Lee Lee's mother, Evie. I walked into Lee Lee's bedroom. She was sitting up in her wheelchair. Her aide was helping her look through a photo album.

In some ways, I thought, Lee Lee looked like herself again. She had gained back all the weight she'd lost after her accident. Her hair had grown back in, and it now grazed the nape of her neck. The color was back in her cheeks. When her eyes met mine, she clearly recognized me. Her face looked almost like the face of the girl I had fallen in love with.

I thought about before the accident. The way Lee Lee lit up every room she walked into. The way people were irresistibly drawn to her. When she smiled, it was like the air warmed by ten degrees. She was radiant. Enchanting. She was the most joyful person I'd ever met.

I still loved her. In fact, I loved her more than I had loved her before. I loved her beautiful, beautiful face. I loved her strength. I loved her determination. But the consistent joy she once exuded was now rare. It had been replaced by anger. By sadness. By frustration. Her smiles were fleeting and often tinged with pain.

I thought I could sing or pray that pain away. I thought I could wait it out. I thought that if I showed up every day, if I held her hand, if I told her about my day, if I militantly hid my own fear and sadness, if I showed her pictures of us together—if I just tried harder—I could fix it all for her.

That had always been my job: to fix things.

But this isn't that kind of story.

I SAT DOWN NEXT TO LEE LEE. I kissed her cheek hello. I took her hand in mine. And when the time came—even though I felt like it might kill me—I forced myself to my feet. And I left ten minutes early.

Part One

Chapter 1

WHEN I FELL IN LOVE WITH LEE LEE, she taught me about one kind of love. She taught me about the kind of love that I didn't actually believe existed. The kind of love you hear about in songs or see in the movies. First love. Big love. Eternal love. The kind of love I never thought I wanted or could actually have.

But even before Lee Lee, there were always other kinds of love in my life. Sometimes it was a hard love. Sometimes it was a messy or confusing or sad love. Sometimes it was love that was paired with the worst kind of loss. But there was always love in my life for the taking. Even if it wasn't the easiest kind.

"GRANDMA! GRANDMA! Let's go! The hack man is here!"

It was three days before Christmas 2001, I was eight years old, and we were standing on my grandma's front porch, shouting through the open door, waiting for her to come out of her house so we could go get our Christmas tree. There were six of us in the family, plus my mom: me; my older brothers, David and Bee; my twin sister, Kareema; my younger brother, Gerb; and the baby of the family, Washika.

There was an empty lot a few blocks away. Usually it was filled with people drinking or buying drugs or just hanging around, but every winter a few old heads from the neighborhood would clear it out and then refill it with evergreen trees in all different sizes.

We didn't have a car, so we had to find a hack man, a guy who drove an illegal cab (pretty much the only kind of taxi that would venture into our neighborhood). He'd wait around for us to pick out our tree, and then he'd cram it into his trunk or tie it to his roof and deliver it back to our house on Viola Street.

I was excited and impatient. I loved everything about Christmas, and getting the tree marked the beginning of the season for us. But my grandma was taking her own sweet time.

My mother sighed. "Reem," she said. "Go on in and get her. We don't have all day."

I nodded and stepped inside my grandma's house, leaving the rest of my family waiting on the front porch.

I paused in the entrance for a moment, letting my eyes adjust to the gloom. It was always dark in that house, even during the daytime. My grandma kept her curtains shut and had only one or two lamps, but half the time they were barely working.

"Grandma?" I called. Not too loud. I didn't know who else was there, and I didn't want any extra attention.

No answer.

I walked a few steps in, heading for the living room behind the stairs. I took shallow breaths, only through my mouth, because I long ago had decided it was better to taste the way my grandma's house smelled than to inhale it through my nose. The house smelled like spilled beer, unwashed bodies, weed, and the distinct burnt-plastic-cat-piss-sulfur smell of people lighting matches and smoking crack. Dirty. Bitter. Acrid. Smoky. I could usually spit that taste out of my mouth once I left the house, but if I got even the smallest whiff of it through my nose, I knew I'd be smelling it for the rest of the day.

I peeked into the living room and saw the outlines of a few figures reclining on the floor and smoking (there was pretty much no furniture in my grandma's house—just walls and floors and dying lamps). I could see at a glance that none of the figures were my grandma, so I stepped out and checked the kitchen. Empty. Out of curiosity, I opened the fridge. Also empty. In fact, it was warm. Not even working. I shut the fridge and left the kitchen, walking back toward the front hall.

"Merry Christmas, Kareem!"

My grandma was coming down the stairs, a big smile on her face. She was wearing her red wool coat and carrying the oversize, black leather purse she never left home without. I knew that the purse was mostly full of junk: pieces of paper with phone numbers on them, and empty coke bags, and napkins that my grandma would use to blow her nose and then tuck back into her bag again to use later. But I also knew that my grandma always had candy in that bag, and whenever I asked her for a piece, she'd hand one right over.

I grinned back at her, happy to see her and equally happy that I wouldn't have to go look for her upstairs, where most of the action took place. "Merry Christmas, Grandma!"

She stepped off the last stair and gave me a hello squeeze on the shoulder. Then she reached over and straightened the collar on my coat. "You ready to go get that tree?"

I nodded eagerly.

"Well, then, better quit standing around, boy," she teased, hooking her arm in mine. "You're gonna make everyone late!"

LIKE MY GRANDMA, my mom was also an addict, but she was much more functional. She always had a job, usually minimum wage. Sometimes even two at a time. She was our only parent—my siblings and I have three different fathers, but none of them were consistently involved in our lives—and she worked hard to make sure that we had our basic needs met. Unlike my grandma's house, our house on Viola Street was well lit and had a decent amount of furniture (even if I always had to share a bed with at least one or two of my siblings). There wasn't a surplus of food, but there was enough to keep us fed. And the lights and heat and hot water were on, at least, most of the time.

My mom kept an open-door policy similar to my grandmother's, but the people my mother let in the house were relatives and friends, or, at the very least, acquaintances. Our house on Viola was always stretched to its limits, but my grandmother's house was a classic crack house free-for-all. She was extremely lax about letting just about anyone wander in off the street, whether she knew them or not. As long as they wanted to party, they were welcomed.

My grandmother would use right in front of us, but my mother was less obvious about her addiction. That didn't mean that she was exactly private about her habit, though. We were too young to be left behind, so if she wanted to get high, she'd have to take us along with her to my grandma's house to score. If the weather was nice, she'd leave us on Grandma's front porch while she went upstairs to get what she needed. If it was raining or snowing or too bitter cold, we'd wait in the hallway or the kitchen, standing around because there was nothing to sit on. But once we were back home, Mom did her best to hide things from us, stepping into the other room, distracting us with the television, or sometimes waiting for us to go to bed.

But we knew. Of course we knew.

ONCE THE TREE WAS DELIVERED, we had to find something to prop it up with. My mom had stashed all our presents in the basement, and none of us kids were allowed to go down there, so Mom trudged down the stairs herself, emerging after a few minutes with a broken Christmas tree stand, a metal bucket, and some plastic twine. We'd picked a good tree that year; not too tall—we could never afford the really big trees—but it was fat and bushy, and it wasn't going to be easy to get it to stand up straight.

My mother fiddled with the tree stand. "Dang . . . stupid . . . thing . . ." she muttered, unable to get it to lock together. Finally she dropped the stand and held the bucket up instead. "Someone take this outside and fill it up with rocks."

Washika and Kareema were helping my grandmother cook in the kitchen, so David, Bee, Gerb, and I headed outside to gather up rocks and broken bricks and pieces of cinder block.

Gerb and I paused a minute to watch some kids playing curb ball just down the street.

"Christmas ain't coming if you two don't start picking up some rocks," chided my brother David.

After we finished, we went back inside and wedged the tree into the bucket, tied some twine around it, and then attached it to the wall.

"Y'all go ahead and add some water to the bucket," said my mother. "Then help me put up these lights."

After we decorated, we ate our first big Christmas meal, chicken and potatoes and peas and a macaroni salad. An apple pie with whipped cream for dessert. This was the first miracle of Christmas: the house was full of groceries. Mom always made sure there was plenty. More than enough. Which was a big deal, because Christmas was the only time of year when things ever really felt that way.

MOM DIDN'T USE MUCH AT CHRISTMAS. She drank, usually beer, but she stayed away from the harder stuff. I think it was because she loved Christmas, too. My mom was young. She'd had my eldest brother, David, when she was fourteen years old and her last baby before she was thirty. In many ways, she was still a kid, growing up right alongside her children. So I think she liked to be present at Christmas. She liked to participate. She worked so hard to make it special, so she wasn't tempted to check out and miss any of it.

BY CHRISTMAS EVE, we were almost frantic with excitement. We'd been watching our mom take mysterious bags and packages down to the basement all month long, and it was another small miracle that we had resisted the very real temptation to sneak down those steps and rip through everything in a frenzy of curiosity.

Around ten thirty that night, my mom stood up. "Time to go to bed," she announced.

We didn't usually have a bedtime. In fact, we generally didn't have any real rules at all. But we did have one hard-and-fast rule at Christmas: no presents were allowed to be opened until exactly one minute after midnight on Christmas Eve. So we knew that if we wanted Christmas, we had to troop upstairs, pretend like we were going to sleep, and give Mom the time to create her magic. None of us believed in Santa Claus. We had always known exactly who was responsible for our presents: it was our young, beautiful, hardworking Black mother. No way were we going to give some fat, old white man the credit our mother so richly deserved.

———————

"WHAT DO YOU THINK WE'LL GET THIS YEAR?" said Gerb after we had all slipped into bed.

I poked him with my toe, too excited to keep my distance. "I hope it's Rollerblades," I said.

"Don't count on it," said David. He and Bee were in the bed next to ours. "Rollerblades are expensive. We don't have that kind of money."

"Maybe we'll just get underwear," said Bee. I knew he was teasing, but he sounded serious enough to fool Gerb.

"No way!" yelped Gerb. "You don't actually think she'd do that, would she?"

"At least if you got some new underwear, maybe you'd change them once in a while," I said to my little brother. "Then you wouldn't stink like a dirty butthole."

"You're the one who smells like a dirty butthole!" said Gerb. He shoved me so hard, I practically fell out of the bed.

"You gonna get it now, bro," I said as I rolled back toward him, planning on flattening him right under me.

"Come on! Come on! It's time!" said Kareema. She was standing in our doorway, holding Washika. "It's midnight, you guys!"

We all jumped up, trying to shove past one another, whooping and hollering as we ran down the stairs at top speed.

Mom had piled the gifts so high that we could only see the star on the very tip of the Christmas tree. We tore into the presents, searching out our names and ripping off the wrapping paper. Most of the toys were cheap, but we didn't care. And she almost always managed to get us at least one good thing that we really wanted. Scooters one year. Bikes another one. And this year: Rollerblades. I don't know how my mother did it. I have no idea how she managed to scrape up the money year after year. I've never asked her. I've just accepted it as yet another Christmas miracle she managed to manifest.

It was past two in the morning when we finished opening all our presents. It was also about ten degrees outside. But we didn't care. Everyone but Washika—who was too little to skate—strapped on their blades and trooped out the door to try them out on the icy streets. My mother carried out all the boxes and torn-up wrapping paper and ribbons and bows and set them on the curb. Then she sat on our stoop, a beer in one hand and a bundled-up and sleeping Washika in the other, and watched us as we stumbled and splayed like newborn colts, and then slowly, slowly, learned to glide and fly.

We didn't sleep for the next twenty-four hours. We stayed out skating almost all night long. We skated until our toes and ears and noses went numb. Until I couldn't feel my fingers or my feet. Then we rolled back inside (we'd all mastered the blades by then and kept them on in the house as well), ate the pancakes and bacon that our grandma had whipped up, and then went straight back to the pile of candy and our new toys and started rediscovering them all over again.

Once the sun came up, people started dropping by to say Merry Christmas—aunts and uncles and cousins and friends. Some brought more gifts. Some brought food. Some didn't bring anything, but my mom happily offered them anything we had.

My mom and my grandma were in the kitchen all day, making Christmas dinner while we continued to play. We were verging on out of control now, punchy from lack of sleep, hyper from all the candy we'd consumed. We played too hard and started to break some of the cheaper toys. Or if something needed batteries and my mom had forgotten to get them, we'd get impatient and damage it by doing stupid stuff, trying to force it to light up or move and then crashing it or dropping it when it didn't do what we wanted it to. Destruction felt almost as satisfying as play.

"Y'all better calm down!" my mother called out from the kitchen. "Once you break it, you're not getting anything else. This is it!"

But we never listened. We just kept on doing what we were doing, alternating frantic joy with an exhausted peevishness, desperate to milk every moment that we had left in the holiday. By the time we all sat down for dinner, we could barely see straight, we were so worn out.

Still, every mouthful of ham, corn bread dressing, sweet potatoes, and green bean casserole tasted extra good because we'd been stuffing ourselves with nothing but candy all day. Eating a plate of food with actual nutritional value gave us a second (or third, or fourth) wind, and after dinner, we all pushed back from the table, ran back to our toys, and started to play again, not stopping until our mom and grandma had cleaned up the kitchen and started turning out all the lights except for the ones on the Christmas tree.

"Good night, y'all," my mother said before she climbed the stairs to go to bed. "Merry Christmas."

Then, and only then, would we admit that Christmas was over.

"YOU GOING TO STAY DOWN HERE with me tonight, Reem?" asked my grandmother as she laid a sheet, a blanket, and two pillows down on the living room floor.

My mom and the other kids had gone up to their bedrooms, but Grandma always slept on the floor when she stayed over at our house. Any of us would have gladly given up our bed for her, but she insisted that she liked the floor. She said that was her spot.

I nodded eagerly. I liked sleeping with my grandma. It was way better than sleeping with Gerb, who always kicked and hogged the covers. Sleeping with my grandma felt like a treat.

"Come here, then," she said, patting the place next to her. "Cuddle on up."

I lay down next to her and, as instructed, cuddled up. She put her arm around my shoulders and pulled me in closer, giving me a kiss on the top of my head.

My grandmother smelled like her house. She smelled like dust and weed and alcohol and the burning ammonia smell of crack cocaine. The scent was so strong that it had seeped into her clothes, her hair, the very pores of her skin. She carried that same terrible, chemical smell with her no matter how far from her home she traveled.

It was strange, though; I didn't mind that scent so much when I smelled it on her. In fact, I really didn't mind it at all. My grandmother had her weaknesses. I understood that about her. But that didn't change the fact that she was also funny and strong and smart and a wonderful cook. Her addictions and compulsions didn't ever stop her from being there for us. She always showed up when she said she would. They didn't change the fact that—even though I was sad that Christmas was truly over—I also felt a delicious kind of sleepiness, sweet and safe and loved, as we lay on the floor together and looked up at the twinkling lights on the tree.

Chapter 2

MY MOTHER HAS A SCAR that runs diagonally through her eyebrow. The tiniest slash. It's faded and faint now. Decades old. Honestly, I wouldn't have even noticed it if she hadn't taken the time to point it out to me.

"Your father gave me this," she said.

She sounded casual. Like she was commenting on the weather.

"He gave me this scar when he hit me so hard that he knocked me out cold."

That's all I know of the incident. I don't know what they were fighting about. What made him so angry. I don't know if it was the first or the last or the fiftieth time that he hit her. I have no memories of my mother and father together. He was permanently out of our lives before I learned to crawl.

I could ask my mother, of course. And I'm certain she would tell me every detail. But a big part of me doesn't want to. I don't like the thought of making her relive a moment like that.

I suppose I could ask my father, but that would involve finding him first. Checking the vacant lots and street corners in my old neighborhood. Nudging over passed-out drunks so I could see their faces. And even if I could actually find him, who knows if he'd remember how it happened.

He is not the one who carries that scar.

WHEN I WAS GROWING UP, I thought I had a pretty clear idea of what love looked like. And also why it was something I didn't particularly want or need to have.

My grandmother and grandfather loved each other. They were partners for more than thirty years. I remember my grandma sitting on my grandfather's lap at backyard barbecues, his arm looped around her waist. I remember the way they always kissed hello and goodbye. The way they held hands. She cooked for him, and washed his clothes in the bathtub, making sure he always had a clean outfit to put on. He brought her gifts. Sometimes they would visit us on Viola Street and stay over, curled up together on the living room floor.

But I also remember the endless fights. Ones that usually started out verbally abusive, my grandmother swearing and screaming, "Fuck you, Jeffrey!" and almost always ended up getting physical.

I don't remember what those fights were about. Maybe drugs. My grandmother liked crack, but my grandfather was more dedicated to drinking. Maybe infidelity. They both had children with other partners. Maybe money. Maybe nothing much at all.

I remember one time on Viola Street. My grandpa showed up on the front porch. I didn't know where he was coming from, but he was dressed really well: gator shoes, a nice leather jacket, his meticulously trimmed mustache that always tickled my neck whenever he gave me a hug. Before he even made it through our front door, my grandmother flew out onto the porch, yelling and screaming, calling him every name you could think of, telling him to get the hell away from her.

My grandpa tried to calm her down. Reaching toward her, murmuring, "Sheila, Sheila, come on now, baby. Take it easy."

But she wasn't having it. She batted his hands away, and suddenly, things switched into high gear.

I was used to grown-ups fighting. Sometimes I thought of myself as an expert on the different types of domestic violence. The various shades of pain and fury. Certainly, I knew far more about it than I wished I did.

My grandparents fought like siblings. Grappling and wrestling. Pushing and slapping. No weapons. No guns or knives. And like siblings, they usually stopped before anyone got really hurt. Things always ended before anyone had to call the police.

My mother finished it that day. Shoving herself in between them. Pushing them apart. All of us kids stood watching through the screen door as our mother shouted, "You two get the hell out of here! Don't you bring this bullshit into my house!"

BUT OF COURSE, that bullshit was already in our house. My dad wasn't the first man to hit my mother and he wouldn't be the last.

MY AUNT LIVED ON OLIVE STREET, a few blocks from Viola, right next door to an elderly woman named Miss Mary. My mother liked to visit her sister, and so we would walk on over to Olive Street every week or so. One day, after we'd finished visiting with our aunt, for no reason I could figure out, my mother brought all of us kids next door to visit Miss Mary.

We sat in Miss Mary's dim living room, eating stale cookies and drinking flat, lukewarm soda, while my mother attempted to chat with the older woman. My mother asked about Miss Mary's health, she brought up a friend they had in common, she even talked about the weather, but Miss Mary wasn't very communicative. She just sat there in a big chair, kind of crumpled up, grunting in response. It seemed like she could barely lift her head.

Miss Mary was very old and very ill. I didn't know it yet, but she was dying.

My siblings and I had finished our cookies and were getting restless. The house smelled funny, like damp and rot and lemon Pledge. We wanted to leave, but our mother kept talking, and Miss Mary kept kind of sliding toward the edge of her chair. She didn't seem to have the strength or the weight to grip herself into one place. I watched them, wishing I could make a bet with my siblings about which would happen first: my mother running out of boring things to say, or Miss Mary hitting the floor in a puddle of old bones and floppy blue cardigan.

Then a stranger walked into the room. He was one of the biggest men I'd ever seen. Dark and tall, six foot five, and easily 280 pounds. He stopped when he saw us. His eyes went wide for a moment.

"What's all this, Mama?" he said to Miss Mary. His voice was surprisingly soft for a man that big.

Miss Mary edged her head up to look at him, and her face split into a wide grin. "There's my boy," she said to my mom. "You know Marcus, don't you? Marcus, this is Sheila's girl, Lazette, and all her little kiddies."

My mom looked up at Marcus through her eyelashes and smiled her beautiful smile. "I've seen you around," she said.

Marcus stared at her for a moment and then slowly nodded. "Yeah," he said. "That's right. I've seen you, but I don't think I met your kids before now. Nice of you all to come visit my mom." He turned toward his mother, bent over, and swept her up into his arms. "Time for your nap, Mama. I'll take you up to bed, now, okay?"

Miss Mary gave us a cheerful wave over her son's broad shoulder. We all watched the big man tenderly cradle his tiny, wizened mother as he carried her up the stairs. To me, she looked like a wrinkled-up toddler being carried around by her daddy.

I looked at my mother. Her mouth had dropped open into a little *o*. Then she blinked and seemed to remember herself. "You have a good nap, Miss Mary," she called after them. "Thank you for the hospitality!"

She shot us all a look, and we remembered our home training.

"Thank you, Miss Mary!"

"Thank you for the cookies!"

"Thank you for the visit!"

Marcus turned around and looked back at my mom. "I'll be seeing you around, Lazette."

I THINK MY MOTHER REALLY LOVED MARCUS. He was quite a bit older than her, savvy and experienced, and she told me once that he was the first man who cared enough to take the time to teach her "the game," meaning how to survive in the streets and hustle. He provided for her, too. Gave her money for groceries and things we needed. She could count on him in a way that she had never counted on any man before.

When he was at our house, my mother would fuss over him. She cooked for him, and he'd sit at our kitchen table and eat, and then they would retreat to her bedroom. Marcus liked cocaine, and he and my mom would get high together. But Marcus had no interest in us kids. He never sat on the couch with us. He didn't want to watch TV. He sure as hell never cooked us a meal or brought home groceries. And we all learned very quickly to never go into our mother's room without knocking first.

Things were okay for a while. My mother would hum and smile to herself while she was doing dishes. Or she would sit and watch Marcus eat, her eyes locked on his fork as he lifted it from the plate to his mouth, making sure he finished up every bite.

Then Marcus cheated on her. And my mom found out.

This wasn't the first time this had happened to her. But maybe it was the first time that she really cared. If it had been another man, maybe my mother would have come out swinging and swearing. She would have thrown pots and pans. She would have called him every name under the sun. But with Marcus, she was quiet. She followed him around with her big, hurt eyes. She seemed to be holding her breath. She went to bed with him. And then came back out in the morning, silent and still. She made him breakfast. She watched him eat. She waited for him to leave the house. Then she walked right outside and slashed the tires on his Pontiac with a butcher knife. She put a brick through his windshield. She keyed off a strip of paint that stretched from hood to bumper.

He came home hot. He knew exactly what had been done and who had done it. My mom turned to run as soon as he slammed open the door. As soon as she saw his face. But he had his hands on her before she could take even one step.

I'd seen my mom get physical with other men, but I'd never seen my mom scared like that. With other men, their fights seemed to be an even match, something she fully participated in. She always gave as good as she got.

With Marcus, she was just trying to survive. You couldn't really call them fights. There was nothing mutual about what happened. They were beatings. And the beatings were gruesome. Terrifying. Marcus broke bones. Marcus busted open her lip. Marcus left her with bruises and gashes. Swollen eyes and missing chunks of hair.

Marcus put a gun in her mouth and swore to God that he'd blow her fucking head off.

Marcus never laid a hand on us kids. He'd give us money after it was over, sometimes even apologized, saying that he was sorry that we had to see what our mother made him do.

We took the money.

We hated him the way children hate the man who leaves their mother broken and bloody and sobbing on the floor.

We whispered to one another that Marcus might kill her someday.

I was sure it would happen.

Every time I heard him stomping up our stairs, making the boards groan and squeak under his weight, I would close my eyes and beg for mercy.

AS A KID, IN MY MIND, sex was never really connected to love. Sex was just sex. Something to look forward to. Something that I had been told would feel good. Something that I planned on doing as much as possible as soon as I had the chance.

Nobody was shy about sex in our neighborhood. No one thought it was something children needed to be protected from knowing about. People practically lived on top of one other. There were no private spaces. We shared rooms and beds and a single bathroom. If there was porn in the house, you can bet every kid knew where to find it and that we generously shared it both near and far. If the adults were having sex, they might close their bedroom door, but the walls were thin, and we all knew exactly what was going on. Nobody really dated or wooed anyone. There were no movies or coffee dates or proms or homecomings. Somewhere around middle school, kids in our neighborhood would just find other kids in our neighborhood, and they would talk and maybe flirt a little, and then hook up. As soon as my older brothers realized that they had penises and that they could do things with them, they headed on out to enjoy themselves. Then they came right back home and told the rest of us exactly what they'd been doing. In our neighborhood, sex was just about as casual and commonplace as shaking someone's hand.

I couldn't wait to become a man. I started to grow pubic hair, and I was practically dizzy with pride. I ran around the house with my pants half pulled down, gloating about those ratty little tufts. When I was thirteen years old, I lost my virginity to a girl who was two years older than me, and you'd think I gotten an A on my report card. I told everyone I knew.

People in my neighborhood almost never thought about the consequences of sex. We rarely used birth control. When yet another thirteen-year-old girl got pregnant in our neighborhood, no one blinked an eye. And when yet another fifteen-year-old boy got that girl pregnant, that certainly didn't mean he was going to marry her. Or even stay around to meet the baby.

No one was thinking about marriage. No one was thinking about love. No one was thinking about the future. We lived in the moment. We grabbed at what felt good whenever it was offered to us. We did it wherever we could find a dark corner. And we didn't worry about what might happen to us after.

Because who could think about their future when your grandmother was in the next room getting her fix? When your auntie was dying of AIDS? When your best friend was shot in the head in her basement? When your brothers were going to prison? When your grandfather was drunk, face down on the floor? When a faded, half-inch-long scar was the only thing your father ever gave your mother to remember him by?

YEARS LATER, I was in the room when my grandfather died of cancer. I was holding his hand. My grandmother was on the other side of him, rubbing his arm, talking him through.

When Grandpa stopped breathing, my grandmother's breath caught in solidarity. When his heart stopped beating, I could see her heart slowly shatter in response.

She was gone less than a year later. Sheila never wanted to be where Jeffrey wasn't.

Where we came from, their kind of love was rare. It wasn't perfect, but it lasted decades. It weathered all the things that should have crushed it: poverty and infidelity and addiction and violence and loss. Their love continued to exist even as they fought, and hurt each other, and broke up and came back together more times than I can count.

Despite all the nonsense and noise, my grandparents always had each other. And they managed to hold on to that until the very, very end.

WHEN I WAS GROWING UP, I thought I had a pretty clear idea of what love looked like. And why it wasn't something I particularly needed or wanted to have.

But maybe I was wrong. Because love looked like betrayal. Love looked like violence. Love looked like fear. But love also looked like my grandmother sitting on my grandfather's lap at a backyard barbecue. His arm around her waist. Her smile so big, it lit up the sky.

Chapter 3

MY BROTHERS AND I had been part of Lezlie Hiner's equestrian program, Work to Ride, since David and Bee had stumbled across the run-down horse barn in a hidden corner of Fairmount Park when I was eight years old. Lezlie was a stern-looking white lady who became like a second mother to almost all the children she worked with, but most especially to us Rosser boys. Every day after school and most weekends, my brothers and I came to the barn to clean stables, shovel shit, groom the horses, and, in return, we learned how to ride and play the game of polo.

Over the years, we had become good riders. Very good, in fact. And polo was slowly but surely changing our lives. There were plenty of other kids from the Bottom who were in the program, but we were also exposed to a whole new class of people.

Barn rats. That's what the kids at Work to Ride who were from my neighborhood called the girls who drove in from the Main Line to take lessons from Lezlie. These girls' parents paid for their lessons. Sometimes they boarded their horses at the barn. They were rich (or at least had much more money than any of us had ever seen), usually went to private school, and were mostly white. They had big houses with their own bedrooms, and fenced yards with green lawns and rosebushes. Sometimes a pool. They had nice, expensive clothes and even nicer cars. Their parents were usually very friendly, donated money to the program, and were maybe a bit naive about who we were and what we could get up to with their daughters.

These Main Line barn rats were sheltered, innocent, and of great, great interest to all of us kids from the Bottom.

Work to Ride had changed my life in almost every way possible. Lezlie had reams of rules that we had to follow if we wanted to ride. We had to attend school, get decent grades, and show up at the barn every day, on time, ready to work. We couldn't swear or fight. We had to stay away from drugs. We had to keep our assigned horse groomed and fed and well cared for. In return, Lezlie not only taught us to ride and play polo but she also kept us off the streets, provided a safe place for us to go every day, fed us, helped us with our homework, sometimes met with our teachers, and even let us stay at her house when we had nowhere else to go.

Not all of us could follow the rules. Not all of us stayed on at the barn. But for those of us who did, Lezlie and her horses almost single-handedly changed the trajectory of our lives. Before I met Lezlie, I was barely making it to school even a couple of times a week. I had no ambitions beyond hanging out in the street and following my big brothers around into whatever trouble they were getting up to. Being part of Work to Ride set me on a path that would eventually lead me out of the Bottom, give me a college education, and introduce me to the world of professional polo. A world that I had no idea even existed before the day my big brothers finally allowed me to join them at the barn. Before that day, I was just a scrubby, insecure kid with a deep need to prove that I was as cool as my older brothers.

But everything changed the day that David lifted me onto my first horse.

I WAS NINE YEARS OLD, and we were in the teeth of summer. It was the point in the season where there was no discernible temperature change between the steaming-hot days and leaden, humid nights. That afternoon, the house on Viola felt like an oven. But it was even hotter outside. So Gerb, Bee, and I were lying spread-eagle on the living room floor, in front of a small rotating fan, each of us impatiently waiting for a little puff of sodden, slightly cooler air to come our way.

We were talking about polo. Because polo was just about all we talked about in those days. Bee was beginning to show his true potential on the field. He was a rising star on the Work to Ride team, and people in the horse world were beginning to talk about him with a lot of excitement. He was considered a prodigy. Lezlie said that if he kept it up, he could get a college scholarship or even go pro someday.

Lezlie was planning a big game and fundraiser in a few months' time, and Gerb and I were speculating about the team we were going to play against.

"Doesn't matter," said Bee. "We gonna win. Because I'll be on the field."

Gerb laughed.

I shook my head. "You got a big head, bro."

Bee shrugged. "You know I'm right, though."

He probably was right, and it was too hot to argue, so I shrugged back at him.

Just then our front door banged open and Kareema, who was being held at the shoulders by a girl I didn't know, practically fell into the room.

We all sat up.

"Shit," said Gerb. "What happened to your face, Reema?"

Kareema's lip was split, and her eye was almost swollen shut.

The strange girl helped Kareema to the couch. "She got jumped," she said.

Bee stood up. "Who did it?"

"That Jeremy kid and his sister," mumbled Kareema through her bleeding lip.

"Fucking Jeremy," said Bee.

Jeremy was a kid Bee's age who lived round the block. He and his family had only recently moved to the neighborhood, but he was an endless source of trouble.

"Thanks for bringing her home, Ashley," Bee said. Apparently, he knew the girl. "You okay, Reema?"

Kareema touched her mouth. "I think he gave me a loose tooth."

"Reema wasn't even doing nothing!" said Ashley. "They just got mad because she beat Jeremy's ass at H-O-R-S-E!"

Bee shook his head. He turned to me and Gerb.

"Let's roll," he said.

I HAD BEEN IN FIGHTS BEFORE. You can't grow up where we grew up and avoid being in fights. Didn't matter if you were old or young, male or female. Everyone threw down in the Bottom. And since I grew up with three brothers, I had been wrestling and scrapping since I could walk. But this was the first time that Bee had included me and Gerb in something like this. Usually, he and David worked as a team if they needed to teach someone a lesson. They always said that Gerb was too young and that I was too scared. But David had gone away to juvie a few months before. So Bee took what he could get.

"He'll be at the schoolyard," said Bee.

Gerb nodded. "He's always hanging out there."

"Yeah," I said. "That asshole."

I knew I should be excited. This was the right thing to do. Me and my brothers riding together to avenge our sister. I knew it was correct. But I was also scared as hell. I didn't like violence. I didn't want to get hit or hurt. In my family, I was the weak one. The sensitive one. I was teased for being soft.

I loved my sister, but I kind of wished she'd found someone else to play basketball with that day.

We saw Jeremy as soon as we walked onto the blacktop. He was standing with his back to us, watching some little kids play hopscotch.

"He's gonna try to run when he sees us," whispered Bee. "Gerb, you circle 'round and cover the back exit." He pointed to a corner of the yard. "Reem, you stay here. I'm gonna go after him first, and if he tries to get away, neither of you let him through. Got it?"

I nodded. My heart was beating so hard, I wondered if my brothers could hear it.

Bee ran to Jeremy, grabbed him by the shoulder, and met him with a punch to the jaw. Jeremy didn't try to get away. Instead, he jumped on Bee and knocked him right over. Bee was tough but he was small, and Jeremy must have had twenty pounds on him.

As soon as they hit the ground, I saw Gerb go running to join in. But my feet felt like they were glued to the blacktop.

"Reem!" yelled Gerb. "Come on!"

I took a deep breath and propelled myself forward. By the time I reached them, Gerb, who was known to go pretty much insane when he got angry, had peeled Jeremy off Bee and was hitting him wherever he could reach. Bee jumped back up and joined in.

Jeremy put his hands up, trying to protect his face, and I swung for his stomach. I'm not gonna lie, I felt proud of myself when he doubled over. And then Gerb kicked him in the ass and sent him sprawling onto the ground.

The three of us continued to kick at him for a few moments as he curled up into a fetal position.

Then Bee put his hand up. "Okay, enough," he said.

I stepped back, but Gerb kept kicking at him.

"Enough, Gerb," said Bee, and gently pushed him back.

Gerb went still.

"That's for Reema," said Bee to Jeremy. "You better not fucking mess with our sister ever again."

Jeremy just groaned.

Bee shook his head, disgusted. He shoved at him with his foot. "Go on. Get up."

Jeremy slowly got up, then spit on the ground. I wrinkled my nose, looking at the little coin of blood and saliva he'd made.

"Get the fuck out of here," instructed Bee.

"And don't fuck with our sister no more!" yelled Gerb as Jeremy jogged away.

KAREEMA AND ASHLEY were still sitting on the couch together when we got back. Kareema had an ice pack that she kept moving between her lip and her eye.

My mother and Marcus had come home in the meantime. Marcus was sitting at the dining room table, eating a sandwich. My mom came out of the kitchen, wiping her hands on a dish towel.

"Where you boys been?" she said.

"We were taking care of Jeremy," said Bee.

My mother nodded once, satisfied. "Good," she said, and went back into the kitchen.

Marcus looked up at us. "You teach him what he needed to know?"

"Yeah," said Bee; Gerb and I nodded in agreement. "He got the message."

"He better have," Kareema slurred through her ice pack.

Marcus smiled and went back to eating his sandwich.

For a moment, I felt a little glow of pride. Then it made me uneasy, to feel good because Marcus approved of our violence.

Ashley stood up. This was the first time I had really looked at her since she had come in the door with Kareema. She was older. Maybe David's age. Fifteen or sixteen. She was dressed in a baggy T-shirt and shorts, but I still noticed her curves.

I had just started really noticing curves on girls.

"Since you're okay, I guess I'm gonna go, then," she said to Kareema.

Kareema nodded. "Thanks for helping me out," she said. "You didn't have to."

"Sure I did," Ashley said. "Nobody likes that asshole Jeremy." She grinned then, and I blinked. Her smile was wide and beautiful.

Just then, there was a sharp knock on the door.

"Police!" a voice announced.

My breath caught in my throat. I turned to look at Bee and Gerb. They stared back at me.

My mom came out of the kitchen and met Marcus's eyes. He slowly stood up and walked to the door.

"I got this," he said.

Marcus opened the door a crack, then slipped outside and shut it behind him. We could hear voices through the door but couldn't really make out what they were saying.

My knees were shaking. I looked at Bee. "You think they're here for us?"

Bee looked grim. "Maybe."

I swallowed hard, trying not to throw up.

Gerb took a step closer to me and plastered himself against my side. "I don't wanna go to jail," he whispered.

"Shush," said Bee. "That ain't gonna happen."

The door opened. "Bee," said Marcus. "Come on out here. They just want to hear your side of the story."

Bee stared at Marcus for a moment and then slowly walked to the door.

The second he stepped outside the threshold, the cop grabbed Bee's arms behind his back, shoved him against the side of our house and slapped a pair of handcuffs around his wrists.

Bee turned his head toward me. His eyes were wild.

I wanted to say something, but I opened my mouth and all that came out was a little squeaking sound.

"Yo!" said Marcus. He sounded furious. "You said you were just gonna talk to him!"

The cop pushed Bee around to face the street. Jeremy and his mother were standing there watching the whole thing.

"This him?" asked the cop.

"That's him," said Jeremy.

My mom went to the door. "You can't just take him!" she said. "That boy went after my daughter first!"

"Yeah!" said Kareema as she joined my mom at the door. "He attacked me!"

The cop ignored them and marched Bee down the stairs.

"We'll meet you at the station!" yelled my mom to Bee.

I ran to the door. "Bee!" I shouted. "Bee!"

Bee tried to look back at me, but the cop opened the door to his cruiser and pushed Bee's head down as he shoved him into the back seat.

"BEE!" I started to cry. "BEE!"

DAVID HAD GONE TO JAIL BEFORE. Multiple times at this point. He was no longer showing up at Work to Ride. He had started hustling on the streets.

But Bee had never been arrested.

Bee, I thought, was different. Bee was special. Bee was a natural, according to Lezlie. She said that he was the most promising young polo player she'd ever met. She said he was destined for huge things.

Bee and Gerb and I had been going to the barn every day for years now. We groomed our horses. We practiced polo. We talked about how, someday, we were going to have a family team.

Bee would be our captain.

Bee was not supposed to go to jail.

My mom and Marcus left to see if they could have Bee remanded into their custody. I wanted to go with them, but Mom said I had to stay home with Kareema and Gerb.

I watched them climb into Marcus's car and drive away, and then I sat down on the front steps and started to sob.

"Hey," said a voice behind me.

I turned, wiping my nose on my arm.

Ashley gave me a little smile. "Hey. You okay?"

I sucked back my snot and tears. "Yeah," I said. "I'm fine."

She sat down next to me. Close enough that I could smell her. Clean sweat and cocoa butter.

"I'm sure they'll get him right out," she said. "He'll be okay."

She wrapped her hand around my bicep. Gave it a little squeeze. "I'm gonna go to the papi store. You want to come? I'll buy you a soda."

———

BEE WAS GONE FOR WEEKS. They didn't let him come home with my mom and Marcus. He would have to wait in custody until his court date. And we would have to wait for that court date to be set.

I felt horrible. I missed Bee. I had fantasies of me turning myself in to the police, telling them it was all my fault. That Bee was innocent. I worried that he wouldn't be home for the Work to Ride fundraiser and game.

I worried that he wouldn't come home at all.

The only thing that made me feel better was Ashley. I started to walk past her house a few times a day. I never had the nerve to actually knock on her door, but sometimes I'd get lucky and she'd be sitting on her stoop. I thought I was playing it cool, but I'm sure my feelings were pretty obvious. She always smiled at me. That killer smile. Sometimes we would walk to the papi store on the corner and she'd buy me a Popsicle or another soda, and that felt like all the encouragement I needed to keep coming back 'round the next day. She wasn't interested in me romantically. She definitely saw me as a little kid. But she indulged my crush. She paid some attention to me. She probably felt sorry for me. But I didn't care. She made me feel better.

Sometimes, late at night, after the air cooled down a bit, Ashley would play basketball with the boys at the schoolyard. Sometimes, if she was feeling especially benevolent, she'd let me play, too. After the game was over, we'd go sit on the steps to cool down. She'd sit and talk smack with the boys, laughing and teasing. Maybe they'd all smoke a little weed together. But while she was talking to the boys, Ashley would let me settle between her legs and then she'd play with my cornrows, undoing them and then braiding them up again. Maybe scratching my scalp a little bit. I'm sure she wasn't thinking about how it affected me. I'm sure it was just something to do with

her hands while she was shooting the shit. But I'd close my eyes and
feel her fingers in my hair, and for just a moment, I stopped worrying
about Bee. I felt taken care of. I hoped that she never stopped.

This felt a little like love to me.

BEE WAS RELEASED the day of the Work to Ride fundraiser. He
came straight from Saint Gabe's, the local juvenile detention hall
(which would be closed down many years later surrounded by less
than pleasant rumors). He was still wearing the gray sweat suit
that he'd been forced to wear while he was inside. He showed up,
changed into his polo uniform, swung up on his pony, and led the
team to victory.

ONCE BEE WAS SAFELY BACK HOME, I didn't feel the need to
go by Ashley's house so much anymore. I still saw her around, of
course. Sometimes I even played a little ball with her. But after Bee
came home, I was able to accept that nine-year-old me was probably
not going to get with a sixteen-year-old girl.

But Ashley had changed something in me. I now noticed girls in
a way I hadn't before. And after a while, I actually started making
inroads with some of the more age-appropriate girls in the neighborhood.

I only thought about the sweetness of Ashley's hands lingering
in my hair once in a while. It was a feeling that I would chase until
I found it again.

Chapter 4

I'M SURE JUST BEING BORN into the Bottom left me immediately vulnerable to a whole list of mental health issues. Certainly, being a constant witness to the domestic violence my mother endured hadn't exactly provided me with the most solid emotional foundation, either.

But really, I'd always felt slightly different from all the other kids I knew. Especially my older brothers. Hard times often seemed to make most people in my neighborhood harder. But hard times just made me all the more timid and fearful.

This did not go unnoticed. I was teased and bullied. Called a mama's boy and a sissy. Left at home when my brothers were out running the streets. Sometimes the teasing was good-natured. My family seemed to think it was funny that I was such a scaredy-cat. But I knew that I was expected to grow out of it. That I wouldn't be considered a real man until I toughened up. But I truly didn't know when, or if, that was ever going to happen.

The world I lived in was scary. I didn't like guns. I didn't like fighting. I didn't like seeing the crosses and the memorial flowers and piles of sodden teddy bears that marked yet another street-corner killing. I didn't like the turf wars and weapons at school. I didn't like that I was confined to a few specific blocks because straying out of the safe zone was an open invitation to getting jumped. And even if I stayed home, where it felt relatively secure, I was constantly worried about the safety of my mother and my siblings, who were all much braver and more reckless than I would ever be.

I never spoke about this to anyone. I wouldn't have even known how to start that conversation. People from my neighborhood just didn't talk about mental health. We pretty much all suffered—not only from the day-to-day violence and poverty but also from decades of generational trauma—and we were taught to keep our pain to ourselves. If someone wanted to escape the hardships and fear we lived with every day, there was basically a choice between drugs and prayer and not much else. Neither of those solutions were going to work for me.

But riding helped. Once I started going to Work to Ride, things got a little better. The barn quickly became my sanctuary. Horses, riding, and polo became a central part of my identity and my biggest release valve. My neighborhood and my home life still frightened me—I wasn't really any tougher—but I felt safe on my pony. Long before I learned the vocabulary of mental health, the barn was the one place I experienced peace.

ONE DAY, a year or so after I started to ride, a new girl walked into the barn.

Mecca Harris wasn't like any of the other girls I knew. She was from the hood, so she wasn't like the barn rats, with their money and expensive riding gear. But she wasn't like my sister Kareema and her friends—girls who liked to giggle and gossip and dress up—either. Mecca was a tomboy. She dressed in big, baggy clothes and didn't wear makeup. She had learned to ride from the Black cowboys in the streets and vacant lots of West Philly. She was tough and fearless and could already outride just about anyone at the barn.

And for some reason that I didn't really understand, Mecca liked me right away. She was three years older than me—twelve to my nine—and a far superior rider. Much cooler, much smarter. Way stronger. But on that first day, she ignored everyone else and walked right up to me. She asked me a bunch of questions about my horse and the barn and if I liked polo, and then announced that we were going to ride together. After that, we became inseparable.

Before Mecca, I'd never had a best friend. I had my siblings, and I had a few buddies from our block (mainly my brothers' friends when they were willing to tolerate my hanging around), but I was shy. If I couldn't be with my brothers, I preferred to spend time with my dog, Tummy, and whatever random animal I had coaxed out of the street and stashed in the shed behind our house. I wouldn't say I was alone—because who could be alone in a tiny house with six kids and only two bedrooms—but sometimes I felt lonesome. Like an afterthought. I was nobody's one and only.

When I was smaller, I'd gravitated toward women and girls. I liked spending time with my mother, my grandma, my aunties, and my girl cousins. I would have happily tagged along with Kareema and her friends if they had let me. To me, girls were safer. Easier. Warmer. I felt at home with them. But in the Bottom, little boys who were comfortable with little girls were suspect. If a man in our hood passed by and saw me jumping rope with a neighbor girl, he wouldn't think twice about calling me a fucking pussy and telling me to go find some boys to play with. Even my mother scolded me when I hung around her too much. She'd tell me it wasn't good for me, that I should go outside and find my brothers.

But for some reason, nobody seemed to care when Mecca and I became friends. Maybe because she was a tomboy and I was just a goofy little kid. Maybe because both of us had trouble making friends and our parents were just relieved that we had anybody at that point. Or maybe people did have opinions, but Mecca and I were so deep into our own private world that we didn't notice or care about what anyone else thought.

Having a best friend, especially a best friend like Mecca, made everything better. The barn had always been my favorite place, but now, knowing that Mecca would be there with me, it was straight-up heaven. I was still a weird, sensitive little kid, but nobody teased me anymore because if they did, Mecca would get right up in their face to defend me. I became a better rider and polo player because Mecca's natural skills inspired me to work harder and ride more. I was braver because Mecca was brave and she expected me to accompany her wherever she wanted to go. We snuck into the barn after dark and had sleepovers in the hayloft, joking and teasing about who was the better rider, who was the better polo player. Mecca was someone I could finally talk to. She listened. She cared. She might occasionally tease me a little, but she never made me feel less than. She was tough and strong, she could stand up to just about anything or anyone, but scratch the surface and she was as soulful and sweet as anyone I ever knew.

We slept together in the same bed. We walked down the street with our arms around each other. We would wrestle and play fight. But our love was completely platonic. I had no romantic feelings toward Mecca. And I am certain she had none for me. Maybe because she was a late bloomer, or maybe for other reasons that ten-year-old me didn't understand just yet—she did not seem romantically interested in boys. When I'd admit to an occasional crush on a barn rat, she'd just laugh and give me a little shit about it, but she never confided that she had any crushes of her own. When Bee announced that he was interested in her, she completely iced him out. She only wanted me. Not my brilliant brother. She wanted our friendship. And for two years, we were as close as I've ever been with anyone. I loved her so much. Mecca was everything to me.

"YO, I THINK I MIGHT be going to this school in California," Mecca said to me.

"What?" I said, turning to her. "What are you talking about?"

We were sitting up in the hayloft at the barn. Our favorite hiding place. We'd made a little nest in the middle of some hay bales, feet up, heads back, shoulder to shoulder. We each had a barn cat in our laps.

Mecca didn't look at me. She just kept looking up at the rafters in the ceiling. "Lezlie says there's a real good boarding school called the Thacher School I could go to. She says it would help me become a veterinarian. She thinks I could get in. Get a scholarship."

I blinked. This was unfathomable. I was already dealing with the idea that Mecca was about to enter high school and leave my scrawny middle school butt behind, but the idea of her moving all the way across the country didn't make any sense at all.

"What does your mom say?" I finally asked.

Mecca was an only child, and she and her mom were close. I couldn't imagine that her mother would let her out of her sight.

Mecca shrugged. "She wants me to go. She thinks it would be a good opportunity." She sounded flat. I couldn't read her voice.

"Well, what do *you* think?" I said. "Do you want to go?"

Mecca was quiet for a moment. "Well, Lez says that getting into vet school is even more difficult than getting into medical school. So anything I can do to make it easier is worth thinking about."

I looked at her, feeling lost. Unlike me, Mecca made really good grades. She was street smart, but she was also school smart. She'd talked a lot about wanting to become a veterinarian someday. But I thought that was like me saying that I wanted to be a superhero. Kids from the Bottom didn't go to college. They didn't go to medical school. And they certainly didn't fly across the country to live at a fancy boarding school in California.

"You sound like a whole-ass adult." I imitated her voice. "'Vet school is more difficult than medical school.'"

She swiveled her head toward me, annoyed. "Well it is. No fucking joke."

"So what?" I said. "What about the barn? What about polo?" I wanted to say, *What about me?* But the words got stuck in my throat.

"There's an equestrian team at the school," she answered. "It's one of the reasons Lez thinks they'll want me."

"But no polo?"

She shrugged. "No polo. But other stuff. Western. Like I used to ride."

"Are their horses as good as ours?" I said.

She nodded. "Fancier, anyway. And they got a big indoor arena. They win championships." She poked me in my ribs. "Besides, if I leave, you'll get to take my place on the polo team. It's all good news for you, bro."

For a moment, I felt a little jolt of excitement. That *was* good news. I had been riding the bench on the second string all season, and I was dying to get out on the field more. But then I thought about being on a team without Mecca, and I shook my head. "The team will suck without you."

She smirked. "Well, ain't that the damned truth."

I shoved at her with my foot. "Fuck you. I take it back. It'll probably be way better. We won't miss you at all."

She laughed, kicking me back. Then she looked up at the ceiling again. "I'd miss the barn," she said softly. "My mom. I'd miss you, Reem." She turned to me and met my eyes. "For real. But you know what Lez always says to us, if we find a way out, we take it and we don't look back."

I felt tears sting at the back of my eyes. "But you gotta at least look back sometimes." My voice was scratchy and sounded small, even to me. "'Cause I'll still be here."

Mecca wrapped her arm around my shoulders. "Maybe you can come out and visit me in California. Or even go to the same school once you're in high school."

This cheered me up a little bit. I imagined visiting with Mecca. The palm trees. The beach. Good horses and championships. The idea that I could be reunited with my best friend somewhere warm and safe down the line.

"What kind of grades do you gotta get to get in?" I asked.

She laughed. "Well, I'd say you'll have to work a little bit harder, that's for sure. But maybe it'll give you some inspiration."

I frowned. I didn't like school much, and I certainly didn't get the kind of grades Mecca got.

"Anyway," she said, leaning back again, "nothing is decided. Who knows if I'll even get in. Don't need to worry about it right now."

BUT I DID WORRY. All that night, and the next and the next. I lay in my bed listening to my brothers breathe and thinking about how only Mecca really understood me. How lonely my life had been before she'd come along. How empty it would be if she left.

Still, I knew that it was a good opportunity. A big deal. I knew that getting out of the Bottom was kind of the point of being part

of Work to Ride. Something we were all supposed to be moving toward. And I knew that if I was a good friend, I would support her. If
I had the same chance, she'd tell me to grab it and never look back.

"YOU HEAR FROM THEM YET?" I asked her a week or so later as
we were walking back from the barn together. "That school?"

She looked away from me. "Yeah. They said I'm in if I want it.
Full scholarship."

I swallowed down my surprise. I tried to keep my face neutral. I
waited. But she didn't say anything else.

"So?" I finally said.

She shook her head. "I don't know."

I took a deep breath. *She'd do it for you.* "I think you should go," I
said so fast and low that I wasn't even sure she heard me.

She slowly turned her head. "You think what?"

I took another breath. "I said, I think you should go."

She squinted at me. "Why?"

"Because . . . because it's an opportunity, like Lez says. Because
you're too smart for the schools around here. Because you want to be
a vet, right? Because California is sunny and there are beaches and
it's safe. You should go, Mecca. You should go."

She stared at me for a moment. Then she slowly shook her head.
"Naw," she finally said. "Naw." She gestured around her, at the street
we were walking down. At the little houses with their peeling paint
and broken windows. At the garbage in the gutters. "I don't want to.
I don't care what Lez and my mom say. I don't care how good it is
there. This is my home. This is where I belong. I'm not going to do
it. I'm not going."

I knew I should argue. Try to convince her. I knew I could parrot everything that Lezlie had ever said to us and maybe get Mecca to change her mind. I knew that if I was a better friend, I wouldn't let her make this mistake.

But I didn't. Because I was filled with relief. Because I was filled with joy. I wouldn't lose my friend after all. Me and Mecca, we'd always be together.

BUT IT WASN'T FOR ALWAYS.

Two months later, Mecca Harris, along with her mother and stepfather, was brutally shot and killed in her own home.

I had been with her hours before. We had been riding together at the barn, and she had invited me over for dinner because her stepfather had just won a big chunk of money throwing dice, and they were getting takeout Chinese food to celebrate. I turned her down. I wanted to stay late and keep riding.

And while I was still at the barn, before I even made it back to the Bottom, someone broke into her house, probably looking for the money that Mecca's stepfather had just won. He found them at their kitchen table, still eating their meal. He forced Mecca and her parents down to the basement. And then he lined them up and shot Mecca's mother and Mecca's stepfather execution style. And then, after he made her watch her parents die, he killed Mecca. He shot her in the head. My best friend.

He took the person I loved most in the world.

MECCA'S DEATH UNLEASHED something new in me. I had already lost a lot of people in my life. You can't grow up where I grew up and not know people who have died violently. But Mecca's death was different. Not only because I loved her so fiercely and needed her so much. But also because she was still a child. And up until then, I had understood that I lived in a dangerous place, a place where I could be hurt, but I had assumed it was only truly deadly for adults. Who would bother killing a kid?

After Mecca, I knew better.

I'd always been timid, but now I was paralyzed by fear. I didn't want to go to school. I didn't want to go out to play. I couldn't even walk to the corner store. And even when I was home, I was constantly thinking about how Mecca's killer (who was never found) had come right into her house and taken her life in the place she should have felt safest.

If it could happen to her, it could happen to my siblings, to me.

WHEN I HAD MY FIRST PANIC ATTACK, I had no idea what was going on. After Mecca died, I had nightmares and I developed a fear of the dark, even curled up with all my siblings in our shared bed. I would make just about any excuse to avoid turning out that light. But eventually either my mother or my siblings would insist on it, and so I would lie there in the dark, with my eyes wide open, my mind whirling, trying not to fall asleep, trying not to think or feel too much about anything.

One night, after the light was out, and everyone else was asleep, I got back up and went downstairs and turned on the TV real low, hoping that it would help me stay awake.

And then, all of a sudden, just sitting there on the couch, I couldn't breathe.

My lungs seemed to tighten, and my heart started to race and my joints and spine felt like they had been encased in ice. I sat there with the light of the TV flickering over me, and I panted and gasped and was absolutely certain that I was going to die.

Eventually, whether from lack of air or pure exhaustion, I passed out. And the next morning, amazed to find myself still on the earth, I told my mother what had happened.

My mother decided I had asthma. She took me to the doctor, who listened to my lungs and made me blow into a machine, and then he told her, "No, your son is totally fine."

He sent us home, assuring us that no further help was needed. That it was all in my head.

And then it happened again that night.

And the night after.

And again and again and again.

I had never even heard the words *panic attack*. I didn't have any concept of trauma or anxiety or depression. Nobody was talking about any of that. And so, when the feeling didn't stop, I decided I was crazy. And I didn't tell anyone about it again. I decided it was my burden to carry alone.

Sometimes it was worse. And sometimes it was better. A few years later, I received a polo scholarship to go to Valley Forge Military school, and, unlike Mecca, I left the Bottom.

And maybe because I worked so hard at that school, both mentally and physically, maybe because I was too exhausted by the time taps finally played at night, or maybe because I'd finally left the immediate threat of real violence behind, I rarely felt the claws of that particular panic anymore.

But I still worried. And I still had the occasional nightmare. And I was still scared about a lot of things. And sometimes that old feeling would well up and surprise me. Sometimes, even when everything seemed good—even perfect—I would be gripped with that same helpless, frozen misery. That inescapable feeling of a catastrophe. And the only thing I could do was close my eyes and wait for my own death.

Chapter 5

"REEM LIKES SARAH! Reem likes Sarah!"

I was thirteen years old, and my little brother Gerb was getting on my nerves as we walked home from the barn.

I pushed him into our neighbor's azalea bush. "Shut the fuck up, Gerb."

"Ow! God dammit, Reem! You're a fucking asshole!"

After keeping it clean at the barn all day, it always felt good to let the curses fly.

"You like that barn rat, little man?" asked David.

I raised up my chin. "No way!" My voice sounded squeaky. Even to me.

"Aw, c'mon, bro. You totally into her," said Bee. "And she follow you around like a little puppy. The only question is when you're gonna stop being such a pussy and make your move."

"Shut up," I said. "You the pussy, bro!" And then I took off laughing and running for home before my big brother could push me into the azaleas.

Later on, after we all went to bed, I listened to my brothers' chorus of snores and thought about what they had said. Honestly, I didn't know if I did like Sarah. She was both bossy and clingy. Bee was right; she loved to follow me around at the barn, but it mainly seemed to be so she could tell me everything I was doing wrong. But she was pretty, with long dark hair and a nice smile. And she was strong. She was an athlete, playing soccer and lacrosse. And she was fucking brilliant on a horse. When we first met, she could literally ride circles around me on the polo field.

Off her horse, Sarah was just another rich, slightly annoying white girl, but on her horse, I knew she was something incredibly special.

Like Mecca had been, I thought as I listened to my brothers' snore. It had been years, but I still desperately missed Mecca. I felt the hole she had left in my life every single day. I was lonely all over again.

Gerb turned over and kicked at me in his sleep.

So maybe I can like Sarah now, I thought, edging away from my brother's sharp toenails. I made myself take the deep breaths that sometimes helped me sleep. *Maybe I will like her. But only if she likes me back.*

TURNED OUT SARAH DID like me back. And so I kissed her in the hayloft.

And then I found out that Lily liked me, so I kissed Lily in her bedroom while sitting at the end of her pink canopy bed.

Michelle straight up told me that she was into me. So I kissed her in the corral, when I knew that Lezlie was in her office and not looking.

I kissed Alex after Gerb told me that Regina told him that Alex thought I was cute.

Then Michelle told me she actually liked Bee. And Alex started dating my friend Brandon. And Lily's family moved to Florida to train, but not before she had a little something going with my teammate Dre.

The barn was a hive of preadolescent puppy love. Everyone had a new boyfriend or girlfriend every other week. We were kind of like a family. But the kind of family who played doctor behind bales of hay. By the time we were in our teens, everyone had pretty much paired up with everyone else. In some ways, it sort of felt like the Bottom to me: a small, enclosed community filled with girls I'd basically grown up with. But unlike the easygoing girls I knew from my hood who never seemed to expect anything serious, some of the barn rats seemed to want something else from me. Something I couldn't even pretend I knew how to give them.

I WAS SEVENTEEN.

"Hey!" Sarah popped her head into the stall where I was grooming my favorite pony, Cholo. Her cheeks were red, and her nostrils were flared. She waved her cell phone in the air. "What the hell is this?"

I inwardly flinched. I was home for the weekend, and I'd been taking my time with Cholo, combing over every inch of his coat, hoping that I could avoid this exact scenario.

"What's what?" I said, deciding to play dumb.

"This text," Sarah said. "What the hell is this text saying you don't want to go to prom?"

I turned my eyes back to Cholo. Shrugged. "I don't know. I'm just not into it."

Sarah took a step into the stall, and Cholo huffed his disapproval. He didn't like to be crowded. Without missing a beat, Sarah stepped back out. She could speak horse as well as I could. But that didn't mean she was done with me.

"What do you mean, you're not into it? It's prom, Kareem. Are you my boyfriend or not?"

I almost laughed. Was I her boyfriend?

When I was in the eighth grade, I left my home to attend Valley Forge Military Academy. A year later, Sarah started at an all-girls private school a mere ten minutes away from my campus. Since then, it had been nothing but drama.

First Sarah broke up with me because she didn't like the way I looked at another polo girl at a match.

Then we got back together, but after another few months, Sarah told me that she was interested in a boy she'd met at a private-school mixer.

Then she called me up a few weeks later and said she wasn't interested in that boy after all, and we should get back together.

After that, we had a screaming fight when she saw me helping another barn rat put a girth on a cinchy horse while I was at the stables for the weekend.

Since then, a cadet I knew told me that he'd heard Sarah was talking to a friend of his. I didn't say anything to her about it. I didn't want another fight. But when she asked me to prom, I'd texted her that I didn't want to go.

I was lonely at Valley Forge. Especially the first couple of years I'd been there. It was a harsh, demanding all-boys school. I missed my family. I still missed Mecca. I missed Lezlie and the barn.

And sometimes, when I was with Sarah, it felt like I had a little bit of home. But mostly it felt like this; it felt like shit.

"If you don't go to prom with me, Kareem, that's it! It's over! We are so fucking done!"

"Language!" yelled Lezlie from her office.

Sarah rolled her eyes.

I put down the currycomb. Rubbed Cholo on his nose.

I knew why I needed horses. I needed them to help me work through the fear and anxiety that I had carried with me since I lost Mecca. I needed horses to get over growing up in a place where gun violence was as common as rats. I needed them so I didn't have to think about my mother's addiction all the time. I needed them to help me manage my guilt about moving away from the hood to Valley Forge and leaving my family behind and in constant danger.

I never told any of this to Sarah. I'd never invited her to my house on Viola Street. I'd been to her beautiful home countless times, but I couldn't even begin to imagine her visiting the Bottom.

I looked up at Sarah. She was still glaring at me, but she had tears in her light blue eyes.

I shook my head. "I'm sorry," I said.

"You are such an asshole, Kareem."

"Language!" yelled Lezlie again.

As Sarah walked away, I suddenly wondered what she would say if I asked her why she needed horses.

Her life always seemed so easy to me. But there was no doubt that Sarah did need the horses. That they must have provided her with something necessary.

Because Sarah was a horse girl through and through.

AND WHEN I WAS NINETEEN: "No way," Amy yelped as she grabbed at my sleeve. "No way are you leaving!"

"Amy," I said. "I promise I'll call you later. Just let me out the door."

"No!" she said. She dropped my sleeve, yanked my backpack from my hands, and took off at a run for the bathroom. "I'm going to drop it out the fucking window!" She slammed the door shut behind her.

I felt like crying. It was one in the morning, we had been fighting for two solid hours, and I still wasn't sure over what. After years of dealing with my mother's addictions, I didn't really touch alcohol or drugs, but Amy had been slowly emptying a bottle of vodka since three o'clock that afternoon, and it had made her nastier and nastier as the evening progressed.

"Amy, c'mon," I begged through the door. "Just give me my bag."

"No!" she shouted back. "Not unless you promise to stay!"

I tried the door and almost laughed. She hadn't actually locked it. I stepped into the bathroom and grabbed the bag out of her hands.

"Hey! HEY!"

I ran for the front door, threw open the dead bolt, and dashed for the elevator.

"No!" she screamed from behind me. "Kareem! Stop! Don't you dare!"

I changed directions, ran for the stairs.

We were ten stories up, but I didn't care. No way was I waiting for the elevator. I burst through the exit and started down the stairs, taking them two at a time, grateful that I'd been training horses all summer and was in relatively good shape. At some point I looked back. She wasn't there. I stopped for a moment and took a deep breath, glad that she had come to her senses and gone back to her apartment.

I hit the bottom floor. Burst out of the stairwell and then forced myself to walk slowly through the lobby. I didn't want any trouble from the doorman.

I pushed through the front doors.

"KAREEEEEM!"

Shit. There she was. Standing in the street. Wearing nothing but her short satin robe. No shoes even.

"Jesus, Amy. Go home."

"Kareem! Don't you dare go! I am not finished with this fight!"

"But I am," I said.

There was a subway station a block uptown. I turned toward it and started to walk. I was sure she would come to her senses and go back. But Amy was a horse girl, too. A jumper. She matched me stride for stride.

I headed down the stairs into the subway station. A wave of summer heat engulfed us.

"Ugh," said Amy. "So fucking gross. Smells like piss. Come on, let's go home."

"You should definitely go," I said. "But I'm going back to the farm."

She shoved me, almost pushing me down the stairs. "No! No! No you're not!"

"Amy," I said, grabbing at the slimy metal banister just in time. "Just stop." I tried to keep my voice low. I didn't want to make a scene. "You're barefoot. You're not dressed. Go home."

I stepped out of her grasp and slid my metro card through the meter. She jumped the turnstile without missing a beat.

"Don't go," she begged as she grabbed my arm again.

There were only a few people in the station. But they all turned to look at us as I made my way closer to the tracks.

"Come on," I said. "Come on. Please. This isn't safe for you."

The train was coming. I could hear the brakes squealing.

Amy leaned in close to me, dropping my arm and clutching at my shirt front instead. "You know who this isn't safe for? You know who this isn't safe for, Kareem?" Her eyes were bloodshot. Her breath smelled rank. "This isn't safe for the Black guy with the white girl who's barely dressed. This isn't safe for the Black guy if the white girl screams."

I felt sick. "Don't," I said. "Please. Don't."

She smiled at me, triumphant. "Now you have to come home with me."

The train pulled up behind us. I could hear the door open. I counted to five in my head. Waited for that little ding that signified the doors were about to close.

"Fuck you, Amy," I said, and tore out of her hands, stepping backward onto the train as the doors shut between us.

Her face contorted into a howl. She reached to pound on the door, but then we were moving and she was gone.

No more, I thought. *No more crazy fucking horse girls.*

A YEAR LATER, I was visiting the barn on my winter break from college. Outside, it was snowy and cold like only Philly gets cold, but inside the barn, it was warm and dry. It smelled like sweet hay and damp horses. Lezlie and I were standing side by side—catching up as I leaned over the stall door and fed Cholo an apple—when a small swarm of the Work to Ride kids came running over, trying to get my attention.

I was used to this. Even though I'd been in college for a couple of years now, the kids at the barn all knew who I was, and they knew that I was always happy to take some time to clown around with them a little bit.

"Hey, Reem!" piped up one little boy as he tugged on my pant leg. "You meet Lee Lee yet?"

I shrugged. "Nope. Who's Lee Lee?"

"Ooooh, Lee Lee!" said one of the little girls. "Lee Lee Jones! She's a white girl, and all these dumb boys be in love with her!"

"Shut up," said the boy. He turned back to me. "She's so pretty, Reem."

"She smells like a flower," said another little guy, with a sigh.

"Yeah, and she dresses real good," said a third kid.

"And she so nice!"

"Nicer than Lezlie, anyway," teased the little girl.

I shot a look at Lezlie, who was standing there with an amused look on her face. She raised her hands, palms up. "They're not wrong," she said.

"A patron?" I asked.

Lezlie shook her head. "A volunteer. Your age. Great kid. Excellent rider. Her stepdad is Phillip Dutton."

I raised my eyebrows. Everyone in the horse world knew who Phillip Dutton was. "The Olympic eventer?"

She nodded. "Yup."

"So she's a barn rat. A horse girl."

Lezlie shook her head at me. I'd told her about the oath I'd made when it came to crazy horse girls, and she had rolled her eyes and told me to stop being such a sexist pig.

"Sure," she said. "If that's what you want to call her."

I curled my lip. "So what's she doing around here?"

Lezlie shrugged. "Doing what we all do. Shoveling shit. Grooming the horses. Teaching little kids to ride." She grinned at me. "She's pretty spectacular, Reem. Even for a crazy horse girl."

Chapter 6

THAT DAY AT WORK TO RIDE was just the start of my hearing about Lee Lee Jones. She came up again and again at the barn. The kids couldn't seem to shut up about her. *Lee Lee this* and *Lee Lee that*, and *Oh, Kareem you should have seen Lee Lee riding yesterday*, and *Do you wanna know what Lee Lee said?* . . . And it wasn't just the kids; Lezlie seemed to find a reason to bring up Lee Lee at least ten times a day, too.

I started hearing her name in my social circles beyond the barn as well. I was at a party when an older woman, a benefactor of Work to Ride, leaned over her plate of paella and asked me if I knew a girl named Lee Lee Jones.

I laughed out loud.

The woman raised her eyebrows at me.

"Sorry," I said. "It's just that you aren't the first person who has mentioned her to me lately."

The woman nodded knowingly. "She's a lovely girl," she said. "A great rider, too. Aren't you single, Kareem?" She winked at me. "You two would be absolutely amazing together."

I smiled politely. "I'm not really looking for anything right now. Just concentrating on school."

But maybe I was lying. Because that night, my interest was finally piqued enough that I looked up Lee Lee Jones on Facebook.

Her profile picture was of her wearing a red hunting jacket and making a dramatic jump on a large chestnut warmblood. I couldn't see much of her face under her helmet, but the horseman in me admired her perfect form.

Her account was public, which meant that I could see every post, every picture, every comment. As I scrolled down, there were more photos of her caught mid-jump while competing. I could tell that she was a serious rider. The horses she rode were beautiful, and she looked more than worthy of them. But it was the pictures of her clowning around that really made me catch my breath: Her laughing with friends. Her posing with her arms around her family. Her dressed in a tight black formal gown for a school dance, absolutely eclipsing all of her equally dressed-up classmates. She had long brown hair, a playful look in her dark eyes, and a wide, gorgeous smile. Simply put, she was stunning; the kids at the barn hadn't been exaggerating about that.

After I saw a picture of her giving her horse a giant kiss on the nose, I couldn't help myself. I clicked on the Friend button.

The next day, I was having lunch with Gerb when I got a message in return:

Lee Lee Jones has accepted your friend request.

"Bro, why you smiling like that?" asked Gerb.

I quickly flipped my phone back over. Made my face go blank. "Nothin'," I said. "Eat your sandwich."

WHEN I RETURNED TO SCHOOL THAT FALL, Lee Lee and I started chatting online. First it was just some Facebook conversations about the barn and who we knew in common. Then I liked a picture on her Instagram, and she liked one of me back. Eventually we started Snapchatting. I'd ask her about her eventing competitions, and she'd ask me about polo. Sometimes we'd talk about school. She was finishing up her undergrad in Delaware but was planning on pursuing her master's of social work after she graduated, hopefully at UPenn. I was going to finish my BA at Colorado State University (CSU) at the same time as her, but I thought I might work a while before going back for my MBA. We talked about our families. She had five siblings, too. Younger twin sisters from her mother and stepfather, and three little brothers on her father's side. We exchanged dorky memes and silly selfies. It was fun and harmless and definitely a bit flirty.

I was still talking to other girls at school, but I found myself thinking about Lee Lee more and more often. I'd compare her to the other girls I was hanging out with on campus. Sometimes, late at night, I'd scroll through her Instagram just to see her face before I went to sleep.

When I'd first started college, I'd been less than confident when it came to women. Between my romantic misadventures at the barn and spending five years at an all-boys' military academy, I wasn't exactly smooth when it came to the opposite sex. But over the next couple of years at CSU, I'd gained some experience and become a little more self-assured.

I was perfectly happy with casual flings and hookups, nothing serious. I believed in enthusiastic consent, and I did my best to make sure anyone I was with had a good time, but I didn't like to cuddle or be touched outside of the bedroom. I thought the idea of a life partner or a soul mate was a fairy tale at best, and I was pretty sure that the quickest way to getting hurt was through falling in love. I reasoned that if you kept someone at a certain distance, there was no way they could hurt you when they inevitably left. I was honest about this from the jump with girls. I never stayed around long enough for anyone to get attached. I rarely hung out with a girl more than a few times before I'd move on to someone new.

But with Lee Lee, it was already starting to feel different. I truly looked forward to her messages and pictures. I'd catch myself smiling every time I saw her name on my phone. I wanted to get to know her, and I was beginning to realize that my interest was about more than just sex.

On the way back to Philly for Thanksgiving break, I decided to ask her if she wanted to hang out while I was home.

I remember typing it out, then erasing it, and then rewriting a few more times before I was satisfied with my message.

I was surprised by just how nervous I was while I was waiting for her answer. And just how relieved I felt when she texted back: *When and where?*

THE NIGHT BEFORE what was supposed to be my first date with Lee Lee, I got a call from Gerb. I was staying with Lezlie.

"Hey, bro," I said into the phone. "What's up?"

"Tyree's in the hospital," Gerb told me. "Nick stabbed him."

Tyree was a childhood friend. A boy from the Bottom I had grown up with. He had been shot when he was sixteen. Lost an eye. And then he was shot two more times over the next few years. But he'd survived all that. Our families were close. His father had been killed when Tyree was a baby. His mother had disappeared not long after that. He'd grown up with only his grandmother taking care of him. He had run with me and my brothers all those years we lived on Viola Street.

I knew the guy who stabbed him, too. Nick. My brothers and I had spent countless summer nights sitting on his front porch playing video games, chatting with his father, Mr. Henry, who was a warm and welcoming man. Nick and his brother were rough, though.

They always had been. But they were also our neighbors. They were familiar. They were part of our crowd.

And now Tyree was in intensive care and Nick was in police custody.

"Tyree gonna make it?" I asked my brother.

I heard him sigh. "I don't know, man. It don't look good."

THE NEXT MORNING, I woke up and groped for my phone. There was a text from Gerb. Tyree had died during the night.

I stayed in bed for a minute. Closed my eyes and took some deep breaths, tried not to cry. These kinds of deaths didn't surprise me anymore. But that didn't mean they didn't hurt all the same.

I thought about canceling my date with Lee Lee. But I wanted to get out. Be distracted. Not have to think about all this. So I borrowed Lezlie's car and started driving.

Halfway to Lee Lee's place, my phone rang again. It was an unknown number.

"Is this Kareem Rosser?"

"Yes?"

"This is Lou D'Angelo at the King of Prussia mall. I have your mother here. Lazette? She, uh, seems to be quite upset. She wanted me to call and ask you to come and get her."

My mother worked as a janitor at the mall.

"Can I talk to her?"

I heard him pass the phone over.

"Reem? Reem?"

She sounded frantic. Out of breath.

"Mom? You all right?"

"No. No, I am not. I am not okay. Can you come and get me, Reem?"

Drugs, I thought.

"Just hold on," I told her. "I'll be there soon."

I TEXTED LEE LEE on the way to the mall. Told her that I was really sorry but that I couldn't meet her that day because something had come up.

She was nice enough in her reply, but I could tell she was waiting for me to explain further.

I didn't, though. I just told her that I'd message her again next time I was in town.

I didn't want to lie. And I didn't really know what the truth was yet, anyway.

WHEN I SAW MY MOTHER, she didn't seem high. She was something else. Frantic. Gasping for breath. And in between her gasping, she was talking. Talking. Talking. She grabbed my arm. Clung to me as I helped her up.

"I'm not right, baby," she said. "Something ain't right. I gotta go to the hospital."

I told her it would be okay. I walked her to the car, buckled her in.

"Mom?" I asked. "You take something?"

"Noooo," she moaned. "No. I'm not high. I swear it. I just ain't right."

"Okay," I said. "Okay. Hang on now. We're going to the hospital."

I started the car. She kept talking. "This never gets easier. This never gets any easier. I can't keep doing this, baby. I can't stand this no more. Tyree's gone now. Kids keep getting killed. Tyree gone. It hurts so much. I don't want to keep doing this."

"Doing what, Mom?"

"Living, baby. I don't want to keep living and hurting like this."

"Mom—" I said.

She groaned and clutched her chest. "I can't breathe. I can't breathe. I can't breathe."

I reached over to take her hand. She twisted away from me, scrabbled at the car door handle. "I swear to God, baby, I gotta get out. I can't breathe! I don't want to keep doing this! I don't want to live no more!"

She opened the door. Fumbled at her seat belt.

"Mom!" I shouted, reaching across her and slamming the door shut. "Mom! Stop! Stop!"

SOMEHOW WE MADE IT TO THE ER. I half dragged, half carried her in.

"Something's wrong with my mom," I said to the woman behind the check-in desk. "She can't breathe."

The woman looked up at us. "Fill out these forms and take a seat," she said.

"But my mom—"

"We'll get to her as soon as possible. Take a seat."

Mom seemed to settle a little when we sat down. Her breathing slowed.

I squinted at the papers I had to fill out.

"I gotta go to the bathroom," she said.

I looked at her. "You okay to do that?" I asked.

She nodded as she stood up. "Yes. I'm okay. Thank you, baby. I'm okay."

I watched her shuffle toward the bathroom, disappear behind the door.

This never gets easier, she had said.

We had talked about this before. We had talked about the weight we carried. The fact that she and I both existed in a state of constant and horrible expectation. Waiting. Waiting for yet another person we loved and knew and needed to die. Today it had been Tyree. Tomorrow it would be someone else. And then someone else. And then someone else again.

I looked at the bathroom door again. Stood up.

She was crumpled on the floor. Curled up in a fetal position.

"Mom!" I choked out, reaching for her.

She shook her head. Tears leaked down her cheeks. "I can't breathe," she whispered.

I had helped my mother up off the bathroom floor before. I had helped her up after her boyfriend had beat her and held a gun to her head. I had helped her up when she was bleeding and broken and crying. But this time felt different.

I can't breathe.

In that moment, I was just scared. I was scared to hear her talking about wanting to die. Even at the worst of times, she had never done that before. And I was scared that maybe she really had taken some sort of drug—the kind that brutalized your mind so much, you never came back right. Just became a shadow person. Never the same.

I held her, and I was scared to lose her. I loved her. I needed her.

"I still gotta pee," she mumbled.

"Well, I'm not leaving," I said fiercely.

She laughed. A small giggle. Which immediately made everything a little bit better.

"I think I need your help," she said. "I'm feeling dizzy."

I stood her up, walked her to the toilet.

She looked at me. "You really not leaving?"

I shook my head. "No way."

She laughed again. "Then I guess you can just turn your back
and listen to me pee, baby," she said.

SHE SPENT SEVENTY-TWO HOURS in the hospital. She wasn't allowed visitors, but I talked to her on the phone multiple times a day.
Every time we talked, she sounded better. A little bit calmer. A little
stronger. More like her old self.

There was nothing wrong with her physically, the doctors had
told me. Her heart and lungs were fine. She was healthy. They only
admitted her because she had talked about wanting to harm herself.

When seventy-two hours passed, she was discharged into Kareema's care.

And I went back to school.

She's okay, I told myself. *She's okay. She's okay.*

Chapter 7

AS SOON AS I RETURNED to Philly for the summer, I sent Lee Lee a selfie of me standing in front of the LOVE statue. She'd immediately replied with laughing and heart emojis, and then wrote, "So is this really going to happen? Are we finally going to meet up?"

I was interning at an asset-management firm run by a man named Joe Manheim, who I knew from the Work to Ride barn. He was a prominent supporter of Lezlie's organization. I had sublet an apartment downtown. This version of Philly was almost entirely new to me; it wasn't the Bottom, or even Lezlie's neighborhood, and I was feeling both proud of myself and a bit like an impostor.

But mainly it felt like a great time to finally meet Lee Lee Jones.

So when Joe, who also played polo, invited me out for a practice game at his club, it seemed like the perfect opportunity. I knew that the club was just around the corner from Lee Lee's farm. And even if I wasn't always completely smooth with girls on the ground, I was pretty confident I could impress if I was on the polo field. Being good at riding is a guaranteed attention getter, like being able to dance or do a backflip. And I figured it might work particularly well with a girl who obviously loved horses as much as I did.

I WAS ON A CITY BUS on my way to the barn. Joe boarded his polo ponies with Lezlie and had asked me to meet him there to help load them up before we drove out to the club together.

I was nervous. Scrolling through my phone. Reading old messages from Lee Lee, tracking the evolution of our acquaintance. We had started out lighthearted and flirty. But at some point, things had changed. Something more intense and honest had grown between us in the past few months.

I knew that meeting a woman I'd known only online was tricky. I'd had incidents in the past where I'd felt a connection based on photos and texts but then something ended up being off when we finally met in real life. Sometimes the girl didn't look anything like her photos. Sometimes her personality was nothing like I'd expected. Sometimes it was something as ineffable as the way she smelled, or an unpleasant tone of voice, or a mysterious lack of chemistry. Sometimes she'd say something borderline problematic or simply too ignorant to ignore, and I'd immediately know that I'd made a mistake in taking our relationship off the screen.

I didn't think anything quite that dramatic was likely to happen with Lee Lee. I didn't think she was going to catfish me or anything. But I did wonder if she could ever hold up to the image of her that I had in my head.

The bus stopped a block from the barn, and I got off. I helped Joe with his ponies, and then we were on our way.

I didn't tell Joe that Lee Lee was going to meet us at the club. Keeping her a secret had become habitual at this point. I wasn't sure why I felt that way. Maybe I didn't want to raise anyone's expectations. Maybe because things might be no more than one or two dates. A hookup. And if that's all it was, I didn't want to have to explain myself to all the people who knew us both.

But then we parked our trailer outside the club barn, and Lee Lee Jones came sauntering up to us wearing these red booty shorts and a black tank top and a pair of little flip-flops, her hair still wet from the shower and held back with a pair of Ray-Bans she had pushed onto the top of her head.

She smiled at me, and I swear I almost forgot my own name.

"Hi, Kareem," she said.

"H-hi, Lee Lee," I stuttered in return.

And then we went in for a hello hug, and I remember thinking that it was weird because it didn't feel weird at all.

It felt natural.

It felt right.

I introduced her to Joe, and he shot me a look like, *Where the hell did this girl come from?*, and I shrugged, playing it cool, acting like she'd somehow just fallen from the sky.

We didn't have any grooms, so it was just the three of us there to unload and get the ponies ready to play. I tried to multitask. I tried to have a conversation with Lee Lee, while at the same time I was also trying to get ready to ride, and also making sure I was helping Joe with whatever he needed. But clearly I was distracted, and nothing I was doing was getting done particularly right. And so Lee Lee, like she naturally did anywhere, just found a way to fit in and help. She helped us lead the ponies out. She walked into the trailer and grabbed polo wraps and saddles. Polo equipment was a bit different from the eventing tack she was used to, so she asked me a couple of questions, but in no time at all she was wrapping legs and strapping on the saddles. All the while keeping up a steady stream of conversation with both me and Joe. She was so at ease. It was like we were all already old friends.

I DON'T REMEMBER MUCH about the practice game that day. But I do remember other things. I remember how I teased Lee Lee about wearing flip-flops to a barn. I told her that any horse girl should know better. But I also remember, despite the dangerous footwear, how happy it made me to be around a woman who really knew her way around a pony. I remember how, when we were switching out our ponies, I would swing off my mount and Lee Lee would hand me my water, and we would have a quick conversation while I was changing my horses, and then I'd gallop back onto the field, pleased that she could see me ride but kind of wishing that I could just keep talking to her instead. I remember thinking that I should feel nervous with her, but marveling at how I absolutely didn't.

I remember how she immediately made me feel comfortable, like we'd known each other for years.

I remember the moment when our shoulders brushed as we were grooming together, and the way I felt that touch rocket through my whole body. And from the way she sucked in her breath, I was pretty sure she could feel it, too.

Lee Lee had to leave right after the game, so we didn't really have any time to hang out or talk. She thanked me for inviting her and told me she had really enjoyed watching me practice, and she gave me a big smile and walked back out of the barn, and all I could think was, *How soon can I see this girl again?*

I CANNOT BEGIN TO DESCRIBE the impact that Lee Lee had in real life. I never should have questioned it. Because *of course* she was even better than anything I could have conjured up in my head. Better than her photos. Better than her texts.

The sound of her laugh. The way she moved. The way she absolutely shined.

And it wasn't just her legs or her smile or her big brown eyes; it was this indescribable something, a kind of glow—an energy—she exuded. I would later witness the way that Lee Lee could walk into any room and folks would just stop and turn and stare. You could see people falling like birds shot out of the sky—mouths hanging open, eyes gone all out of focus—already halfway in love with her as she crossed the floor and moved past them.

And I'm not going to lie; on that day, standing on the polo field, watching her effortlessly help with the ponies, I was definitely one of those people. But I didn't stop at halfway in love. From the moment I laid eyes on her, she had me. I was completely in. I had no doubt that I wanted Lee Lee Jones to be my person.

Chapter 8

"I THOUGHT YOU WERE GOING TO show me around, not get us lost!" Lee Lee teased me after we took yet another wrong turn. "I thought you said you knew this city!"

I laughed and squinted at my phone, trying to ascertain where we'd gone astray. "Oh, I do." I took her arm and steered her in the opposite direction. "Just not this part of the city."

Downtown Philly is fifteen minutes from the Bottom. A direct shot on the train. When I was growing up, it was a field trip. A destination. A once-in-a-very-long-while treat. In some ways, it may as well have been the moon.

We always got plenty of notice if we were going downtown. My mother treated it like it was a vacation—one we had to plan and save for.

"Well," she would say as we were all sprawled around the living room, watching TV. "Well, I was thinking that we should go downtown in a couple days. What do y'all think?"

"Yes!" we would cheer. "Yes! Yes!"

"Hmm." She'd pretend to frown. "Hmm, y'all don't sound that excited. Maybe we should just stay home."

"NO! NO! NO!" we'd yell back.

She cocked her head. "Wait, what was that?" She gave a long-suffering sigh. "'No'? 'No' you don't want to go? Well, if you really feel that way. We'll just stay home, then."

"Mooommm," we'd groan. "Please! C'mon, Mom!"

Then she'd flash us her big, beautiful smile and say, "Oh . . . okay. I guess we can go."

And we'd jump all over her like a bunch of hyper puppies.

Downtown meant the Liberty Bell. Chinatown. The LOVE Park. It meant winding our way through a packed Reading Terminal Market, sniffing and salivating over every food booth. It meant hoagies or water ice or maybe a cheesesteak or soft pretzels that were smeared with mustard and bigger than our heads.

It felt like another world from the four-block radius I had grown up in.

So the fact that I was now living and working in downtown Philly for the summer felt a little bit like I had suddenly moved to Paris. This was not Viola Street. This was not the Philly I knew so intimately. But I was eager to explore it. And the idea of doing that with Lee Lee made it even more appealing. She wasn't one of those people who says they're from Philly but really lives in the suburbs. She loved the city and definitely spent time there, but she didn't claim it as her own. At least not yet. I thought maybe we could discover it together.

"I FEEL LIKE A TOURIST," I admitted as we walked down South Street, cherry water ices in our hands. "I wanted to be all cool and show you Philly, but honestly, this is not my hood. I barely know this area at all."

Lee Lee took a bite of her water ice. "I've been to West Philly," she said. "In fact, I've seen your mural. I drove by it and then parked and got out so I could see it better."

I laughed, surprised. Philly is known for its murals. And there was one on Cambridge Street—not far from where I'd grown up—

that had been painted in honor of Work to Ride. It depicted my teammates and me in mid-gallop, three stories high, playing polo in the streets of West Philly.

"You got out of the car?" I asked, trying to imagine this pretty, young white girl wandering around the Bottom. "Weren't you scared?"

Lee Lee shrugged. "No one bothered me. There were just, you know, kids and families and stuff. I liked walking around. It was a really interesting neighborhood."

I studied her face for a moment, trying to see if she was fucking with me.

She looked sincere.

"Huh. Okay." I tipped my cup back and drank some of the sweet melted ice. "How did you even hear about that mural, anyway?"

"Oh, Lezlie told me. But I admit that I drove out to see it only once you and I started talking."

I ducked my head to hide my smile. "And did you like it?"

Lee Lee met my eyes. "How could I not?"

BECAUSE THE POLO PRACTICE GAME had been more of a meetup, I considered this to be our first official date. I had planned it out meticulously, so happy that I was interning downtown, that I was subletting a nice apartment, that I had all these markers of success I'd never been able to offer a girl before.

It wasn't that I thought Lee Lee was materialistic. In fact, if anything, she was the complete opposite. Her main concern in life truly seemed to be finding ways to help people out. She volunteered at the barn, and she planned to have a career in social work so she could continue working with vulnerable kids. But I had spent a good portion of my adolescence with very mixed feelings about the fact that I had grown up in West Philly. When we traveled for polo and I'd met all these other kids my age who came from a world of money and privilege, I sometimes felt like a curiosity. A freak. People were always perfectly nice to us Work to Ride kids, but there were moments when I could tell that we were there not because they recognized that we were good polo players, but because we were a novelty. I often found myself feeling—not ashamed exactly—but protective of where I came from. I didn't want to talk about it, and I didn't want to put it on display for people I was certain could never understand what it truly was.

I thought that maybe I'd feel the same with Lee Lee. I thought that I wanted to impress her more than I wanted her to know who I really was. And I thought that maybe if I could offer her downtown Philly, with my cool new apartment and my job in finance, I could keep her distracted from the topic of where I grew up.

What I hadn't counted on was the fact that she would be interested enough to ask. Not in a condescending or snobby way. Not in the way I was used to being asked about my childhood home. There was nothing exoticizing about the way she was looking at me. Her questions felt rooted in true and sincere curiosity.

And what I really hadn't counted on was the fact that I'd feel comfortable enough to tell her about any of it. Being this vulnerable with a woman was new to me. Holding nothing back felt great. Not having to code-switch or play macho or wear a mask or feel like I was somehow responsible for representing all of West Philly felt even better.

"Do you want to go back to my apartment?" I asked her.

And she smiled and said, "Why not?"

———————————

WE WALKED HOME TOGETHER, talking about our respective childhoods, our parents, and our siblings. Lee Lee told me about her parents' divorce, which had been a difficult time for her. And I told her about some of the ways my family had struggled as well. I loved the way she listened. I loved her intelligent questions. I felt like I could trust her enough to tell her just about anything. And I wanted to know everything about her in return.

As we walked, I noticed other men's eyes on her. I didn't really blame them. She was, of course, shockingly beautiful, and I'm sure I would have turned my head to watch her go by if I hadn't known her, either. In a way it just made me feel even prouder to be with her.

But sometimes those kinds of looks went over the line.

One guy started following behind us, catcalling and asking her why she was with someone like me.

"Hey! Hey, sexy! Hey, girly! What are you doing with a loser like that?"

I honestly don't know if this guy was being straight-up racist or just letting Lee Lee know he thought she could do better, but I was beginning to lose my cool. I didn't want to do what I'd been raised to do, which was turn around and get in his face and defend my own manhood. That seemed ridiculous and dangerous and not how I wanted to spend our first date.

But he kept at it. He wouldn't back down. And ignoring him was not working.

"Hey, girl! Hey, girly! Why don't you see what it's like to be with a real man?"

I felt my stomach tighten and my hands curl into fists.

I stopped walking.

But it was Lee Lee who finally solved the problem.

"Hey!" she said, spinning around to face him. "Hey! Listen to me! You have got nothing on this man I am with. Nothing! So just shut your dumb mouth and mind your own business!"

The guy stopped in his tracks. His mouth was hanging open like his jaw had been broken.

I looked at Lee Lee. Her cheeks were flushed, and her eyes were glittering, and she looked like the type of person you would never, ever want to fuck with. She was magnificent, furious, beautiful, and simply winning at everything. I looked at her, and I was washed with the strongest feeling; I didn't want to be anywhere else but there at her side.

That was the moment.

That was the moment that I fell in love for the first time in my life.

AFTER THAT, we made it back to my apartment without further incident. I was so excited to show off my new place. It was only temporary, of course, but it was my first truly adult living space. All my own. And Lee Lee was pretty much the first person I got to show it to.

Neither I nor Lee Lee was twenty-one yet, and once we got back to the apartment, I wished I could smoothly offer her a nice glass of wine to go with the cheesesteaks and water ices we had consumed earlier, but since I didn't have that, I decided that we should crack open a dusty bottle of Malibu rum that the owner of the apartment had left behind.

"Would you like a drink?" I asked as Lee Lee made herself comfortable on the couch.

Lee Lee nodded brightly. "Sure!"

"On the rocks?" I thought that sounded cool.

She nodded again. "Absolutely."

I went into the kitchen, where I opened the bottle and sniffed the contents. I didn't have any mixers, but I figured that it smelled sweet, so it would probably be okay straight up. I took down two water glasses from the cabinet, dropped a couple of ice cubes into each, and poured half a glass of the suntan-oil-smelling drink into each cup.

"Cheers," I said as I handed her the glass and sat down next to her on the couch.

"Cheers," she said back, clinking her glass to mine.

We each took a big gulp. Then another. It was coconutty and sweet and went down easy.

Before I knew it, I had drained the entire glass.

It took only about ten seconds to realize I'd made a huge mistake.

I've always had a weak stomach. I think it's because it's where I carry most of my stress. As a kid I was constantly complaining about bellyaches, spending all sorts of time curled up in bed or on the couch, my arms wrapped around my middle like I had 24-7 appendicitis. And when I ate something that disagreed with my stomach, it was like my stomach had a memory. I never wanted to touch that food again.

I had recently started drinking a bit at school, and I'd had a particularly unfortunate night with way too many whiskey and Cokes.

I thought rum would be different enough from whiskey, though. I thought I was a grown-ass adult who could hold his liquor with dignity.

Instead, I felt the telltale rumble deep in my belly. I felt saliva pooling in the corners of my mouth. I stood up, desperate to make it to the bathroom.

"Are you okay?" asked Lee Lee.

I opened my mouth to answer, and then I projectile vomited all over the coffee table and the floor.

"Oh my God!" shrieked Lee Lee, scrambling to get out of the line of fire.

I groaned and took a step away from her. And then I threw up again.

The Malibu. The water ice. The goddamned cheesesteak. Splattered all over the apartment.

"Oh my God!" Lee Lee was laughing. "Oh my God, Kareem, are you okay?"

I was done puking, but I was humiliated. I wanted to die right on the spot.

"I'm sorry," I managed to choke out. "I'm so, so sorry."

"No, no," said Lee Lee. "It's okay! It's . . ." She was laughing, but she looked kind of wild-eyed. "Can I get you a glass of water?"

I shook my head. "I'll get it myself."

I practically ran into the bathroom, desperate to get away from the disgusting scene of my disgrace. I violently brushed my teeth, rinsed my mouth with mouthwash. I thought about losing Lee Lee's number. I thought about never leaving the bathroom again.

There was a gentle knock on the bathroom door, and then, when I didn't answer, Lee Lee slowly opened it. "Hey," she said. She was smiling, but not in a mean way. "Do you have, like, some paper towels or something?"

"What?" I was horrified. "Oh God, no! Don't do that!" I didn't want her to clean up my mess.

She reached out her hand and tentatively patted my shoulder. I felt both soothed and terribly childish. "I can't hold my liquor very well, either," she said. "I throw up all the time. It's no big deal at all. Seriously. Once, I was so hungover, I threw up at a competition while I was still on my horse."

I barked out a laugh, surprised at the visual.

She grinned at me. "But I still won the blue ribbon."

WE DIDN'T SHARE our first kiss that day. I mean, of course we didn't. Cleaning up puddles of puke didn't exactly set the mood.

But when Lee Lee was ready to go, I walked her back down to her car, prepared to accept the fact that even though I already knew that I was desperately, unbreakably in love, I would most likely never see this girl again.

But Lee Lee surprised me. That was something else I learned that day, that Lee Lee Jones would constantly and always surprise me.

We got to her car, and I started to say goodbye. And it was absolutely killing me, but I had already decided that I wasn't going to ask her out again. I didn't think there was any chance I was coming back from the catastrophe of puke. I thought I would let her off the hook and just say that I hoped to see her around the barn someday soon.

But before I could start talking, she slipped into my arms and gave me a long, warm, lingering hug. She pushed her body fully against mine. She wrapped her arms around my back and held on to me in an almost fierce kind of way.

We stood that way for a moment. Her head on my shoulder. My

hands on the small of her back. I felt high from being so close to her. I felt ill thinking that this might be the last time this would ever happen.

Then she whispered into my ear. "Best first date ever."

And the thing was, she actually sounded like she meant it.

Chapter 9

I WAS NOT IN THE HABIT of keeping track of "firsts." At least, not in the romantic sense of the word. I understood that some people liked to commemorate the milestones of their relationships. I'd dated more than a few girls who suggested we celebrate a one-month anniversary or speculated about how meaningful a specific date or a place might be to us someday. But I never felt the need to collect memories, or glorify a certain day, when, honestly, I could never bring myself to visualize a future.

All that said, I will never forget my first kiss with Lee Lee Jones.

It was at the end of a party. The kind of crossover celebration that regularly happened between the Work to Ride folks and the horsey set who had farms and estates outside of Philly.

There had been a time, when I was younger, when these kinds of parties worried me. It wasn't anything the people who threw the parties did. They were almost all perfectly nice, perfectly welcoming. It was just how I felt about myself. I was sure they would find me too loud. Too wild. I didn't know what to do with my hands or when to say please or thank you. I was constantly concerned that I was letting Lezlie down with my table manners or how I chose to speak to adults. Even worse, I was convinced I was letting West Philly down. I knew what people thought about my neighborhood. I knew what they must assume about me, and so every time I stumbled over a question of etiquette, I could only imagine them judging not just me but also my mother, my family, my entire upbringing.

But now it was different. I had grown up. I had attended what felt like hundreds of these parties. I had learned to code-switch as naturally as taking off my jacket or putting on my riding boots. I knew what was expected of me. I could, almost instantly, put people at ease. I knew the patterns and the etiquette. I knew how to make small talk. How to gracefully put down a drink with one hand and pick up a canapé with the other.

I didn't feel like I was one of them, exactly. At least, not all of the time. But I no longer felt permanently outside the circle.

And now, I thought, as I watched Lee Lee move around the room, leaning in here, smiling there, lighting up people's faces as she passed by, *now, I was in love with one of them.*

I knew my chance to kiss Lee Lee wouldn't happen until the end of this party. I wasn't twelve years old anymore. I wasn't a little kid running around the farm. I knew I couldn't just pull her behind a stack of hay bales and expect people not to notice. I wanted to take her aside. I wanted to text her to meet me somewhere. But people never took their eyes off Lee Lee. They would notice if she and I walked out the door together; we would never hear the end of it.

So I also knew I would have to wait. But this party felt like it was happening in slow motion.

IF YOU HAD TOLD ME that there was such a thing as a mudroom when I was an eight-year-old on Viola Street, I would have looked at you like you were speaking Russian. *What the hell?* I might have said. *An entire room, just for mud?*

But now, of course, I knew what a mudroom was. I understood its purpose. I kind of even wanted one of my own, someday. And in this specific moment, I was very grateful for this particular mud-room's existence.

"Thank you, thank you! I had such a great time! I'll see you next week at the show!" I could hear Lee Lee making her goodbyes from the kitchen.

I had already made all my goodbyes. And now I lingered in the mudroom, taking my sweet time pulling on my jacket. Slowly but-toning every button even though it was a warm summer night.

"There you are." Lee Lee appeared on the threshold of the room. Her dark hair was backlit gold at the edges. I watched a flush creep over her cheeks as she met my eyes. "I thought you'd already left," she said.

I shook my head. "Nah, I wouldn't have left without saying goodbye."

"Good," she said. She took a step toward me. Then hesitated.

It had been a week since our first date in Philly. We hadn't seen each other again, but we'd been texting and calling multiple times a day. When we'd realized we'd been invited to the same party, I'd been delighted. I'd imagined we'd get to spend the whole evening together. But because we were still keeping whatever it was between us private, I'd barely spoken to her at all. I'd just watched her. And wished. And waited.

I closed the space between us. She put her hand on my arm. I put my hand on the curve of her waist. I couldn't tell you who leaned in first, whose lips outpaced the other's.

I can only tell you that what happened next was entirely new to me.

I always told girls that—just like I didn't like cuddling or PDA—I didn't like kissing. I mean, I understood it as a preliminary necessity. I knew it was an important point of initial contact. But I'd never felt like it was particularly essential or enjoyable. (And I fully realize that this reluctance says way more about me than it does the girls I kissed.) Before that first kiss with Lee Lee, if you had asked me what I thought about kissing, I would have shrugged and made a face and said something incredibly dumb like, "It's just something to get out of the way."

This kiss, though? This kiss was different.

Our lips met, our bodies touched, and I was taken somewhere completely unknown to me.

This kiss wasn't just sexual. Although I had been filled with a drumbeat of sexual attraction for Lee Lee from the moment we first met.

This kiss made me want more. It made me want to learn every single thing there was to know about this girl. But, at the same time, this kiss was not something that needed to lead to anything else.

This kiss was singular.

It was uncharted.

It was sacred.

And then, this kiss was over, as we heard people leaving the kitchen and heading our way.

We slipped apart, retreating toward opposite corners of the room. We walked out into the night, herded through the door by the small crowd of chattering guests pressing behind us. We couldn't touch again. We barely even had the chance to look at each other before we went our separate ways.

I drove home that night, replaying that moment over and over in my mind. It felt like a song that I would never stop humming. I realized that I would never forget that moment, this day, or the future anniversary of our kiss. I suddenly understood that you can never disregard what truly changes you.

MY BOSS BECAME ENAMORED with polo that summer, and because I was his intern, his schedule was my schedule. He practiced three afternoons a week, and it was my job to go with him. I didn't mind, of course. I was always happiest on a polo pony. And it certainly didn't hurt that the club where we played was right around the corner from Lee Lee's farm.

The more time Lee Lee and I spent around horses, the more I realized just how deep her equine knowledge actually ran. Unlike me, she had been born into a horse family. Her grandfather and father were polo players. Her mother was a jumper. And her stepfather was one of the preeminent eventers in the world. There had never been a time when world-class horses weren't as familiar to Lee Lee as the family dog might be to the rest of us.

Lee Lee came to our matches and seemed more than happy to watch me and my boss play. At first, I was flattered, but then I came to realize that her interest in watching me ride was not just about me. A serious horse person likes to watch. A pro rider knows that they can learn just as much watching another person ride as they could if they were in the saddle themselves. After I rode, Lee Lee always took the time to pick my brain, to ask me questions about the choices I'd made, the way I had handled certain moments. I realized that she wasn't just admiring my form. She was using me for her own improvement.

I HAD THIS SILLY LITTLE FANTASY we used to joke about. At the polo club, we'd always see the stick chicks grooming for their boyfriends. They'd set up the ponies between chukkas (that's polo vocabulary for periods of play). Get the horses brushed down and tacked up and then stand back as their man swung up on his pony and raced off.

I liked to imagine doing that for Lee Lee. I always told her that when I finally got to see her compete, I was going to be her groom. And she always shook her head and told me no way. That I didn't pay enough attention. She said that I'd put the horses' boots on wrong or screw up her tack. That I was too slow.

And I always laughed at her and thought she was joking.

I knew that Lee Lee was good on a horse. But I admit, in those early days, I used to wonder how in the hell she won so many blue ribbons. She was an eventer, which meant that she competed in dressage, jumping, and cross-country, often all in one day and all on the same horse. I would never admit this out loud, but eventing was more dangerous—and took even more skill—than polo. You had to be a brilliant athlete to master all those disciplines. And you had to have incredible stamina and strength to perform them all in one day.

Still, I just didn't see Lee Lee as having the killer instinct that the pro athletes I knew naturally seemed to have. Lee Lee was sweet and warm to just about everyone. She smiled all the time. She never used foul language. She was smart and funny and charming. She wasn't a pushover; she challenged me sometimes, she didn't let me get away with any bullshit, but it was always in a calm, kind of amused, way. I didn't doubt that she was brilliant and disciplined, but I'd never really seen the necessary bloodthirsty competitive side to her nature. I wondered if she really had what it took to be a pro.

"GET OUT OF MY WAY, KAREEM!" she growled as she slammed past me.

I stepped back, blinking my eyes in shock. We were at Plantation Field, a horse farm around the corner from her parents' place, and she was competing in an ODE (one-day event) where they crammed all three disciplines into a single day. She had just finished her dressage competition and had not done as well as she had hoped to.

I had made the cardinal mistake of reaching for her hand and trying to give her a consolation kiss after she got off her horse. She shook me off, shoved right by me, practically baring her teeth, and then turned around and whipped off her riding gloves and threw them in the dirt with a curdled little scream of rage.

"Whoa!" I held up my hands. "Hey, you didn't do that bad. I mean, at least you were way better than that one lady with the bright pink—"

"Don't. Joke." She was dead serious. "Not now. I don't have time for any of—" She waved her hand in a circle indicating *this*. "I need to get ready for the next event. I need to change. I need to tack up. I need to focus." She turned her back and started to walk away. Then she looked back at me, her chin held high, her eyes drilling into mine. "I need to *win*, Kareem. *I am going to win.*"

And I stood there, and I watched her march away, and I don't think I'd ever been so turned on in my entire damn life.

Like recognizes like. It turned out that my sweet, warm, cuddly Lee Lee was actually a super competitor. And I recognized that, because I was one, too. I knew exactly how she felt. I had jumped off my pony a hundred times with precisely that same look on my face, that hot feeling in my chest, raging at my failure, utterly determined to do better. I understood why she had thrown down her gloves. I was not insulted at all about her pushing me away. I got it. I absolutely accepted and deeply appreciated this version of her. Lee Lee was an athlete. Lee Lee was a champion.

LEE LEE AND I WERE DRIVING BACK to her family farm after a polo game.

Chester County is horse country. All rolling green hills, red barns, and white-fenced pasture upon pasture upon pasture. If you drive out there anytime between October and March, you stand a good chance of seeing a foxhunt. It looks like something out of a painting: The master of the hounds leading the charge, wearing his bright red coat and black velvet riding helmet, everyone else in their pinks and britches. All ripping down the country roads mounted on their field hunters, chasing after the baying dogs.

About forty-five minutes outside of Philly, we made the turn toward her house. We drove down the long driveway, lined with neat, even hedgerows, up the hill toward a medium-size, modern house that overlooked seventy acres of pristine pastures, multiple riding rings, a cross-country course, three barns, and at least two dozen grand prix–level horses.

"During the day," said Lee Lee as she made her way down the driveway, "there's pretty much just birdsong and the sound of the horses calling to each other. At night you have to drive with your high beams so you don't hit the deer—or sometimes even bears— that wander into the road." She pulled up in front of the house, put her car in park, and turned and smiled at me. "It gets so dark here. There's almost no light at all but the moon and the stars."

We got out of the car, and I stood there looking up at her house. Lee Lee hadn't been exaggerating. All I could hear around me was the sound of the wind in the trees, birds singing, and the distant sounds of horses. It was green and lush and private. Flawlessly peaceful.

I was a world away from Viola Street.

LEE LEE HAD INVITED ME OUT to spend the night at her house. Her parents were in Germany, she had said. "They'll never even know you were here."

This didn't exactly sit right with me. I knew that we still hadn't told anyone about our relationship—or even defined what was going on between us *as* a relationship—but I didn't like sneaking behind her parents' backs. I knew what I wanted from Lee Lee. I wanted her to be my girlfriend. I wanted to tell everybody that we were to-gether, to have her standing proudly at my side. I wanted to declare that I was in love with her. But I was afraid that it was too soon. I was afraid that if I was honest, if I blurted it all out, I would scare her away.

As we climbed the steps up to her front porch, I reminded my-self that even being a summer fling was no small thing when it came to a woman like Lee Lee.

Take whatever she's willing to offer, I told myself.

Lee Lee opened her front door, and we were greeted by what felt like a small flood of friendly dogs, followed by a nonchalant cat named Nala, who I would soon learn was Lee Lee's favorite animal in the world. I sank to my knees, scratching and patting, perfectly happy to be engulfed by all the fur and slobber. In my opinion, an-imals make a home, and I was glad that Lee Lee and her family seemed to feel the same way.

"Do you want a tour?" Lee Lee offered me a hand to pull me out of the dogpile.

"Absolutely."

We walked the house hand in hand. It was newly built and a bit more modest than some of the other houses I'd visited in the area, but it was comfortable and homey. I could tell that the family—kids and pets and all—really lived in every inch of it.

Lee Lee's bedroom was on the basement level, removed from the rest of the house. As she showed me around, I couldn't help but notice her bed and imagine how amazing it would be to spend an entire night with her in my arms.

"Wanna visit the stables?" Lee Lee asked me as we clomped back up the basement steps.

The horses were incredible. I'd been around ponies since I was little, but the horses at Work to Ride were donated and rescued, often old or ill-trained or quirky. I loved every one of those ponies, but it was quickly apparent to me that the horses on Lee Lee's family farm were entirely different creatures. These were grand prix–level thoroughbreds, at the height of their strength and health, groomed until they were shining. These horses, I understood, were one of the reasons why Lee Lee's family didn't live in a manor or mansion. This was a working farm. The priority was the horseflesh. And horses, especially incredible ones like these, were not cheap.

We walked back up the trail, toward the house. This was exactly what I imagined for myself someday. The horses. The barns. The fields. The warm and inviting house. This was the family farm I had been dreaming about since I was a little kid.

Lee Lee and I sat on her back porch, sipped a beer or two, and watched a spectacular sunset. The early evening air smelled like fresh-cut grass. The cicadas and crickets were singing. The horses were backlit by the sunset, grazing in the distance. Lee Lee stretched out her legs and bumped me affectionately with her foot. And for once, all the nervous energy and worry that tended to flutter around in my mind and my gut went still. I was surrounded by all this beauty and nature. I was with someone who I had come to realize was my absolute favorite person in the world. It was a nearly perfect moment, and I wished like hell I could hold on to it, suspended in time.

THE NEXT MORNING, I rolled over, reaching for Lee Lee, but my hands came up empty. Her side of the bed was cold.

I squinted at the clock and saw that it was past eight, which explained her absence. Barn chores started at 7:00 a.m. sharp. I had offered to help her the night before, but she had obviously slipped out early and left me to sleep in.

I walked up to the kitchen, stretching and yawning as I emerged into the warm morning light. There was a pot of hot coffee, and I helped myself to a cup and sat down at the kitchen table, enjoying the way the soft breeze came in through the open windows and thinking about the previous night.

Sex with Lee Lee was not like any sex I'd ever had before.

I mean, it was great. We obviously had an amazing amount of chemistry and attraction. And we were two young, healthy, willing adults. But sex with Lee Lee was part of a bigger whole. I wanted as much of her as she was willing to give me. I wanted her thoughts and her laughter and her teasing and her affection. I wanted to hear her childhood stories and future plans. And I wanted her body, too. Of course I wanted that. But the way I felt when our bodies met wasn't like the fleeting physical pleasure I had grown accustomed to with other girls. What was between us was so much more weighted and joyful. It was just another aspect of who she was, as important as her sense of humor, or taste in music, or the way she made me feel when her eyes caught mine across a room. Sex between us was incredible, and I wanted more of it. But I wanted more in the same way that I wanted to know her favorite flower, the worst nightmare she ever had, the last thing that had made her cry.

Whatever this woman wanted to offer me, I thought as I took another sip of my coffee, *I would happily take and hold on to forever.*

"Good morning!" said Lee Lee as she walked into the room. She was wearing jeans and a T-shirt that were smeared from mucking out stalls. She bent down and gave me a quick kiss, and I could smell the familiar and comforting scent of sweet hay and horse manure.

"We need to get going," she said. "My parents will be home from the airport in a few hours."

She started to move away, but I grasped her arm and pulled her back down into my lap for a longer, sweeter kiss.

"Good morning," I said back to her.

She smiled at me, kissed me again, and then wrapped her arms around my neck and laid her head against my shoulder.

We stayed that way for as long as we dared, holding on to each other, bathed in the warm morning light, pretending that we had all the time in the world.

Chapter 10

IT WAS NO SURPRISE that Gerb was the first person I told about Lee Lee.

Our family had always been tight. I had close relationships with all my siblings—and my mother, too, of course—but Gerb was more than just a brother to me.

Gerb and I went through it all together. We were only two years apart, and when we were small we were each other's de facto buddy and playmate. Although Kareema was my twin, she made it pretty clear early on that she wanted nothing to do with boy stuff. She and her girlfriends thought Gerb and I were generally stupid and smelly. Way beneath their notice. Washika was a baby. And David and Bee had their own thing going on, a lot of which involved shaking me and Gerb off so they could run the streets.

So that left just me and Gerb. And honestly, most of the time that was more than all right.

Growing up, Gerb and I had a lot of friends in common on Viola Street. We also rode together at the barn. But it was in military school where we truly closed the circle and became a team of two. Gerb arrived at Valley Forge when he was in the eighth grade and I was a sophomore. I had already been through all the hazing and the plebe system, so I knew what horrors were coming for him, and I did my best to both prepare and protect him. I taught him how to finesse the system. How to yield when necessary. Who he had to respect, and who he could ignore.

We went on to play on the Work to Ride polo team together. To be the first all-Black team to win the Open National Interscholastic Polo Championship. And that led to summers training and riding in Connecticut and the Hamptons. We were often the only Black people around for miles, so we stuck together. We protected each other. We had our own little inside jokes; the kind of bond where you can just look at each other and know what the other person is thinking, and then suddenly you're both laughing so hard that you're crying.

Sometimes Gerb felt like my little brother. Sometimes he felt like a peer. And sometimes, because he really didn't have anyone else he could trust or turn to, I felt like I had to be a father figure to him. Our own dad was long gone, and our mother was using for most of our childhood, so we necessarily formed something stronger and bigger between us than the average brothers might. We turned to each other for both understanding and survival.

I had Gerb over to my apartment a couple of days after I spent the night at Lee Lee's house. We were sitting on the couch, watching an old recording of the Heguy brothers tear up the polo field.

I kept opening my mouth to tell him about Lee Lee but then closing it again. I wasn't sure what I wanted to say. I couldn't say she was my girlfriend. We weren't like that yet. But I couldn't say we were just talking, either. She was more to me. And I hoped I was more to her, too.

Finally, I stood up. "You want a snack? Some chips or something?"

Gerb shrugged, never taking his eyes off the TV. "Sure."

I walked into the kitchen, which was only a few steps from the living room. I opened a bag of chips.

"So," I said as I walked back over. "You know Lee Lee Jones?"

Gerb turned his head and looked at me. "That girl at the barn?"

I dropped the bag on the coffee table. Sat back down. Helped myself.

"You hittin' that or something?" said Gerb.

He reached for the bag, but I snatched it back.

"Hey," I said. "Don't talk about her that way."

Gerb stared at me like I'd sprouted an extra head. "Um. Why the hell not? You crushing on her?"

I put the bag down, embarrassed. "We been seeing each other."

Gerb's eyebrows shot so high they practically disappeared into his hairline. "What do you mean, 'seeing each other'? Like, you been talking?"

I shrugged. "More than that."

"Like, she's your girlfriend?"

I shrugged again. "Not quite that, either. We been on some dates. We been hanging out a lot."

Gerb smirked at me. "And you like her. Like, you really like her."

I looked away from him. "Maybe I do."

Gerb smacked his hand on my shoulder. "Hey, man, I get it. I seen her. She's fine as hell."

"She is," I agreed. "But she's cool, too. And smart. And funny."

Gerb shook his head, smiling. "Who are you? What'd you do with my brother Reem? 'Cause I know that my boy would never be talking about no girl like this."

I stood up, shaking my head. "Okay. All right. Never mind."

Gerb grabbed my arm. "No, man, seriously. I never heard you talk about any girl this way before. This serious?"

I sat back down on the couch. "Yeah," I said. "Yeah. I think it is. Or, at least, I want it to be."

"Wow," said Gerb. "No shit?"

"No shit," I replied.

Gerb said, "You tell all those girls back in Colorado? You let them know you're off the market?"

I shook my head. "Naw. I mean, I just haven't been talking with them this summer. I stopped talking to anybody after I met Lee Lee."

"And what about that? She's at school in Delaware, right? What are you guys gonna do when you go back to Colorado?"

I shook my head again. "I don't know. We haven't got that far yet. I haven't even told her that I'm catching feelings." I took a chip from the bag. Crunched down. "But I think I'm going to. I think I have to."

We were quiet for a moment. Gerb crossed his arms over his chest and leaned back, staring off into the distance. I did the same.

Then he looked at me. "Wait a minute. You actually gonna bring her home?"

I nodded slowly. "Yeah," I said. "I think I'm gonna bring her home."

I'D NEVER BROUGHT A GIRL to the Bottom before. Of course I'd been with some girls from the neighborhood who knew my family and had been in and out of my house. But that was different. Casual. We'd just been hanging out. And I'd been with some girls from the horse world who *wanted* me to bring them home, but I never wanted to take it that far.

Taking Lee Lee home to the Bottom was a big leap of faith. But every little thing I learned about Lee Lee only made me fall harder. She was smart. She was driven. She was kind. She had grown up wealthy, but she wanted to give back. She loved hip-hop and Black literature and art, but not in a culture-vulture kind of way. She was just endlessly open and curious. She wanted to know all about where

I grew up, she asked me question after question about my family and what it was like being raised in West Philly. And it never felt intrusive or exoticizing.

It just felt like she wanted to know *me*.

"NERVOUS?" I said to Lee Lee as we pulled up to the curb just down the block from my mother's place. My mother was having a barbecue, and I could hear music and laughter trickling in our direction.

"Well, I mean, I wasn't." Lee Lee laughed. "Should I be?"

"Naw." I grabbed her hand and smiled at her. "Come on. They're gonna love you."

"Okay. Good. Let's go, then." She started to pull her hand away from mine.

I clung to her for a moment. Not quite ready to get out of the car. She met my eyes again and smiled. "What?"

"Nothing," I finally said. I gave her a quick kiss and let her hand go. "Okay, c'mon, let's go."

The thing was, I was absolutely positive my family would love Lee Lee. She was so beautiful. Inside and out. Why wouldn't they love her?

But what I didn't know was what she would think of *me* after she met *them*.

It was one thing to know me from the polo field, or as the guy who was interning as a financial analyst and subletting a nice apartment in downtown Philly. It was another thing to meet the guy with five brothers and sisters, most of whom had been in and out of prison. To see the tiny, run-down house on Viola Street where we'd all grown up. To get to know my mom, who worked so hard to raise us but also struggled with addiction and depression. I was deeply protective of my family, and of my background, and one of my biggest insecurities was the idea that I might open up that part of myself and be judged. Judged as a thug or a criminal, judged as less than, or just not good enough. I'd spent so many years being seen as a novelty act on the polo circuit—the one Black guy in the room—that I was used to being written off for where I was from. In fact, I pretty much expected it.

Lee Lee and I had talked about my family. I had told her about Viola Street. And I'd been open and honest. I'd told her more than I'd ever told any girl. We had talked about race. And class. We had talked about generational poverty and inherited trauma. Lee Lee had good politics and social instincts. She had read widely and thought deeply. I trusted all those things about her.

But it was one thing to have a conversation about the racist nature of the penal system in a sidewalk café on Rittenhouse Square; it was something altogether different for her to meet my cousin who had just got out of prison after serving a four-year sentence for dealing.

I knew that Lee Lee would be nothing but polite and respectful of my mother, but what if my mother wasn't sober? I knew Lee Lee would compliment my mother's home, but how could she see it as anything but a dump compared to the place she lived in? I wondered if, once she saw where I was really from—what I was truly made of—I would be too much.

Or maybe not enough.

Lee Lee turned to look at me with a big smile on her face. She was a few steps ahead, wearing a red tank top and jeans and sneakers, her hair pulled back into a long braid that snaked down over one shoulder. She did a little shimmy, dancing to the beat from my mother's house.

"C'mon!" she said, waving me toward her.

I took a deep breath. I hoped we'd be okay.

IT TOOK HER ABOUT TEN MINUTES before Lee Lee was laughing with my mother, accepting a plate of chicken and potato salad and sitting on the front stoop.

And then she was playing curb ball with the neighborhood kids.

Then she was hanging out with my cousins, sitting on the hood of a car in front of my mother's house while my cousins drank forties and smoked weed and cracked jokes. They were all bullshitting her. Competing to see who could tell her the wildest story. They were cussing and yelling and throwing insults.

And she just sat there and joined right in. She wasn't intimidated in the least. She gave as good as she got. She made them laugh.

"That girl blends right in with this family," said my mother as we stood together on the porch.

I looked at my mom, still a little nervous. "You think so?"

My mother watched Lee Lee as she fell back against the hood of the car, laughing so hard there were tears in her eyes. "Oh, I know so," my mother said.

I looked over at Lee Lee. She caught my eyes and grinned, waving at me. Then she turned away, smiling at Gerb, who had just walked up to join them. He smiled back at her and flashed me a quick thumbs-up.

The people in my neighborhood knew how to guard themselves. They knew when someone was bullshitting them. They knew when they were being patronized or pitied. And I could tell, just by watching them, that they knew that was not what Lee Lee was about. You would have thought she had grown up down the block, she fit in so quick.

My people fell for that girl just as fast and hard as I did.

SHE STAYED OVER AT MY PLACE that night. We lay in bed together on our backs, side by side, our arms and legs pressed together. Breathing in the dark.

"I loved your family," she said softly.

I turned toward her. "You did?"

She turned toward me so we were nose to nose. "I loved everything about today."

I love you, I almost said.

Instead, I smoothed back her hair and gave her a soft kiss. "They loved you, too," I said.

DESPITE THE OBVIOUS JOY we took in each other's company, I spent a lot of time in those early days wondering if Lee Lee's feelings for me were as strong as mine were for her. I'd never felt about anyone the way I felt about Lee Lee. I'd had a habit of dating women for short amounts of time and then inevitably finding a small fault in them that I would eventually convince myself I couldn't possibly endure. I always ended things before they got too serious. It was a pattern, I knew that, even then. And looking back now, I can see that after a lifetime of losing people to gun violence, and prison, and addiction, and always wondering not if, but *when*, someone else I loved might be taken from me, I might have had some attachment issues. I might have been a bit shy about allowing myself to need anyone too much. That it was always easier to leave before I was left.

But somehow, Lee Lee seemed to bypass all that bullshit. I'm sure I probably tried looking, but I couldn't seem to find that fatal flaw. This woman only became more beloved in my eyes with every day and night that we passed together.

If I had been a little older and a lot more confident, I wouldn't have wasted a moment playing it cool. If I'd known what the heck I was doing, I would have just asked her how she felt instead of sitting around worrying about whether I was a summer fling. And if I'd been paying more attention, I would have seen that Lee Lee's feelings were just as strong as mine. She was wondering the same things about how I saw her and what our possible future could be together.

SHE LEFT AT DAWN THE NEXT MORNING. Slipped out of bed and showered and got dressed. She had promised her parents she'd be back at the farm early to help with chores.

"Don't get up," she whispered. "Sleep some more." She kissed me goodbye. Her wet hair smelled like my shampoo. It was cool against my cheek.

I heard the front door shut behind her. I lay there for a moment thinking about the day before. How we had stolen away from the party at one point and gone to the papi store to buy Cokes, and everyone in the store had looked at us, and I had slipped my arm around her waist because I was so fucking proud of her and I needed everyone to see my pride.

I finally got out of bed and took a shower and got dressed for work. I drank a cup of coffee. Ate a bowl of cereal. Picked up my keys to leave, and then my phone chimed.

Made it home safe! she texted. *Yesterday was amazing. Thank you again.*

I love you, I wrote back.

And then, before I could change my mind, I sent the text.

The reply was almost instant.

Oh! I'm shaking right now. In a good way! I'm so happy you finally said it. I've been wanting to say it for so long.

I held my breath for a moment, waiting. And then:

I love you, too!

I WAS BACK ON THE ROAD to Lee Lee's house again. This time alone. It was Evie's—Lee Lee's mom—fiftieth birthday party, and I had been invited to meet pretty much the entire family all at once.

I'd borrowed a car from Lezlie. Dressed up in Hamptons casual clothes: red slacks and a blue button-down shirt. I was pretty sure I knew what kind of party this would be, and as I turned down the driveway and saw the two huge white party tents shimmering in the field next to their barn, heard the sound of live music being played, watched as thin, tan, mostly blond or blondish women in sundresses and straw hats mingled with men in summer-weight linen, I practically nodded to myself in confirmation of what I had been envisioning.

I parked my car in the field, and before I could even open my door, Lee Lee was running up to me. "Kareem!" she yelled.

I smiled to see her so excited. She had been texting and calling me all week, talking me through this first meeting.

"Don't worry," she told me. "They trust me. They trust my judgment. And since I love you, they're going to love you, too."

I got out of the car, and she ran into my arms and kissed me. "Hi! Hi! I'm so glad you're here! Are you nervous? You don't need to be nervous! Everyone's been drinking already!"

I laughed. "Including you?"

She raised her eyebrows in fake innocence. "Maybe a little bit?"

I shook my head and kissed her again. "Okay," I said. "Let's do this."

Lee Lee made a little squeaky sound of happiness. "Come meet my mom," she said, pulling me toward one of the tents.

Even close up, the party was as I had imagined: An overflowing buffet and passed canapés. A full bar and drinks in almost everyone's hands. White-shirted catering and waitstaff. Strings of lights. A dance floor. A band playing covers of 1980s hits. People drinking and laughing and dancing, but nobody too loud or too exuberant or too out of control.

But this party hit different, too. Because even though I knew a lot of the people who were there—years of horse shows and polo games had familiarized me with the community—I also knew that among all these semi-familiar faces were people I didn't know yet—people who meant something special to Lee Lee and therefore were going to mean something special to me.

Lee Lee guided me through the tent toward a knot of people standing by the bar.

"Mom! Mom!" Lee Lee said as the crowd parted. A pretty blond woman in a white dress looked over at me, smiling, and I couldn't help but laugh.

Evie looked at me for a moment, her brows knit, and then started laughing along with me. "Oh!" she said. "Oh, it's *you*!"

IT WAS TWO YEARS EARLIER and I was leaving a horse show outside of Philly. I had stayed late, helping Lezlie load up some of our ponies, and was one of the last people to drive out. It was an autumn evening. No sunset to speak of. Just slowly getting dark and then darker. Raining and muddy and cold. I turned a corner on the long gravel driveway leading out of the farm, and there was a truck and a trailer, jackknifed just off the side of the road, with a blond woman in riding gear standing next to it, getting soaked, looking like she could kick something she was so mad.

I rolled down my window. "Hey," I said. "Do you need help?"

She looked over at me, sighed, and then laughed. "Yes," she said. "I definitely could use some help."

I parked my car and got out. Close up, I could see that the woman was older than I'd thought, but she was still very pretty. She smiled at me and stuck out her hand. "I'm Evie." Then she looked ruefully back at her trailer. "And I seem to be stuck."

BACK AT THE PARTY, Lee Lee ping-ponged her head back and forth as Evie and I laughed. "What?" she kept saying. "What's so funny?"

I turned and explained the story to Lee Lee. Her mother and I had spent a good hour in the mud and rain getting that trailer unstuck.

"But that's amazing!" said Lee Lee. "That's crazy! Mom! I've told you all about Kareem! How could you forget you actually knew him?"

"I *know*!" said Evie. She opened her arms and hugged me. "Well, of *course* you're Lee Lee's boyfriend! It all makes so much sense now!"

I hugged her back, feeling my chest swell at the words *Lee Lee's boyfriend*. It was the first time anyone had ever referred to me that way.

Evie let go and stepped back, beaming at me and Lee Lee. "I'm turning frigging fifty today," she announced. "Let's do some shots!"

AFTER I MET Evie (or rather, met her *again*), I met Lee Lee's step-dad, Phillip. He shook my hand and then clapped me on the back. "How ya doin', mate?" he said in his broad Australian accent.

I have to admit I was a little bit starstruck. I'd met a lot of famous horse people at this point, but watching Lee Lee ride at eventing shows had given me new respect for the discipline. Lee Lee and I spent a lot of time joking around about which was harder, polo or eventing, and even though I was staunch in defending my sport, deep down, I knew that no other version of riding was as challenging as eventing. And Phillip was widely acknowledged as being one of the best eventers in the world. Which, I had recently realized, made him one of the best *riders* in the world.

After Phillip stopped shaking my hand, I steeled myself for the inevitable questions about my background and family. The usual curiosity, sometimes bordering on rudeness, about just who I was and where I came from. After all, I could hardly blame him; not only was I an outlier in the community, I was also dating his stepdaughter. But Phillip surprised me. He didn't ask me a bunch of questions. He just welcomed me to the party. Told me he was glad I was there. That he hoped that Lee Lee and I would have a grand time together.

Lee Lee's twelve-year-old sisters, Mary and Olivia, came over then, smiling shyly.

"Guys, this is Kareem!" said Lee Lee. "Remember I told you about him?"

Lee Lee's little sisters were twins, but they were very different from each other. And not just physically. Olivia, Lee Lee had explained to me, lived for horses just like Lee Lee and her parents. But Mary thought horses were an absolute waste of her time.

I stuck out my hand, sensing that these quiet young girls wouldn't respond well to the usual rambunctious teasing I employed with my own younger siblings and most of the kids at the barn.

"Nice to meet you, ladies," I said.

The girls shook my hand with dignity. Serious and polite.

"You guys want to dance?" asked Lee Lee.

They shook their heads.

"Well, we're gonna dance!" I said, grabbing Lee Lee's hand.

"Ooooh," the twins said in unison as I led a laughing Lee Lee to the dance floor.

LATER THAT NIGHT, Lee Lee led me back to her room. We were more than a little drunk. Definitely very clumsy, as Lee Lee giggled and groped for the light switch, and I stumbled into the foot of her bed and smacked my knee.

"Ow, ow, ow!" I laughed, falling over onto her bed.

Lee Lee gave up trying to turn on the light and dropped down beside me.

"The room is spilling," she said. "I mean, spending. I mean spinning."

"Yeah," I said. "All those things."

She turned toward me and lay her head on my chest. "What did you like best about tonight so far?"

I thought for a moment. "Meeting your family. And the way they obviously all loved me."

She laughed, smacking my shoulder with her hand. "Big head much?"

"Okay, okay," I said, fending her off.

She snuggled back into me. "But yeah. They did love you. I knew they would."

"Actually," I said. "I thought of something I liked even better. I liked it when your mom called me your boyfriend. And how everyone you introduced me to already seemed to know me, so I could tell that maybe you had been talking about me a little bit."

Lee Lee's face was pressed against my chest, but I could feel her smile. "I definitely have," she said. "More than a little bit. How could I not talk about my boyfriend?"

I kissed the top of her head. "I talk about my girlfriend, too."

"Oh yeah?" she said. "Who's your girlfriend?"

"Oh, you know, just some girl I met in Colorado . . ."

She smacked me again. "Reem!"

I laughed. "No, no, it's you. It's Miss Lee Lee Jones." I pulled her tighter. "Of course it's you."

She sighed. "I'm so happy," she said. "I didn't know I could be this happy."

I stroked her hair. "I love you," I said. And I thought to myself, *I will never get tired of saying that.*

"I love you, too," she said.

And I will never get tired of hearing that.

She yawned. She snuggled even closer. I closed my eyes, and we drifted off to sleep in each other's arms.

I WOKE UP THE NEXT MORNING in a little bit of a panic. Lee Lee and I were tangled up on the bed together, still fully clothed. My head was pounding, and my mouth was so dry my tongue felt like sandpaper. And the light slanting in through the window was not morning light. It was late. Like nearly noon late.

I sat up and grabbed my head. "Shit," I groaned.

Lee Lee opened her eyes. Even hungover, with her mascara half-way down her face, she looked amazing to me. "Good morning to you, too?" she asked.

"Sorry," I said. "We fell asleep, and I just don't know if I'm supposed to be here or not. Is this going to be weird with your family? Should I sneak out the back or something?"

She sat up. "What? No," she scoffed. "They knew you were going to stay the night."

"I mean, I knew I was staying over, but I thought they might want me in the guest room or whatever."

She shook her head. "Kareem. I'm twenty years old. You are my boyfriend. I love you. And they know all that. There is no way you were sleeping in the frigging guest room. Now"—she kissed the top of my head—"let's go upstairs and get some breakfast."

Even with all of Lee Lee's assurances, I was still nervous. I imagined them all sitting there, waiting for us, the looks on their faces when they realized we had been together all night long.

Lee Lee opened the door at the top of the stairs, and I was hit with the delicious smell of coffee and maple syrup. The afternoon light streaming through the kitchen windows was dazzling.

"Hi, Kareem!" Mary and Olivia looked up from the table and smiled at me. I'd thought they looked more like Phillip than their mother, but when they smiled, I could see both Evie and Lee Lee in them.

"Hey, girls," I said. "Good morning!"

"Well, it's not really morning," said Evie.

I froze and then looked over to see Lee Lee's mom standing in front of the stove.

She met my eyes and smiled. Then she poured two mugs of

coffee and walked over to hand them to me and Lee Lee. "Take a seat," she said, gesturing to the kitchen table. "I'm making pancakes."

I settled down at the table with a relieved sigh. Phillip wandered in a moment later and winked at me and Lee Lee before silently taking a cup of coffee and practically burying his face in it.

These people were not my family. This was not my culture. But I loved their daughter. And that seemed to be enough for them. As we sat and ate breakfast together in that warm and sunny kitchen, I looked around the table at Lee Lee and her family, and I thought that this place already felt a little like home.

Chapter 11

AUTUMN IN COLORADO was like nothing else. Maybe it was the elevation, or the clean mountain air, but all those fall colors—the blue, blue sky, and the almost psychedelic sweep of yellow and orange and red leaves—practically hurt my eyes with their beauty.

But after leaving Lee Lee back on the East Coast, autumn in Colorado was just not hitting me the same way it had the year before. Saying goodbye had been excruciating. Lee Lee and I'd spent that last week together hoarding time. Of course I still had to work and pack and say goodbye to my friends and family, but I did those things with an efficiency I didn't even know I was capable of. Because any moment that I wasn't with Lee Lee felt like it was time wasted.

The looming fact of our imminent separation colored everything. We couldn't seem to help ourselves; even if we were in the same place, we didn't want to be in different rooms. And if we were in the same room, we needed to be close enough to touch. We were banking time and physical contact and conversation. We were so greedy for each other that even sleep felt unnecessary.

The miracle of Lee Lee being there—in my arms, in my bed, in my life—suddenly felt extraordinarily fragile and temporary.

So we made plans against our separation. We made promises. We wouldn't let more than six weeks pass without seeing each other. We would take turns flying out. We would talk and FaceTime and text every single day. Lee Lee promised that I would be the last person she spoke to every night. I vowed that she would be the first thing I thought of every morning. We were determined to make long distance work.

Still, I dreaded leaving her. I loved everything about having a girlfriend. I loved walking down the street arm in arm. I loved cuddling up to her every night in bed. I loved seeing her first thing in the morning. I loved our private jokes and the way she noticed if I was having a bad day just from the look on my face. I loved how I could tell if she was tired or hungry or needed an iced coffee. I loved how Lee Lee really knew me. I loved how I could let down my guard, take off all the different masks I had to wear, and just be the real me with her.

And I worried that with seventeen hundred miles between us, we could lose everything.

WHEN I TOUCHED DOWN in Colorado, I kept repeating one thing to myself: *Four weeks. Four weeks. Four weeks.* Lee Lee was flying out in October for a long weekend, and I would see her then. And that helped a little bit, knowing that there was an end in sight. It gave me something to look forward to.

In the meantime, I told my friends and polo teammates all about her. Showing them pictures of her on my phone.

"Wait a minute, Kareem, you said this is your *girlfriend? You* have a *girlfriend?*"

I suppose I deserved their disbelief, since I had always sworn up and down that I didn't want anything serious. That I wasn't interested in anything but casual.

But I was proud of Lee Lee. I wanted to show her off. I shoved my phone back in their faces.

"Yes, bro, this is my *girlfriend*."

And they whistled and made impressed faces and then laughed at me, telling me I must be whipped.

But I didn't care. Because I wanted everyone to know that Lee Lee was mine. And that I was Lee Lee's.

BEFORE LEE LEE, I had spent time with a few different girls at school. Nothing serious, but there was a girl named Lizzie who had been a little more. Lizzie and I had talked on and off during my first year at CSU. She was sweet and funny and very pretty. A nice person. I knew she wanted more from me than I was willing to give. I knew that every time we slept together, she hoped it would change from something that was casual into something permanent. Sometimes she'd talk about her desire to have a boyfriend. To have a partner. To have something serious in her life. And I wasn't stupid. I knew what she was getting at, but I pretended I didn't. I hated to disappoint people. I never wanted to hurt anyone's feelings. I didn't like conflict. But I also knew I didn't want to be with her that way. So I would change the subject and just hope that she'd get the hint.

We're friends with benefits, I'd tell myself whenever I'd start to feel guilty. *I never promised her anything else. She understands that.*

Still, even though I told almost everyone else about Lee Lee, I didn't tell Lizzie. I didn't want to see that flash of pain in her eyes.

Instead, I avoided her, hoping she'd get the unsaid message and understand.

WHEN MY WEEKEND WITH LEE LEE in October finally arrived, I was so excited, I could barely stand still. It had been an interminable four weeks; every day that Lee Lee and I had counted down together felt like forever.

I double-cleaned my room at the apartment I shared with my roommates. I bought new sheets. I asked to borrow my roommate's Jeep, and I thought long and hard about what I'd wear when I picked her up from the airport. After all the time away, it felt like a reset, and I wanted everything to start from perfect.

THERE IS A MOMENT that is unique to long-distance relationships. That moment when, after days or weeks or even months of longing, you have your beloved in your arms once again. It's an unbelievable rush. It's the sweetest thrill. It's always a new beginning. It's your body and soul rejoicing in the physical return of something that felt like it had been lost to you.

Lee Lee walked off the plane and into my arms, and I could feel her whole body shaking with the excitement and pleasure of being reunited with mine.

We practically ran out of the airport together, our arms entwined, big, goofy smiles on our faces, feeling like we were complete once again.

It was raining as we drove up I-25. We were talking and laughing. Lee Lee was sitting as close to me as possible, touching my arm, my wrist, my shoulder. I pointed at the mountains and the trees all bright with fall colors, peeking out behind the mist and gray clouds.

Lee Lee sighed happily. She grabbed my hand and brought it to her mouth for a kiss. "I've missed you so much," she said.

I squeezed her hand in mine. "Me, too."

I'D ALWAYS TOLD THE GIRLS I was seeing that no way was I down for any PDA. I had my reasons for this. I wasn't raised in that kind of family. My mom showed us love by working her ass off to keep us fed and clothed and a roof over our heads, but she almost never gave us kisses or hugs. I knew she loved me, but I would have probably dropped dead in shock if she actually said it out loud. My siblings and I weren't physically affectionate, either. We wrestled and pushed at each other, we teased and gave each other shit. We only curled up close at night when the heat had been shut off and we might freeze to death otherwise, but that was about the only physical contact we had. The older I got, the more I had decided that kind of affection was weak and silly. Especially for a man. So when a girl tried to get too clingy with me like that, I'd shake her off. Tell her that it wasn't me.

But Lee Lee blew right past that pretty much right away. And that night—and actually, the whole visit—she couldn't keep her hands off me, and I don't just mean that in a sexual sense. She smacked my butt as we walked to the bathroom on the way to brush our teeth. She draped her legs over mine as we sat on the bed. She squeezed my arm to make a point. Rubbed my back. Pressed her shoulder to mine. She pulled my head down into her lap and scratched my scalp, her nails lightly combing through my hair, and I closed my eyes, thinking of being a kid again with Ashley, feeling that sensation for the first time.

I was absolutely helpless when it came to all the little ways Lee Lee showed me she loved me. And the way she made me want to turn around and do the same for her. Suddenly I was the one hooking my arm in hers as we walked out the door. Suddenly I was playing with her hair, tracing the curve of her neck—not even aware I was doing it—as we sat around talking to my friends. I was the one standing there with my arm around her waist as we waited for a table at a restaurant, pulling her close, closer, close as I could get.

It was a revelation, everything that I'd been wanting. I hadn't even realized how much I'd missed it until I had it back again. I couldn't get enough.

I CAME HOME TO PHILLY for Thanksgiving. Usually my family and I spent the holiday with Lezlie, but that year I found myself up early in the morning at the Kimberton Hunt Club for the Blessing of the Hounds and to watch the annual foxhunt that followed it—an event that Lee Lee assured me her family never once missed. I felt like I was in the middle of an old oil painting. Everyone was dressed up to the nines. Some men were even wearing top hats and tails. It was a cold, snowy day, and Lee Lee and I stood together, watched the baying hounds race off into the woods followed by the riders in their red hunting jackets, atop their galloping horses (the fox was never harmed).

Later that night, I sat surrounded by Lee Lee's family at their long, laden dining room table, and we laughed and drank red wine and ate our holiday meal and I wondered if this was what Thanksgiving would be for me from now on: the hunt club, the snowy farm, and Lee Lee Jones always at my side.

AFTER THANKSGIVING, Lee Lee and I managed the next six weeks of our separation by obsessively planning our winter break together. Every night, I'd call Lee Lee just before she went to bed (she was two hours ahead of me, so she always fell asleep first) and after declaring how much we missed and loved each other, and telling each other about the minutiae of our days, we'd talk about Christmas and New

Year's and what the time surrounding those holidays would be like for us.

Though Lee Lee invited me to her home for Christmas Eve, I knew I couldn't miss Christmas with my family. And I couldn't quite see Lee Lee holed up in my mother's two-bedroom house with all my siblings, waiting for the clock to hit that minute after midnight.

"I'll come for Christmas dinner," promised Lee Lee. "After all, you spent Thanksgiving with my family."

I knew that her family's Christmas dinner would probably be more lavish than my family's, but I was glad that she didn't automatically assume that the holidays would always be with her folks.

"And after Christmas I want you to be my date for the debutante ball in Wilmington. So you'll need a tux."

The what?

I almost said it out loud, but I didn't want to sound ignorant, so after we said our good nights and put down our phones, I googled. And the next night, I had more questions.

"So, uh, are you actually, what do they call it, 'coming out' at this thing?"

Lee Lee laughed. "No, no. I was already presented."

"So you're a debutante."

She laughed again. "Not anymore. That's all over. This is the fun part. We watch all the new girls come out, and then it's just drinking and dancing all night long. It's like a big, fancy party."

"Right," I said slowly.

I'd been to plenty of high-society functions, but a debutante ball was something I'd never even heard of. I already suspected that I'd be the only Black person in the ballroom. And despite all my internet research, I thought that there was a very high chance I'd make a total fool of myself.

Lee Lee must have picked up on my hesitation because her voice dropped low and sweet. "Don't worry, Reem," she said. "You in a tuxedo? You're going to be the sexiest thing at the ball."

MY FAMILY AND I GOT CALLS from David and Bee, who were both in prison, on Christmas morning. It felt wrong to be standing in front of our tree, looking at the opened stack of presents, without my older brothers. My mom got choked up talking to them, and Gerb, Kareema, Washika, and I did our best to cover up her sadness by making jokes and teasing and trying to chatter even louder than her tears. We knew it didn't make our brothers feel any better to hear our mother missing them so much.

Lee Lee joined us for Christmas dinner, which we'd started having at Lezlie's sister's house after my grandmother had passed. We all ate and drank and laughed, just like we had at Lee Lee's house on Thanksgiving. But it was different with us because there were empty places at our table. I watched Lee Lee smiling and laughing, and I was glad that she was there, but I wondered if she regretted not being with her own family. I wondered if she noticed the slight feeling of melancholy that hung over the holiday for us now, thinking about the people who should have been there with us, thinking about the way Christmas used to be, and knowing that our family would never be quite the same again.

Later that night, after we exchanged presents, Lee Lee and I lay in Lezlie's guest room together, spooning in the narrow bed.

"It's crazy that Lezlie let you stay the night," I said into the nape of Lee Lee's neck. "All those years she spent trying to keep me and the barn rats apart—and here we are with her blessing."

Lee Lee laughed softly. "I guess this means you're all grown up."

I smiled. "Or that Lez just really likes you."

Lee Lee laughed again, and I wrapped my arms even tighter around her.

"Our first Christmas together," she murmured.

I kissed the top of her head. "Merry Christmas, Lee Lee Jones."

She scooted back until there wasn't any space between us at all. "Merry Christmas, Reem."

WE GOT READY FOR THE DEB BALL together in our hotel room. Pregaming with a bottle of champagne that Lee Lee had brought in her suitcase.

It was the first time I'd ever worn a tuxedo, and Lee Lee had to help me tie my bow tie. She was ridiculously beautiful in a floor-length, curve-hugging silver sequined dress that covered her all up in front, but draped in a deep cowl down her back, exposing a long swath of her perfect skin.

"There," she said, straightening my tie and then running her hands down my lapels. "You look so good."

I smiled, shaking my head. "Nobody is gonna be looking at me, girl."

She met my eyes and tipped her chin up toward me.

I laughed. "Don't tempt me. I'll mess up your lipstick," I warned her.

One side of her mouth quirked up. "So mess up my lipstick. I've got more."

So I kissed her, loving her scent and warmth. I ran my hands down the bare flesh on her back as we came up for air. "I approve of this dress," I said.

She grinned at me. "How's my lipstick?"

"You still have some on. I guess I should do a better job."

She laughed as I bent my head to kiss her again, but we were interrupted by a knock on the door.

"Lee Leeeee!" the voice of her friend came through loud enough to sound like she was already in the room with us. "I know you have champagne! Let us in!"

THE PRESENTATION ITSELF was a mystery to me. It honestly felt like rich, white nonsense. And there were more than a few moments as I was sitting there with Lee Lee, politely clapping as my champagne buzz wore off, when I wished I was just about anywhere but there. But after the last girl in the last white dress made her last bow, Lee Lee grabbed my hand, and she and her friends jumped up out of their seats, and started racing as one toward the back of the ballroom.

"Open bar!" said Lee Lee, dragging me along with her.

I ROLLED OVER THE NEXT MORNING and looked at the naked back of the woman I loved, and I felt the way my legs ached from dancing for five hours straight, and even though my head was pounding and my mouth was bone-dry because *open bar*, I thought, *Perhaps there is some joy to be found in rich, white nonsense after all.*

WE SPENT NEW YEAR'S EVE in Wellington, Florida. My boss, Joe, was putting together his first string of ponies, and since Wellington was the center of horse culture in the United States, and I had worked a few summers there, he had hired me to come down to guide him through the process. He'd rented a big house right on the beach, and since he was bringing his wife and daughter, he told me that I should bring along Lee Lee as well.

Lee Lee was delighted to come. She was even more familiar with Wellington than I was. She had been going there since she was a little girl, and she and her family often spent their entire winter break in the area.

I was technically working, though going to horse shows and trying out polo ponies and laying out on the beach every day while staying in a beautiful house with my beautiful girlfriend sure as hell didn't feel like work. It felt like a vacation. The first real vacation that Lee Lee and I had ever experienced together.

On New Year's Eve, Lee Lee and I left the party we'd been invited to so we could be alone on the beach. We took off our shoes and waded into the surf up to our knees, and turned on our phones, and counted down to midnight, and then kissed as the waves crashed around us and fireworks exploded above our heads.

As 2015 began, I was in the arms of the most beautiful girl I had ever seen, and I thought, *This is my future.*

I thought that Lee Lee and I would have a horse farm in Pennsylvania, and a winter home in Wellington. Maybe even an apartment in Philly, too. I thought that we would have a bunch of gorgeous children who would be as easy at the Blessing of the Hounds as they would be at my mother's backyard barbecue. I thought that we would have Christmas with my family. And Thanksgivings with Lee Lee's. I thought that I would go to so many debutante balls that they would become second nature and I would stop thinking about how I was the only Black man in the room.

I held this woman who I treasured, and I thought that I was surely the luckiest man in the world. I thought that nothing could ever touch us. I felt like we would always be young. We would always be beautiful. We would always be happy. And we would always be in love.

Chapter 12

I HAD A HANGOVER.

Not a particularly bad one. Maybe a six on a one-to-ten scale. Dull and rhythmic headache. Dry, dirty-tasting mouth. Queasy stomach. I figured I could probably avoid puking if I mainlined some coffee within the next fifteen minutes.

My phone rang, and I answered without looking. Lee Lee called me every morning, and since she was two hours ahead of me, I was usually still in bed when I first heard her voice.

"Hey, baby," I croaked.

"Kareem?"

It wasn't Lee Lee.

"It's Lizzie."

Lizzie. My heart started to race. I sat up.

"Hey. Lizzie." I did my best to sound cool. Friendly but disinterested.

"Listen," she said. "I was just on Facebook . . ."

Oh fuck. Oh fuck. Fuck. Fuck. Fuck.

I'd forgotten about Facebook.

"GIMME YOUR PHONE," said Lee Lee when we were in Wellington.

"Why?"

She reached out her hand and beckoned. "Just gimme."

I rolled my eyes but handed it to her, watching as she swiped her finger over the screen.

She handed it back to me, beaming. "There!"

I looked at the screen and saw the words, *In a relationship with Lee Lee Jones.*

She looked so happy. "Now we're Facebook official!"

"Perfect," I said. "I love it."

And I did.

"SO YOU HAVE A GIRLFRIEND?" Lizzie's voice was hard.

I took a deep breath. "Yes."

"And you guys are exclusive?"

Another breath. "Yes."

"And you were together with her when we hooked up last month?"

I closed my eyes. "Yes."

I WAS AT A PARTY. It was the kind of party where you were forced to jump in place instead of dancing because the crowd was so dense. The kind of party where it was only halfway through the night and I couldn't count how many red plastic cups of beer I'd already swallowed down.

I felt a playful tap on my shoulder. Someone whispered in my ear. "Hey, stranger."

I twisted around and there was Lizzie.

"YOU REALLY HAD ME FOOLED, Kareem. I thought you were better than this shit."

I was silent.

"And I really don't appreciate being put in this position. I wouldn't have ever even thought about sleeping with you again if I'd known you were involved with someone."

"I know," I said "I'm sorry."

Lizzie ignored my apology. "I just feel sorry for her. I feel sorry for your girlfriend."

LIZZIE LOOKED AMAZING. I mean, she always looked good, but I don't know if it was the beer, or the dress she was wearing, or the fact that I suddenly felt very, very lonely, but I couldn't seem to tear my eyes away.

"Hey," I said back to her. "It's been a minute."

She smiled at me. Oof. I'd forgotten that big, sexy grin.

"I can hardly hear you!" She leaned in, putting her mouth so close to my ear I could feel her breath blow warm across my cheek. "You want to get out of here?"

"AND I'M GUESSING you haven't told her."

"No." My voice sounded like a scared little kid's. I fucking hated myself.

Lizzie sobbed. Just once. Harsh and angry.

I'D FORGOTTEN JUST HOW MUCH I liked Lizzie. She was smart. And she could always crack me up. We found the same things funny. Especially when we were both drunk.

We were walking back to her place. Laughing hysterically at a story she was telling me about a professor in one of her classes who had farted in the middle of a test.

Lizzie slipped on a patch of ice and yelped, almost falling.

I grabbed her, helping her stay upright. "Whoa! You okay?"

She kept laughing, still in my arms.

That's when I kissed her.

"I MEAN, WHAT WERE YOU THINKING? What the hell were you thinking?"

"I don't know."

THE TRUTH WAS, I wasn't thinking. I wasn't thinking about right or wrong. I wasn't thinking about the repercussions. I wasn't thinking about any promises I had made.

I wasn't thinking about Lee Lee at all.

I WALKED BACK HOME to my apartment a couple hours later, still drunk. Still high from the sex and the companionship. Feeling good.

I shivered. The winter air was so cold, it burned my lungs. I dipped my face into the collar of my jacket, smelled my own breath. Smelled my body. Smelled Lizzie.

I would eat something, I decided. There was leftover Chinese food in the fridge. And then I would sleep in the next morning.

"HEY, BABE!" Lee Lee sounded happy. Happy to hear my voice. Happy to be talking to me.

For a moment, everything was okay. For a moment, I didn't remember what I had done.

"So what did you do last night?"

Then, I did.

"ARE YOU GOING TO TELL HER?" I hated the pleading note in my voice.

Lizzie made an exasperated sound. "You should tell her, Kareem."

"I know, but—"

She cut me off. "You need to tell her."

I COULDN'T SLEEP. I couldn't eat. I could barely concentrate in class. I was shit at polo practice. I kept missing easy shots.

"What the hell is wrong with you, man?" said my teammate Alex. "That last pass was a fucking gift and you missed it by a mile!"

"Sorry," I muttered, reeling my pony around and riding in the other direction.

The thing was, I was pretty sure I had gotten away with it. Nobody had seen me and Lizzie leave together. I had avoided her since that night, making up excuses any time she texted and invited me out.

It was only one time, I told myself. *I'll never do it again. It doesn't need to hurt anybody.*

But every time I got on the phone with Lee Lee, I felt sick.

She was the same. Sweet and warm and loving and curious. And I was the asshole who was lying to her. I was the absolute monster who had fucked someone else.

"I WILL," I promised Lizzie. "I know. You're right. I'll tell her."

Lizzie was quiet for a moment.

I closed my eyes, terrified.

"I really, really liked you, you know?" I could hear the pain in her voice. "I thought you were different."

After Lizzie ended our call, I sat on my bed for a minute. It was an icy, gray day. I told myself I was shaking because it was cold.

I closed my eyes, leaned back against my pillows. Then I picked up my phone again.

We need to talk.

I sent the message to Lee Lee and then ran to the bathroom and threw up.

WHEN I WAS GROWING UP, I was surrounded by people who lied. Everyone was trying to survive, so everyone had a hustle. Everybody was constantly trying to finesse their way into something. It seemed like almost everyone cheated, and they stole, and they lied.

Even my mom used to make a lot of promises.

Yes, I will get you those sneakers, Reem. Yes, I will take you to that movie. Sure, I will buy those cookies that you like so you can have them in your lunch box.

And I would believe her. I would wait for the sneakers. The movie. The cookies. I would wait for her to keep her promise.

But my mom was an addict. And the thing about being an addict is that if you have limited resources—meaning very little time or money—your addiction will inevitably use them all up. And turn you into a liar.

Yes, baby, I know I said I would, but I'm gonna have to get you those sneakers after my next paycheck. Some extra expenses came up this week. Nothing I could do about it.

Eventually I learned that promises were made to be broken. And I hated it.

I hated not knowing who I could trust. I hated the fact that I never knew if someone was just being nice to me or they wanted to use me for something. I hated the pain that I saw all around me when the liar was inevitably unmasked and their lies became clear.

Maybe I especially hated it because I couldn't fully participate in it. I was terrible at lying. I had absolutely no cool and way too much of a conscience. I couldn't even take a piece of ten-cent candy from the drugstore without feeling like I was the worst of the fucking worst.

"I always know when you're lying, Reem," said my brother David. "'Cause you look like you swallowed a mouthful of shit."

I THOUGHT I'D FEEL BETTER when I finally told Lee Lee. I knew that getting it off my chest would be hard. I knew that the conversation would absolutely suck. But I thought that once I'd admitted my mistake, we'd talk about it, I'd say I was sorry, and then we'd move on.

"FIRST OF ALL," I said. "I need you to know that I love you."

"I love you, too," Lee Lee said right back. No hesitation at all.

"I love you, and I know that I'm so lucky to have you in my life."

"Me, too. I feel the same way."

I squeezed my eyes shut. She was making this worse.

"I made a mistake." I took a deep breath and pulled the Band-Aid off the wound. "I slept with another girl. I can't sleep. I can't eat. I feel really bad about it. And I'm sorry. I'm really sorry."

She was silent.

"Lee Lee?"

"Are you serious?" Her voice was shaking. "You're joking, right?"

"Lee Lee, I'm so sorr—"

"Who was it? Was it someone I know?"

"No. Just some girl I know from school."

"Do you love her?"

"No! No, listen—"

"How many times?"

"Wha—"

"How many times did you sleep with her?"

"Once. Just once, I swear. And I don't love her. She doesn't mean anything to me. I just made a mistake. And I'm so sorry."

She was silent again.

"Lee Lee?"

"I need to go to class."

"Wait, come on, I want— We need to talk about this, right?"

"We can talk later. I need to go to class."

And then she hung up.

I WAS FRANTIC. I must have texted her fifty times.

I'm so sorry.

Can we talk more?

I understand if you need more time.

It meant nothing, I swear.

Take all the time you need but just know that I love you. I still want to be with you. That hasn't changed.

Are you out of class?

Can I call you now?

But she didn't answer. Not once.

That's when I realized that it might actually be over. That's when I became sure she was going to dump me. And I felt like the stupidest fucking guy in the world. Stupid that I thought she might forgive me. Stupid that I had even told her about it. Stupid—so fucking stupid—that I had cheated in the first place.

I thought about her family. How she would tell them and they would know that I'd cheated. I thought about my family, and Lezlie, how they would find out what I had done. There was no way I could hide it. I'd been so proud. I'd made sure everyone knew how I felt about Lee Lee. And now everyone was going to know how I had screwed it all up.

I thought about never seeing Lee Lee again. Losing her. And I could barely breathe.

My phone rang. I jumped to answer.

"Lee Lee?"

"What are you going to do to make this better?" Her voice wasn't shaking anymore. She sounded hard. And pissed off.

"Wha-what do you mean?" I was stammering.

"How are you going to fix this?"

"Not—not do it again?"

She huffed out this annoyed little puff of air. "Well. Yeah. That's understood. But what else are you going to do?"

"I mean, I don't have any money right now. I can't get you a big gift or anything . . ."

She laughed, but it wasn't the good kind of laughter. "We are not Kobe and Vanessa. That is not what I'm talking about at all."

"Then what—"

"To rebuild my trust. To make me believe that you won't do it again. How are you going to make it right between us?"

"I'll do whatever you want. Whatever you tell me to." I was frantic.

She started to cry. "Do you have any idea how much you hurt me?"

I felt sick. I hated to hear her cry. "I know. I know. And I'm so sorry. I really am. It was so stupid. I was so stupid."

"But then why did you do it?" Her voice sounded tiny.

"I don't know. I really don't. I screwed up. I just—I screwed up. But it had nothing to do with you. You are perfect. I love you so much. This was all because of me. My mistake. And I will never, ever do it again."

She was quiet for a moment. "I want to believe you. I really do."

I grabbed at this little glimmer of forgiveness. "You can. I swear. I will do whatever you need to make this up to you. Just tell me what to do."

She sighed. "I don't know how long it will take."

"All the time you need."

"And patience. You're going to have to be patient, Kareem."

"Absolutely. I'll be as patient as you want."

She was quiet again. I imagined her sitting in her room, looking at the wall.

"Okay." She sounded defeated. "I guess we can try."

"Yes." I felt like punching the air. "Good. I'm so glad you said that. I love you so much."

"Okay," she said again. Her voice sounded flat. "Okay. I'm tired. I'm going to sleep now. We can talk tomorrow."

"Right," I said. "Good night. I love you."

"Good night," she said. Then she hung up.

HOW LONG WAS LONG ENOUGH?

I wondered this every day when we would talk and she would never fail to bring up what I had done. I wondered this when she told me she wanted me to text when I was going somewhere and then text her again when I got back home. I wondered this when she would ask me for endless details of my evening: Who was I with? How long was I there? What did I do?

I tried to think about how hard it was for her. I tried to remember that I was the one who had screwed up. I tried to tell myself that she would forgive and forget. To imagine what it would be like once we made it over this hill.

But I had very limited resources. No imagination when it came to making things right. I wanted it to be as simple as her telling me exactly what to do, what to say, how to act, and then have her—seeing that I was so willing to do what she asked for—decide to let it all go.

But, of course, I didn't deserve that forgiveness. I hadn't earned it in any way. And it was never going to be that easy.

And that's when I broke another promise. I started to lose patience.

IN MARCH, we met in California for an international polo tournament I was playing in. Lee Lee had bought her airline ticket before I'd told her about Lizzie.

I was relieved that we would finally be able to see each other in person. I'd been toying with the idea of flying back home. I was convinced that if I could hold her, reassure her with my physical presence, literally show her how sorry I was, she would finally find peace with things. I was sure that seeing her in person would remind us both how much we loved each other.

She gave me a quick kiss when we first saw each other. Then she hugged me, and we held on for a very long time. And I thought about how this used to be—this moment of reunion—how sweet and sexy it had always been before. How special and joyous. And now it just felt sad and a little cold and empty.

She pulled away. Wiped her eyes. "What time is the game?"

I KNEW SHE WAS GOING TO END IT. I could tell. We had been quarreling over the phone about things even before she arrived. What I considered to be stupid little fights over my forgetting to text her or not calling her back soon enough. I was sure that those fights would end once we were able to see each other in person.

And in a way, they did. We didn't outright fight. We just went through the motions. We attended all the events together. We went hiking with a bunch of mutual friends. I introduced her to everyone as my girlfriend. My team won the game, and she showed an appropriate amount of public excitement and support. But I could tell it wasn't real. I could tell that she was unhappy. That she regretted coming. That she was done with me.

And honestly, I was almost relieved. I'd imagined that actually telling her what I'd done would be the hardest part. That once I'd managed to get that part over with, it would be easy. I didn't even consider all the work that would come after.

I was young. And stupid. And selfish. And inexperienced in what healthy, monogamous love was supposed to look like.

And I was certain that she would never actually forgive me.

WE HUGGED AGAIN AT THE AIRPORT. This time it was me who pulled away first.

By the time I got back to Colorado, there was a message on my phone: *We need to talk.*

Chapter 13

EVER SINCE I WAS EIGHT YEARS OLD and first entered the Work to Ride barn, horses have made me feel better. They made me feel better when my mom was using and checked out. They made me feel better when she got hurt by her boyfriends. They made me feel better when my grandparents died. When I went away to military school. When my brothers went to prison. When my best friend was murdered in her home.

In the face of pain, horses were always my softest place to land.

So after Lee Lee broke up with me, it's no surprise that I turned back to horses. I had inherited a college polo team that was made up of players who, up until then, had mainly ridden the bench. The two starting players from the year before had graduated. CSU had not won a polo championship in twenty-three years. We had an adviser, not a coach. Nobody thought we had a chance. But what might have felt like an impossible situation to some just felt like an opportunity to me. I was used to being the underdog.

And I was grateful to have a distraction from the fact that I had lost the woman I loved.

I didn't have much of a mental health vocabulary in those days. I couldn't have put a name to my anxiety or panic attacks. I couldn't have explained what growing up in a neighborhood lit with violence and poverty had done to my mind and soul. I just knew that, even when I was seventeen hundred miles away from the place that had shaped me, there were some days when I felt like nothing was safe or good. There were some mornings when it was a struggle to get out of bed. There were some moments when I had trouble breathing. And when those times came, the only thing that helped me get past them were the horses.

So that's what I did in those weeks after I lost Lee Lee. I spent every spare second I had on the back of a horse. I set aside all my frustration and sadness and loneliness as soon as I climbed up into my saddle. I let my brain go blank and my heart go numb and my competitive side have full rein. The team racked up win after win after win.

And in some ways, this worked. If I was on the field, I was safe. She didn't exist. I told myself that if I rode until I was exhausted, I wouldn't have to think about her. If I won enough games, I would feel good about myself again. If I was skilled enough at polo, I might forget about what an ignorant fool I'd been when it came to love.

But off the field, I was haunted. I thought about her before I fell asleep each night. I thought about her first thing in the morning. I thought of her every time something good or bad or beautiful or funny happened, and I was visited by the urge to text her or pick up the phone and call. She had blocked me on social media, but sometimes I would give in to the temptation to ask a friend to check on her for me and let me know that she was doing okay.

LEZLIE DROVE UP to watch me play a game in Massachusetts. She met me in the barn after and watched me pack away my gear.

"So, no Lee Lee, huh?" she finally said.

Before we broke up, this game had been one of the times Lee Lee and I had scheduled as a reunion. She and Lez had planned on driving up together.

I turned and looked at Lezlie, and I knew right away that she knew everything I had done. Sometimes, when I messed up, Lezlie wouldn't have to say a word. She'd just sort of look at me silently, and that was painful enough. It was worse than her lecturing me.

"Yeah," I said. "No Lee Lee."

MY MOTHER CALLED ME a couple of days later.

"Gerb told me what happened, baby." Her voice was warm and sympathetic, which made me wonder if she knew the whole story yet. Honesty and monogamy might not have been a common thing in the Bottom, but that didn't mean my mom didn't wish for them. I'd seen how hurt she'd been by the men who screwed around and lied to her.

And now, I realized, *I am no better than they were.*

I swallowed the lump in my throat. "I cheated on her. Did Gerb tell you that?"

My mother sighed. "He did."

"I'm an idiot."

"You made a mistake. It happens to the best of us."

"I feel like shit."

She laughed. "Well, of course you do. But I suspect that Lee Lee might feel even worse."

"I know. I hate that I hurt her."

She was quiet for a moment. "I liked that girl a lot."

I nodded even though my mom couldn't see me. "Mom?"

"Yes, baby?"

"Do you think I have any chance of getting her back?"

"I don't know, Reem. You hurt her bad, and she's got her pride. But I guess I'd try if I was you. I've never seen you so happy as when you were with that girl. She lit you up from the inside out."

WE ONLY LOST ONE GAME that entire season and made it to the nationals.

During our week in Connecticut, playing the national tournament, I can honestly say that I stayed busy enough that I didn't think of Lee Lee at all. I thought about the ponies and my teammates and tricky shots on the field and what team we were facing next and whether we might go into overtime. I thought about winning and winning and winning and then winning one more time.

And then we won the whole thing. The first time CSU won a championship in twenty-three years. And I stood on the field with my teammates as we celebrated, holding up the trophy and listening to the crowd lose its collective mind. It should have been one of the happiest days of my life, but I looked out into the bleachers and realized that all I really wanted was to see Lee Lee Jones standing out there in the audience, cheering me on.

THE EQUINE WORLD IS SMALL. Horse people always know what other horse people are up to. So when we won the championship, and I received Player of the Year, while I was disappointed that Lee Lee hadn't been there in person to see it, I also knew that there was no doubt she would find out that it had happened. And that she would feel something about it. The athlete part of Lee Lee would never turn her back on this kind of win. She would know just how much it meant.

And I was right, because only an hour or so after the championship game, Lee Lee sent me a text—horse person to horse person, winner to winner—congratulating me on my victory.

I wrote her back immediately. I grabbed that opportunity with both hands. And this time, I didn't hold anything back. I told her how I wished she could have been there. I told her how much I missed her. How sorry I was. How I still loved her.

And then I watched my phone, my heart in my throat, as those little dots danced as she wrote out her message back. I wanted to shout with triumph when my phone finally chimed and the sweet words *I miss you, too* appeared on my screen.

THE NEXT YEAR WASN'T SIMPLE. We were back together, and that felt right, but I had to stay in Colorado over the summer for polo, and Lee Lee was competing, too, and often on the road, so we couldn't see each other as much as we needed to.

Things were still raw between us. Lee Lee's friends all thought she was crazy to return to me (it would be years before they fully trusted me again) and Lee Lee herself, for obvious reasons, veered between affection and suspicion. She couldn't be with me in person, so she still wanted to know where I was, who I was with, and what I was doing pretty much 24-7.

I understood why she needed this. And I knew it was the price I had to pay to earn her trust back, but that didn't make it much easier. I missed the effortless joy we had shared before. I missed our jokes and clowning around, and how easy everything had been between us. I missed the unspoiled certainty of our love. I missed the way Lee Lee had once made me feel; how, through her eyes, I was the man I had always wanted to be.

And, of course, I had absolutely no one to blame for all this but myself.

Still, we hung on. I worked hard to earn her trust back. I did just about everything I could think of. We had these regular and what felt like endless conversations that began to feel Sisyphean—always returning to my betrayal, always reliving the mistake I had made, always apologizing, always promising that I'd never hurt her again. I hated those phone calls, but I knew they were necessary. I knew they were part of the penance I owed her.

There were better moments. I returned home once to surprise her over a long weekend. We hadn't seen each other for months, and I still remember driving down the road to her farm, talking to her on the phone, pretending I was still in Colorado when I was really trying to ascertain where, exactly, she was on the farm. When I walked into her room, still on the phone, she exploded with joy. Just threw herself up into my arms, wrapping those long legs around my waist and hugging me so hard I almost fell backward.

Moments like those sustained us. Reminded us what we were to each other. What we had been. What we could still be if we tried.

IN MAY 2016, I became the first person in my family to graduate with a college degree.

My mother had promised to fly out to see my graduation. She said she would bring her then-husband, Hank, my younger siblings, Gerb and Washika, and my eleven-year-old niece, India (David's eldest daughter). But my mom was forty-three years old and had never been on a plane. Hank, who was fifty-two, had left Philly only once, when he had driven the two hours to New York City and got so carsick he swore he would never leave town again. And they were both active addicts. As I bought their tickets, I wondered if this would turn out to be the kind of promise that was made just to be broken. I reminded myself not to get too excited.

But when I arrived at the Denver airport and saw them all walking out of their gate, I was ecstatic. I could barely believe they'd done it. They greeted me with warm hugs and wide eyes. Everyone was talking as fast as they could. No one but Gerb had ever flown before, and they all felt the need to process their experience as loudly as possible.

"There's no garbage on the streets!" exclaimed India as we drove back to my campus. "Everything's so clean!"

"And no potholes!" said my mother.

"And look at all those volcanoes!" said Hank.

I glanced back at him, puzzled. "Volcanoes?"

He gestured at the Rocky Mountains. "There! Those volcanoes! I never seen so many!"

I coughed to cover up my laugh. "Mountains, man," I said. "Those are just mountains."

He didn't seem to hear me or care, continuing to point out the snow-topped Rockies and talk about them like they might erupt at any moment.

LEE LEE FLEW IN LATER THAT DAY, and Lezlie arrived in her truck, which she had driven all the way from Philly so we could load it up and move my things back home after graduation. That night we all went out to dinner at a local restaurant and bar. We laughed and talked and ate and drank. After dinner, I watched Lee Lee drag my giggling mother out onto the dance floor. They bumped hips and waved their arms in the air. They grinned at each other and rolled their shoulders. They fell against each other, laughing and joyful.

It was the first time all these people—my mother and siblings, Lezlie, Lee Lee, and my friends from school—had all been in the same place at the same time. And it made me feel so rich. Rich in a way that Wellington and debutante balls didn't measure up to. I was rich because I had love and support and laughter. I was rich because everyone I really cared about was there in the same room and we were all celebrating this huge milestone that, for most of my young life, I had never even imagined was possible.

AFTER THE CEREMONY, Lee Lee and Lezlie and my mom helped me pack up the rest of my things and load it all into Lezlie's truck. Everyone was flying out later that evening, and Lezlie and I planned to start our drive home together the next morning.

Lee Lee and I stole a few moments alone whenever we could, laughing and kissing.

"Three more days," I said as we held each other in my half-packed bedroom. "Then we're done with long distance for good."

"I can't wait," she whispered back.

I was finally heading back home to Philly. I had a great job as a financial analyst, a downtown apartment that Lezlie had found for me (and I had seen only through FaceTime), and, best of all, Lee Lee had gotten into the master of social work program at Penn and would be in the city with me full-time. It was everything I had worked so hard for. Everything I thought I wanted. Everything I had dreamed of.

After I drove everyone to the airport and helped them with their luggage and kissed them all goodbye, after Lezlie and I had dinner and she went back to her hotel, after I said goodbye to my roommates, who had also graduated and were heading home with their parents, I sat in my now nearly empty room and found that I couldn't breathe.

Still crazy, I thought as I sat on my bed and gasped. As I tried to force my lungs to expand. As I tried to open my throat back up. As I tried to stop shaking and crying. *Still crazy.*

Still scared.

Still doomed.

Chapter 14

"REEM? . . . REEM? . . . KAREEM? Are you awake?"

I didn't answer. It was early. Very early. And we had stayed out late barhopping. I thought maybe if I didn't answer, we could sleep a little longer.

Lee Lee gently dragged her fingernails up and down my back, but her voice got louder. "Reem? Reeeem?"

I still didn't answer. Though I appreciated the back scratching.

Then she poked me in the ribs. Hard. "Kareem Rosser! I know you're awake!"

I groaned and rolled away from her. "You're evil," I said into my pillow.

She laughed and snuggled up next to me, rubbing her nose against my neck. "Listen, listen. I've got a great idea. We should get a cat today."

I cranked 'round to look at her. "Get a what now?"

She sat up, all enthusiasm. "A cat! A cat! I mean, why not? You're allowed to have pets in this apartment. And cats are easy to take care of. And you were just saying that it was so quiet when you're here all alone—"

"I was just saying how much I *liked* the quiet when I was here all alone."

She charged on. "You need a pet. You need a cat."

I looked up at her. She was practically quivering she was so excited. "I mean, I don't know if I *need* a cat . . ."

"Okay, okay, you *want* a cat!"

"Do I?"

"Don't play! You know you want a kitty!" She poked me again. "Come on, it will be so fun!"

I laughed, shaking my head. "I mean, why not? I guess I want a cat."

WE HIT THE PET STORE FIRST, overbuying on cat supplies. Litter box and multiple bags of litter, food and water dishes, wet and dry food, a pet brush, a light blue collar with a silver buckle, plastic fishing pole–looking thing with a string and a shock of pink feathers attached to the end, a bunch of little rubber balls with bells in the center that jingled when you rolled them.

I was actually getting excited now. Lee Lee was right. I *did* want a cat. Growing up, I was always dragging stray animals home from the streets, and sometimes my mom would even let me keep them. My dog Tummy had been practically as important to me as my siblings. And I loved sitting with a barn cat in my lap at the Work to Ride barn. In a world full of things that were hard, animals were easy. And necessary. It was something that Lee Lee and I both agreed upon.

"So it will stay at your place," said Lee Lee, "but it will be our cat. Equal responsibility."

"Okay," I agreed. Lee Lee had about ten cats back at her family's farm—indoor and outdoor. She loved them all madly, and she basically knew everything there was to know about cat care.

———————————

WE FOUND OUR CAT at the third shelter we visited. He was a silvery gray with bright green eyes.

"A Russian blue," the woman who ran the shelter told us, "and the friendliest guy in the place."

We sat in the visiting room with him for thirty minutes. He spent half the time cuddling in our laps and the other half twining himself around our legs, endlessly purring.

"MURPHY?" said Lee Lee as we lay in bed that night. We were admiring the cat who was nestled between us and trying to decide on a name. "Or how about Mr. Paddles?"

I laughed and scratched him behind his ear. I could tell that he liked it because his eyelids drooped and he looked at me as if he were drugged.

"What about Nolan?" I said. "He looks like a Nolan."

"Nolan," echoed Lee Lee. "I like that." She ran her finger down his spine. He purred even louder. "Do you like that? Nolan?"

The cat yawned and showed us all his sharp little teeth.

"Nolan it is," I said.

Lee Lee nodded. "Nolan. I love it. I love him!" She leaned across him and kissed me. "And I love you, too."

"That's good," I said. "Because I don't want to be replaced by a cat."

Lee Lee laughed and then snuggled back down into the pillows. One hand on me, one hand on Nolan. She yawned. "Mmm, turn out the light, please?"

I reached over and snapped the lamp off, and I was immediately overtaken by that familiar sense of dread.

I slid down under the covers. Tried to block out everything but the sound of Lee Lee's breathing. Nolan's purring.

This, I lectured myself, *is everything I wanted. I have the girl. And the job. And the apartment. And now I even have a damn cat.*

So, then, why did I not feel better? Why did I constantly carry this stone of fear lodged inside my chest?

I HADN'T ALWAYS EXPECTED that I would return to Philly. Growing up, one of the things that had been drilled into my head by Lezlie was that, if I got out of the city, I should stay out. She understood how strong of a pull the Bottom had on anyone who'd grown up there. She knew there was every chance I could end up right back on the streets where I started if I wasn't careful. And she wanted me to put as many miles between my old neighborhood and myself as I possibly could.

I was aware of what Lezlie had been trying to keep me from, and I knew she wasn't wrong to worry, but the longer I was gone, the more I missed my beloved hometown. Once Joe offered me work and Lee Lee was accepted into Penn, there was no rational reason not to return.

But after years of being away, coming back home threw me off-balance. I didn't exactly know who I was supposed to be. I had always been careful to keep my worlds as separate as possible. I had always believed that the Kareem who went to school in Colorado was not the same Kareem who lived in the Bottom. The Kareem rubbing elbows with the rich and connected at his polo games was not the same Kareem who would hang out on the corner with his brothers and crack jokes. And I thought that the Kareem who had been a terrified little boy suffering through panic attacks so bad that he couldn't sleep at night was not the same man who took his girl-friend into his arms, closed his eyes, and slept like nothing bad could ever touch him again. But suddenly, all those different versions of me were in one place: Philly. And they seemed to be converging.

My little sister called me the next morning. "Mom and Hank are fighting again. Can you come over?"

I shut my eyes and sighed. My mom had gotten married while I was still in Colorado, so I hadn't spent much time with my new stepfather. But since I'd returned home, I'd realized that my mother had made another unhappy match.

Hank wasn't physically abusive, so I suppose that was a step up from her past relationships. But he was cruel and impulsive and lashed out at my mother verbally. And his addiction fed her addiction. Their fights were almost worse than the physical ones had been because at least the physical fights always had a definite ending. Without someone interceding, these screaming arguments could stretch forever.

I touched Lee Lee's shoulder. Nolan was now sleeping curled around the top of her head. "Babe," I whispered. "Lee Lee?"

Lee Lee opened her eyes and smiled at me. "Good morning."

I tried to smile back, but apparently she could see the strain on my face.

"What's going on? What's wrong?"

I shook my head. "That was Washika on the phone. Mom and Hank are at it again. I gotta go help."

She put her hand on my arm and squeezed. It wasn't the first time this had happened. "That sucks. I'm sorry. Is there anything I can do?"

I shook my head again. "No, that's all right." I started to climb out of bed. "I don't know how long I'll be gone. Sorry."

Lee Lee nodded. "I'll head back to the farm, then." She plucked Nolan off her pillow and talked to him a squeaky voice. "Will you be okay all by yourself, little boy?"

I smiled as I pulled on my pants. "I think he'll survive."

"Oh, wait," said Lee Lee. "What about our plans for this afternoon? Remember, we were supposed to meet up with Anna and Scott."

I sighed, frustrated. "Right. We better cancel. Or you can hang without me."

Lee Lee frowned. "I mean, couldn't you just tell your mom that you need to be somewhere by—"

I cut her off. "No. It doesn't work that way. I'm sorry. She needs my help right now."

Lee Lee's frown got deeper, but she nodded. "Okay. I get it. That's fine."

AS I SAT ON THE TRAIN heading for West Philly, I tried to figure out what was eating at me. Despite the drama with my family, it shouldn't have felt so hard to be home.

I wasn't living in the Bottom anymore. I had a really nice apartment in the touristy part of South Street. I was making good money, and I was excited about my new job. Things with Lee Lee were good. She was going to get her own apartment once she started school in the fall, but for now, she stayed over nearly every night. We spent our evenings exploring the new neighborhood and trying out happy hour at all the local bars.

But even if I was safely living away from West Philly, my family was still in the Bottom. My brothers and sisters and their kids; my mom was still there, living with her husband and my youngest sister, who wasn't even out of school yet. My mom was still using, and still having issues with her man, which made everything even more precarious. And so, I regularly went back. And even though the Bottom was part of me, even though it still felt a lot like home, it also opened up a wound that I thought I had managed to heal. There was just so much history and loss. Being there could fill me with joy, or it could leave me dizzy and scared and feeling like the helpless little boy I had once been.

I SPENT MOST OF THE MORNING playing referee between my mom and Hank. Trying to calm tempers on both sides. And then, once I managed to cool things down, my cousin came over and asked for money. Again.

It's not that I didn't want to give it to him. When I'd received my first paycheck and saw just how much I had left after paying my own expenses, I'd immediately started thinking about how I could help my family out. It felt so good when someone I cared about asked me if they could hold a few dollars and I could just say yes without having to think twice.

But after I said yes the first few times, it started to get out of hand. I never said no—I didn't know how to—and I was spending all my extra cash.

I didn't blame them. I knew exactly what it felt like to constantly be short on money. And I was glad that I could offer one more line of defense for them in an emergency. But my family needed so much. And I simply didn't have it. I was the first one to get out. The first one to earn a degree. The first one to have a decently paying job. But I was by no means wealthy. And I loved them. I wanted to help them in whatever way I could. But the weight of their expectations and their demands on my attention and resources was starting to overwhelm me.

"What do you need the money for?" I asked my cousin.

I hated myself for asking. I knew I sounded like an asshole. But I'd already loaned out at least half of what I had in my bank account.

My cousin sucked his teeth. "I mean, I got a lead on this new job but I need something decent to wear to the interview. But if you ain't got it—"

I held up my hand. "Nah, bro. I've got it. No worries. We can hit the ATM."

My cousin nodded. "Cool. Thanks. And after that"—he grinned—"I'll buy you a beer."

THE NEXT MORNING, Joe stuck his head in my door and raised an eyebrow just after I sat down at my desk, desperately chugging from a bottle of Gatorade.

"Good morning, Kareem!" He spoke so loud that I worried he must know I was hungover and was punishing me. "Did you finish that report for me?"

For a moment, I froze. Had I finished that report? I couldn't say.

Then I remembered and relaxed. "Yeah, yes. I sent it to your email Friday night."

He nodded and stepped into my office. "Great. I'll look it over ASAP, and we can sit down to go through it after lunch." He picked up my bottle of Gatorade and gently shook it with a little smile. "This won't do a thing for a hangover, by the way. Water, water, some ibuprofen, and more water, my friend."

I looked down, embarrassed to be caught out.

He clamped his hand on my shoulder. "Hey," he said. "It's fine. We were all young once. God knows I've been there. Just try not to throw up in your trash can."

"Thanks," I mumbled. "I won't."

THE THING WAS, I really did not know what I was doing at the job. Not yet at least. I loved Joe, and I was fairly certain that he had faith in me. But the kind of high-level financial analysis we were doing was way above my pay grade. And the company was still very small, so I couldn't hide how green I was. I was forced to learn on the fly every single day, and I felt eternally ignorant.

I met Joe after his wife started taking riding lessons at Work to Ride. He was immediately enchanted by Lezlie and the program, and started donating both his time and money with the kind of wild enthusiasm that I would soon learn he brought to everything he became interested in. He had a horse trailer and he often volunteered to drive our ponies to different events. And I would inevitably tag along with him to help. We hit it off right away. Joe was very smart and successful, and he had grown up wealthy, but he'd had a complicated childhood that reflected my own in more ways than I might have expected. He had struggled. And he didn't hide his stories. He hadn't been a great student in high school and had gone to a small, second-tier college, not the Ivy League one his parents had expected him to attend. He was a recovering addict who was twenty years sober. He had made a ton of mistakes, he told me, but he was always working to correct himself. To become a better man.

The way that Joe was so open with me made it easy for me to be open to him. He was like Lee Lee a little bit, in that he was genuinely and endlessly curious, and he asked me a lot of questions. Not only about my past—growing up on Viola Street, my family, my success with polo, what military school had been like—but he wanted to know about my future, too. He wanted to know what I wanted to do. To be.

When he hired me he had told me that he knew I had less experience than other folks he could have hired, but he truly believed that I had both the drive and the intelligence to master the work. "You're hungry," he said. "And smart. It might take you a minute or two to catch up, but I know you're a sound investment."

Of course I appreciated his confidence in me, but when there was a new task to master every single day—and when I was struggling as much as I was struggling—it was sometimes hard not to feel a debilitating case of impostor syndrome. I was always running behind.

WHEN I GOT HOME THAT NIGHT, Lee Lee was in the kitchen making dinner. She was just learning to cook, so it was basic pasta and red sauce, but it smelled good. She smiled at me and waved a wooden spoon.

"Hello there! Hope it's okay that I let myself in."

Nolan, who had been winding his way around her ankles, strolled over to say hey to me.

I smiled back at Lee Lee and bent over to pick up my cat. "That's why I gave you my spare key," I said. "So you can come over and make me dinner anytime you like."

She snorted and then leaned across the counter to give me a kiss. She smelled like basil and garlic.

"Just let me change out of these clothes," I said as I walked toward my bedroom. "Then I'll come help."

"Hey, my mom was wondering if you wanted to come with us to Martha's Vineyard next week!" Lee Lee called from the kitchen.

I put Nolan on the bed and unbuttoned my shirt. "For how long?" I called back.

"We're gonna be there for two weeks, at least," said Lee Lee. "It'll be fun! The Vineyard is so gorgeous right now!"

I shook my head even though she couldn't see me. I pulled on a clean T-shirt and some shorts and walked back out to the kitchen, Nolan at my heels.

"Here," she said as she handed me the spoon. "Stir this sauce while I make a salad."

I started to stir. "That sounds really nice. But I can't take time off work."

She made a little huffing sound as she chopped a carrot. "I mean, I'm sure Joe wouldn't mind."

"I just started working there, babe. I can't ask for time off yet."

She rolled her eyes. "Oh, come on. He's always been flexible before."

"I was just an intern before."

"But my mom was really hoping you could come. She said we could have the guesthouse all to ourselves! It's practically right on the beach."

I sighed. "That sounds amazing, but no way can I make it happen."

Lee Lee turned her back to me. "Well, maybe I won't go, then. That's too long to be apart."

I looked at her. I knew what she really meant, which was that she didn't trust me to be on my own that long without her. But I decided to let it pass.

"Do whatever you want to do," I said. "I'd miss you, but you shouldn't skip a family vacation just because I have to work."

She shook her head. "Never mind. Forget I asked." She continued chopping the carrot. Then she brightened and looked up at me.
"Oh, hey, I forgot to tell you that I told Min and Jen we'd meet them
at MilkBoy tonight after dinner."

I stirred the sauce a little harder. "Sorry. I can't," I said. "I need
to figure out the Microsoft suite tools. I looked like an idiot at work
today trying to get it all straight."

"Oh, come on," said Lee Lee. "First you can't go on vacation,
and now you can't even go out to have a few drinks?"

I stopped stirring the sauce and held my breath for a moment.
I knew I should tell her how I was feeling. I knew she'd understand
if I told her that I felt overwhelmed at work. I could have told her
how embarrassed I'd been that morning when Joe had figured out
that I was hungover. Or that my family was stressing me out. That I
was worried because my mother was using too much again. That I
didn't have time to meet Lee Lee's friends at a bar, that I didn't really
want to spend the money, and that her buddies would probably be
only lukewarm toward me anyway because no one had forgiven me
for cheating on her. I could have told her how I felt like I was totally
unqualified to be doing the work I was doing, and I was worried that
Joe would come to his senses and fire me. I could have told her even
more than that. And I probably should have.

But I didn't feel like I had earned back the right to dump these
kinds of complications on her anymore. I thought that what she
needed from me was for me to be there for her 100 percent. She
needed me to show her that I still loved her, that I was paying attention, prioritizing her, that I would be faithful and true. I thought it
had to be all about Lee Lee.

I picked the spoon back up. "Okay," I said. "I mean, sure. We
can totally go out tonight."

She smiled at me. "You sure?"

I nodded, and started to stir the sauce again, happy to have ended the argument but uneasy about the fact that I had just pushed something off that I knew would come back in a different way later on.

IT WAS MIDNIGHT. About a week later. Lee Lee was at her farm for the night. I held Nolan in my lap and stared out at the city lights from my living room window. I could hear Philly—but just traffic and the occasional passerby, not the same sounds I'd heard growing up. No kids in the street playing curb ball at all hours. No arguments. No laughing. No music. No gunshots.

So why was I feeling like I was thirteen again, trapped in the dark, unable to breathe?

Waiting to die.

I worked to draw in another ragged breath.

I am safe, I reminded myself. *I am safe. I am safe.*

Nolan squirmed to get down, and I released my grip, realizing that I had been holding him too tight.

He hit the ground and stalked off to my bedroom, shooting me an offended green glare over his shoulder as he slipped through the gap in the doorway.

I BORROWED LEZLIE'S CAR and drove out to Lee Lee's farm the next morning.

I can't quit my job.

I rounded the curve just before her road.

And I can't pull away from my family.

I turned up her long driveway.

So it has to be Lee Lee.

I parked the car.

I knew I was making a mistake as soon as I told her.

I knew that I was turning my back on what had been the best part of my life.

I remember the way she looked at me. The heartbreak in her eyes.

"I can't believe you're doing this," she said.

MAYBE I WAS PUNISHING MYSELF. Maybe I didn't feel like I was worthy of being loved. Maybe I was just burnt out and exhausted and thought that Lee Lee would never let go of the pain of my infidelity. Maybe I thought that I would never measure up to what she really wanted and needed from a man.

Maybe I would do just about anything to avoid feeling the way I had felt the night before.

I reasoned that if I was single, I could concentrate on what I needed to concentrate on and everything would just be easier.

But, of course, it didn't work like that.

When you love someone—like, really love someone—losing them is like walking through flames.

I had loved and lost people in my past. I lost Mecca. I lost my older brothers to prison. I had lost my beloved grandparents. I knew that white-hot, searing feeling of realizing that someone was gone, never to be retrieved. I lived with that fear, that pain, that smothering feeling of sorrow, entrenched into my bones. And when I lost Lee Lee again—even though it had been entirely by my own making—

that loss flared through me and burned so bright that I was truly afraid I would be incinerated within the blaze of my own grief.

I TURNED TO OTHER THINGS.

I stopped drinking almost completely. Instead of barhopping, I went straight home from work, pored over what I had learned that day, went to bed before midnight, and then was up before dawn the next morning.

I was never late for work anymore. I was often the first one there and the last to leave. I decided that I would stop pretending I knew things that I didn't and just ask questions when I needed to. I made a point of spending more time with Joe, really picking his brain. Learning as much as I possibly could.

I set limits with my family. I started to carefully question the urgency of any given situation, and I didn't always come when they called. I told them that I would help them financially when they re-ally *needed* something, not just *wanted* it.

I walked around my new neighborhood. Bought a few things for my apartment. Tried to feel comfortable. Tried to convince myself that I was not standing on shifting ground. That no one was going to take all this away from me.

I spent a lot of time with Nolan, who really hated being left alone all day and was always incredibly needy by the time I got back from work. I held him in my lap. I carried him around like a baby. I slept with him curled up under my chin. I talked to him.

I talked to him a lot.

And slowly—slowly—slowly, the rock in my chest got a little lighter. A little less razor-sharp.

Sometimes I even closed my eyes at night, took a deep breath, and went straight to sleep.

THEN, AFTER A FEW MONTHS, I heard through the grapevine that Lee Lee had found an apartment just a couple of blocks from mine.

"She's here," I told Nolan.

He had settled for my company because he didn't have any other choice, but I knew that he missed her, too.

I couldn't stop thinking about her. I was on high alert every time I left the apartment. I figured it was only a matter of time before I ran into her again. I wondered how I'd feel when I saw her. I wondered what I'd do if I saw her with another man.

I started to feel the burn of her loss again. I started to wonder why I had ever let her go.

What a waste, I thought. *What a loss. What did I do? What a fucking fool I was.*

SHE TEXTED ME. *I miss you.*

And just like that, it felt like someone had pulled me from the fire.

I called her immediately. "We need to stop breaking up," I told her.

She laughed. A little sad.

"Let's meet," I said. "The park near my place?"

SHE LOOKED EVEN MORE BEAUTIFUL than I remembered. Tall and graceful, walking toward me with that confident, sexy, long-legged stride. Seeing her made me feel like I had been gut punched.

"I miss you," I said as soon as she was close enough. "And I'm so sorry. I was so stupid. I need you. So much. We belong together."

She looked at me. Her dark eyes were grave and measured. "If we do this," she said, "that's it. No more breaking up. No more going back and forth. If we are together, Kareem, this time it's for good."

"Yes," I said.

We knew. This was real. This was something more serious—more honest, more certain—than we had ever committed to before.

SOMETHING SHIFTED AFTER THAT. It wasn't the same as it had been in the beginning. It was actually better in so many ways. It was deeper. Much more authentic. We had both gone through it, and we had both grown up. I told Lee Lee why I had left, about work, about my family, how much was on my shoulders, and she understood and consoled me. She didn't try to fix it. She just listened and then offered me a warm place to land.

And, on her part, she finally managed to let go of her distrust. She didn't forget, of course, but I think she really did forgive me. We still had to be tender with each other, careful, but there was joy and relief buoying up that tenderness, not pain and regret.

It never crossed my mind to cheat again. Lee Lee was everything I wanted and needed. I was happy. We lived blocks away from each other. I was excited just knowing that she was there, that we could see each other whenever we wanted. We could hug each other whenever we wanted to hug each other. We could walk down the street, arm in arm. For the first time for a long time—maybe even ever—I felt complete.

We started to talk about the future again, but in a new way. Not just in a "Won't it be great when we can see each other every day?"

way. More like "This is what our family farm will be like. This is where we'll live. Will we have more eventing horses or polo ponies? Will our kids love polo or jumping more?" We talked about how our children would be interracial and need to understand both of the worlds they came from. How I didn't want to raise them in the Bottom but that it was so important to me that they would be comfortable there, that they would be able to understand and accept it as part of themselves. We talked about how we could get my family out. How to keep them safe. Lee Lee understood how vitally important that was to me.

We got a second cat—Nora—to keep Nolan company when we weren't home.

We would lie in the dark next to each other every night, push Nora and Nolan over so we could twine together, with Lee Lee's head on my chest, and we would talk and smile and dream and breathe. We would listen to our cats' purr. We were making a map of our life together. We were taking the first real steps on our path.

Chapter 15

SOMETIMES I THINK OF THINGS as the *before* and the *after*. And sometimes I think of the moment in between, when everything went silent and still.

There was our before. Where we had nothing but time, plans, and dreams. I could look into Lee Lee's eyes and see all the years that were to come, the life that we would build together, the endless days I considered our due. Where I could reach for her, my hands greedy, hardly able to believe that she was finally standing before me, to touch, to hold, to love.

There was the after, where I waited, patiently and not so patiently, for her to come back to me. Where every tiny step forward shot me through with breathless hope. Where the inevitable stumble backward brought me white nights and dull, gray days.

And then there was the moment it actually happened. The moment when a freak accident, a shy horse, a cold day, a twist and a fall, a bitter, unlucky convergence that nobody saw coming, shattered my heart, and reordered the world as we knew it.

THE LAST NIGHT OF BEFORE, I sat at Lee Lee's kitchen counter, keeping her company while she cooked dinner. She was making veggie burgers. Or maybe turkey burgers. (Some memories are indelible. Some are closer to a guess.) In any case, it was something I didn't really consider a burger. But I didn't care. The girl I loved was finally living in the same city as me, we had worked through all the hardest parts, and we were taking every spare moment we had to be together.

We had been playing house all week, moving between her apartment and mine. And I was watching the most beautiful girl in the world dance around the kitchen as she cooked me a meal.

It was four days before Christmas, and the streets of Philly were as cold as a meat locker, but inside her apartment, Lee Lee liked to keep the heat up high and wear as little as possible. Not that I was complaining. She had the kind of grace and faith in her body that could only come from riding, jumping, hacking, and maintaining control over thousand-pound animals on an almost daily basis.

We were talking about our day, work for me and grad school for her, and what we were going to do over our Christmas break. We needed to figure out the logistics of whose family we would see and when. We talked about Christmas shopping, and I admitted that I still hadn't finished buying all her gifts. Lee Lee teased me, calling me out for procrastinating, before laughing and saying that maybe she still had a few things she wanted to pick up for me, too.

All this was new enough that it still felt like a small miracle, these easy and routine day-to-day moments. When we had been apart, I hadn't realized that these mundane things, cooking and doing dishes together, brushing our teeth side by side, deciding whether we'd sleep with the window open or shut, would be the best part of every day. I hadn't known how much pleasure I would take in domesticity.

After dinner, we cuddled on the couch and watched a movie. I don't remember what film it was, but I do remember the way Lee Lee's head fit into the crook of my neck as she lounged against me, the way her long, dark hair spilled over my chest, how her hand was tucked neatly under my thigh. I remember kissing the crown of her head, and the deep feeling of contentment that washed over me. I remember how when the movie ended she yawned and stretched and suggested we go to bed. We both had to get up early the next morning. I had my last day at the office before the holiday break, and Lee Lee was already out of school, so she was going to drive out to her family farm to ride. She was training for an upcoming event in Florida and had been doing the hour-long commute between the city and her farm whenever she could spare the time.

Just sleeping in the same bed together felt like a gift again. As good as it had the first time I had ever held her in my arms. She was the little spoon, her back pressed against my chest, tapping her ice-cold toes against mine, making me jump and laugh as she insisted that I warm her up.

I closed my eyes and pulled her a little closer.

"This is so nice," she murmured.

I nodded as she rolled over to face me. Her eyes gleamed in the half light of the room. "We should just move in together, right?" she said. "I mean, either you're here or I'm at your apartment. It's just stupid to keep two places."

I smiled. It wasn't the first time we had talked about moving in. We had imagined it like a fantasy when we first got together, something to look forward to once we graduated college. And it had become more and more of an actual possibility as we grew older and started really planning our future together. But this felt different somehow. Like a true decision, not just a someday kind of thing.

"Yes," I said. "Absolutely. But maybe we should talk about it tomorrow when we're not so sleepy."

She smiled back at me, that big, gorgeous smile that never failed to make my heart squeeze in my chest. "I'm not that sleepy," she said.

Then she yawned in my face.

"Seriously?" I said.

She laughed. "Okay, maybe I'm just a little bit sleepy."

She scooted up close to me again, wrapping her arms around my neck and pressing her body to mine.

I dipped my face into her hair, taking in her scent. "I mean, we don't actually have to go to sleep."

She snorted. "No, no, you were right. It really is late. We need to sleep."

"Babe, make up your mind."

She laughed and gave me a little shove. "Close your eyes, Reem."

I did as I was told.

She fell asleep first. She always fell asleep first. Her breath grew slower and deeper. I could tell the moment she slipped under, the way her body relaxed and sort of melted against mine as she let go. It only took a few moments for me to follow. Lee Lee pulled me with her and, like always, I was only too happy to follow.

I just wanted to be wherever she was.

I WAS LATE FOR WORK THE NEXT MORNING. My alarm went off, but the bed was so warm, and Lee Lee had rolled over and pressed herself up against me, her legs twining with mine. She buried her face in my neck and whispered that it was still early, that I could stay a little longer . . .

For once, my tardiness didn't really matter. I was the only one in the office that day. As the most junior person on staff, I had been tasked to answer the phones and take messages for the last day we were technically open. But the office was silent. No one was calling three days before Christmas.

I thought about our discussion the night before. About the idea of moving in together. I wished I could call Lee Lee and talk about it some more. Make real plans. But I knew she was riding. No way would she answer her phone. So I opened up my laptop and started scrolling instead, trying to find one last gift for Lee Lee.

I'd already bought her a small stack of lingerie (a box that would sit in my closet, tags on, and unopened, for years after) and a Canada Goose jacket that I knew she wanted (I liked the idea of keeping her warm even when I wasn't around), but I wanted to find something more romantic and heartfelt. Of course, it wasn't the first time we'd spent Christmas together, and it definitely wasn't the first time I'd bought her a gift, but this year was different for a couple of reasons. First of all, I could finally afford to spend some decent cash on her. And second of all, this was the beginning of our grown-up life together. I wanted to find something that would mark this transition. To show her how good it all felt, how our hard work had paid off, how lucky I thought we were.

I clicked over to Pinterest and typed in "Romantic gifts" and scrolled through pages of listicles and jewelry ads, DIY projects that I would have had to start weeks earlier to pull off with any success. Finally, I clicked on a link that seemed like the perfect idea. I could search the address of the first place I had ever kissed Lee Lee—the farmhouse with the mudroom where it all began—and then print out the google capture of that farm, and frame it for her.

I typed in the address and laughed. It sure didn't look like much. The image wasn't the actual house. It was basically a stretch of muddy field surrounding their long gravel driveway. I smiled to myself, imagining how Lee Lee would think I was crazy at first, giving her such a weird gift. But once I explained what it was, I knew she would love it. The lingerie was sexy, and the jacket was expensive, but Lee Lee was sweet and sentimental, and she loved a big, romantic gesture more than anything.

The phone rang, and it took me a moment to realize that it was my cell, not the office phone. I glanced at it and didn't recognize the number, but for some reason I answered it anyway.

"Kareem? It's Phillip."

I went cold. Phillip had never called me before. There was no reason he would ever call me.

"There's been a riding accident. Lee Lee's being medevaced to Christiana Hospital in Delaware."

I caught my breath. Forced myself to speak. "Is she okay? How—how bad is it?"

He paused. Just for a split second, but it told me enough. My heart started to pound out of my chest.

"We don't really know her condition yet, but we're all headed there now. You should come, too, son. You should come as soon as possible."

I DIDN'T HAVE A CAR. That was all I could think about at first. I had been planning to get one, but I had been waiting until I saved up enough to buy the kind I really wanted. Now I felt like a fucking idiot. Why had I waited? I should have bought something cheap. I should have known I might need it for an emergency. Why the hell didn't I have a car?

I called Joe. I told him that Lee Lee had been in an accident and I needed to get to Delaware and that I didn't have a car. He must have heard the panic in my voice, because what felt like a few moments later, I was flying up the stairs to his apartment, grabbing his keys, and then speeding down 95 South.

My mind was heaving as I drove. It didn't seem possible. All equestrians understand how dangerous horses are. Every rider knows someone who has been maimed or disabled or killed while riding. We'd stand around the stables and swap gory stories we'd heard, trying to outdo each other with the terrible details, as if saying them out loud somehow protected us from the possibility of ever having it actually happen to us. Everyone has a favorite horror story about horses spooking, or riders being stupid, or just that moment when someone glanced left when they should have been looking right, and all the disaster that came after. Lee Lee's sport of choice—eventing—was one of the most dangerous of all disciplines. But for some reason, it had never occurred to me, not even once, that she might get hurt.

I had grown up surrounded by death and violence and poverty. In the Bottom, getting shot was a daily possibility. That's no exaggeration. By the time I was twenty-one, I had lost at least half a dozen relatives and friends to gun violence. Because my family was still there, there was always a part of me that was steeled against the inevitable call from home telling me that I had lost yet another person I loved.

But not Lee Lee. I never thought that call would be about Lee Lee. She'd been seated on a pony before she could walk, and she rode some of the best, most expensive horses in the world. As far as I was concerned, her life was as safe and protected as anyone I'd ever met. And I'd be a liar if I didn't acknowledge that maybe a little bit of the reason I allowed myself to fall in love with her—to open up enough to truly need and depend upon her—was because I somehow assumed that she wouldn't be taken from me in the same way so many people had already been. I expected loss from my own family. Not from this golden girl who lived such a blessed life.

I RAN INTO THE HOSPITAL and was directed to the waiting room. I got into the elevator and forced myself to take a deep breath, trying to calm down. All the information I had was that Lee Lee had been trying out a prospective horse for the farm. A young gelding. She was outside, on the exercise track, just trotting. They weren't going fast or jumping. Nothing bigger than a trot. Then the horse tripped, threw Lee Lee, and it rolled and landed on Lee Lee's head. Lee Lee was wearing a helmet, as she always did. The horse was completely fine. It shook itself off and scrambled right back up. Lee Lee was knocked unconscious.

I didn't know more than that.

Maybe it wasn't that bad, I thought as I made my way down the hospital hallways. *Maybe she's already fine. Maybe I'm just overreacting.*

Then I walked into the waiting room and saw Evie and Phillip and her father, Richie, and her two little sisters, Mary and Olivia, people who were usually all smiles and laughter, gracious and warm. They were huddled together, looking pale and shell-shocked and sick with worry. I stood in the entrance, frozen, just staring at them for a moment. That's when I knew it was bad and maybe even worse than bad.

Finally Evie looked up and saw me. She stood right up and came over to hug me, and I could feel her shake a little, like she was trying not to cry. I remember being surprised. I hadn't spent that much time with Lee Lee's family since I had come back to Philly. I was still embarrassed by my behavior in Colorado, by the fact that I had broken up with her again after I'd moved back. I only ever saw them when I was with Lee Lee, and though they were always perfectly nice and welcoming, it still seemed to me that we were all being a little careful, feeling each other out, staying on our best behavior.

But everything changed that day. They could have closed ranks as a family. They could have told me to go kick rocks. I know how hard and terrifying the situation already was for them, and they could have decided that adding their daughter's on-again, off-again boyfriend to the mix was just more than they could deal with. But they didn't. Phillip called me immediately after the accident and told me to come to the hospital. Evie gave me that hug and led me straight into their inner circle. Richie clasped my shoulder and asked me how I was doing. They knew that my pain and fear were as real as theirs. They didn't think twice about acknowledging how import-ant Lee Lee was to me, and I to her. They were so generous that way. And I was grateful.

Lee Lee was already in surgery, Phillip said. The doctor said he would update us as soon as possible.

We sat there for an hour, waiting. Sometimes we tried to make small talk. Sometimes we looked at our phones. Sometimes we just sat silently staring at the door, trying to will the doctor to walk through and give us good news.

But when the doctor finally came out, he didn't mince words. "Lee Lee has suffered a major brain bleed," he said. "We've re-moved the top of her skull to relieve the swelling and pressure. She's now in the ICU. We're hoping for the best. But you should prepare yourselves. I'm sorry to say that there is a good chance that she won't make it."

All of us, as one, burst into tears. It was a horrible, violent ex-plosion of grief and love and fear. Richie's face went white. Phillip grabbed his daughters, who were wailing like they had been stabbed, and Evie kind of fell against me like her knees had given out. We all clung to one another and made noises so raw and hurt that it still gives me shivers to remember it.

I think it was that moment when Evie and I first saw the mirror of our grief in each other—like recognizes like. Maybe it's not fair to compare what I was feeling with a mother's anguish, but as Evie and I held each other and cried, I could feel the waves of pain rolling off her, and I was certain she could feel mine. It felt like there was nothing corporeal between us—just this overwhelming exchange of agony.

After a moment, Evie dropped her arms and turned to her husband, and I dug into my pocket and, with shaking hands, called my mom.

I am normally the calmest person in any difficult situation. My mom always joked that, even though I was such a sensitive kid, I was the one she could depend upon the most in an emergency. She said that she could always count on me to remain ice-cold when everyone else was losing their damned minds. And it was true. I'd lost a lot of people growing up, people I really loved, and I always just sort of went inward when I got the news. It was like my whole body stilled and my mind hyperfocused to a point where I actually felt deeply calm. I might fall apart later, but in the midst of the moment, I was unusually highly functioning. I know now that people who suffer from anxiety can be quite steady when faced with real chaos. We are almost always in fight-or-flight mode—ready for the worst—so when that actually becomes an appropriate response to a situation, we are generally able to spring into action with a helpful and practiced force.

But that was not happening this time. Instead, I was hysterical. I was hyperventilating. I was on the verge of blacking out.

"Baby?" my mom said. "Reem? Is that you? What's happening? What's wrong?"

I managed to gasp out what was going on, and once she understood, she told me to just hang tight. She would get there as soon as she could.

WHILE I WAS WAITING FOR MY MOTHER, the rest of Lee Lee's family slowly started to fill up the waiting room. Lee Lee's three little brothers were brought in. Her grandmother showed up. Family friends. And each time someone new walked in, someone else would have to catch them up. Tell them how bad things really were. It was terrible, hearing "She might not make it" over and over again. Seeing the shock and fresh tears of each new arrival.

Finally, the doctor came back out and said she was stable but that "the next few hours would be critical." He said he couldn't make any promises about her survival yet because they didn't know how her brain would respond to them removing her skull, but that a few people could go in to see her soon.

I know I could have gone in right away. I could have gone in with Evie and Phillip and Richie. But I couldn't bring myself to do it. I was terrified. I kept thinking about how Lee Lee and I had been cuddling on the couch together less than twenty-four hours before this. How she had been joking around in the kitchen in her little shorts and T-shirt. How we had been in each other's arms that very morning. I wanted to think of her that way. I didn't want another version of her to replace the Lee Lee I already knew and loved so much. The doctor kept talking about how she was missing a piece of her skull. That very same head that I had kissed with such tenderness the night before. I didn't know how I would react when I saw her, and though I appreciated how inclusive her family was being, I didn't want to add to their burden by showing them my pain. I didn't want them to feel like they had to take care of me, too.

"You go ahead," I told them when we were finally told that she was able to have visitors. "I'm going to wait for my mom."

It was past ten when my mom finally arrived with Gerb. She walked straight over to me and gathered me up in her arms. I broke down again. There was some comfort, of course, having her there, but not as much as I had hoped. I was broken in pieces, torn apart. A mother's love is powerful, but it can't change the reality of a situation like that.

Finally my mom stepped back and looked into my eyes. "You ready to go see her?"

I wasn't. But I nodded. I knew I had to do it.

THE FIRST THING I NOTICED when we walked into the ICU was the smell. There is a smell that permeates every intensive care unit I've ever been in. That so-clean-it's-almost-empty smell. It's not even bleach or Lysol. It's that air that breathes out when they open a packet for a tube or tool that's going to be used. It's the smell of hospital sheets and rubber gloves. It's the scent of sterility. I hate that smell.

When we walked into her room, at first I couldn't focus on *her*. All I could see were the machines that were attached to her, down her throat, her nose, through the veins in her arms, breathing for her and keeping her blood pumping, and giving her life. And then I saw the towel they had draped over her head to cover the place where they had removed her skull, and there were all these bloodstains seeping through. And there was an aluminum safety blanket draped over her body because she was shaking uncontrollably.

"She's storming," the nurse told us. "Her brain is firing but not connecting; her body still thinks it's under attack."

That's when I finally saw her. I saw Lee Lee lying in that hospital bed. She was hurt and broken and struggling, but she was still the girl I loved. I lost it then. I fell to pieces. I had the urge to gather her up, pull her to me, somehow make it all better, but instead I gently kissed her face over and over and I bargained with her. I told her that if she decided she wanted to make it—if she fought and pulled through—I would be with her forever. I would never leave her side.

"And no matter what," I said. "No matter what, I'm here. I'm with you. This is not going to change anything about us or our relationship. I am yours, Lee Lee, and I love you, no matter what."

THAT DAY FELT LIKE A YEAR. That night felt like a lifetime. I sat with her as long as they would let me. Watching the nurses and doctors come and go as they leaned over her and said her name and asked her if she could move her eyes.

"Lee Lee? Can you hear us? Move your hands if you can. Blink your eyes, Lee Lee."

But she didn't move. She didn't blink. So the doctors would try other tests, shining light in her eyes to see if her pupils responded, dragging a pen down her bare foot to see if she would react.

There was just enough response to indicate that she wasn't brain-dead. There was that little bit of hope. The doctors didn't know if she'd ever walk or talk again. They didn't know how bad things really were yet. But she was still there. That spark that made her Lee Lee Jones hadn't entirely disappeared.

I wanted to stay the whole night. I didn't want to leave her side. But Evie and my mother finally convinced me that I'd be more useful if I went home, got some sleep, took a shower, and came back the next day. Lee Lee's parents said they would stay with her, and Phillip and Richie promised to call me if anything changed at all.

"I CAN DRIVE," I told Gerb when he insisted that I give him my keys. "I can drive."

"No, you can't, bro," said Gerb, and stretched out his hand.

I shook my head. "I'm fine. I can do it."

"Come on, man. Don't make me fight you on this. You're in no shape to be behind the wheel right now."

"I said I'm fucking fine!" I was getting mad.

My mother stepped between us. "Don't be a fool," she said. She plucked the keys out of my hand and gave them to Gerb. "You take him home, and you stay with him tonight, you hear?"

Gerb nodded. "Yeah. 'Course I will."

I deflated. They were right. I was too exhausted to drive, and I didn't even know why I was arguing about it. I let my mom lead me to the car. I let Gerb take the driver's seat, and I sat with my head pressed against the cool glass, watching all the Christmas lights blur on the side of the road as my brother drove me home.

MY FRIENDS FROM THE BOTTOM, Dre, Brandon, and Kevin, were waiting for us outside my apartment when we walked up. Since I was one of the few Black people living in that building, they were probably scaring my neighbors, looking all thugged out and waiting around in the hall like that, but I didn't give a fuck. This was my family. These were my boys. The call had gone out. They knew I needed support, and they were there, in the middle of the night. There for me.

"Hey," I said when I saw them. I gave them a weak smile. "Y'all didn't have to come."

They stepped up, shaking their heads like I was an idiot, each of them taking me into their arms, building me this wall of comfort. "Love you, man," they whispered. "She's gonna be okay, I know it." "Don't worry, bro. We got you."

They gave me just a few moments of that, and it shocked me how much it helped. Then they followed me inside, sprawled out on my couch and my floor, raided my fridge, and started laughing and teasing me, and doing their best to lighten the mood a little to keep my mind off things.

"I gotta go to bed," I finally said. "Thank you for coming, but you know, you guys don't need to stay."

"We're not going anywhere," said Dre. And then he called dibs on the couch.

I TOOK A SHOWER, trying to wash off that hospital smell. I brushed my teeth. Then I slipped into some clean sweats and a T-shirt and plugged my phone in next to my bed.

I was hoping it wouldn't ring. I kept remembering the doctors saying, "We'll know more in two hours, in ten hours, in twenty-four hours." They never said she was in the clear. They never said she would stay. And I somehow knew that if I got a call that night, it would only be the worst kind of news.

"Scoot over," said Gerb as he slipped into bed next to me. "I ain't sleeping on your living room floor."

I laughed. Gerb and I hadn't slept in the same bed for years, not since we were kids. But I didn't mind. It felt different, of course. We were two grown-ass men and two cats in one queen-size bed, and it was a squeeze. But it felt good. I was relieved that he was there. I didn't want to be alone.

"Hey, man," I said. "Thanks for everything today."

He shrugged. "Of course. I'm here for you. Whatever you need, bro."

I reached over and turned out the light.

I fought sleep. I was afraid to close my eyes. I thought I would be back at the hospital. I thought I would see her family crying. The doctor giving us horrible news. There would be blood and the machines pumping air into her lungs, forcing her heart to beat. I was afraid I would see her strong, beautiful body, rigid, shivering, storming.

Close your eyes, Reem.

I was exhausted. And eventually I couldn't help it; I shut my eyes.

And there was Lee Lee.

Lee Lee dancing in the kitchen. Lee Lee stretched out, all long legged and sprawling on the couch. Lee Lee teasing me, poking me in the side with her elbow as we brushed our teeth together, fighting for room at the sink. Lee Lee smiling that heart-stopping smile as she turned toward me in bed and tenderly put her warm palm against my cheek.

Lee Lee was there. She was still there.

And like every night, she took me with her. And I did my best to follow wherever she wanted to go. Because I never wanted to be where Lee Lee Jones was not.

Part II

Lee Lee's proud graduation day at the University of Delaware.

Photo Credit: Evie Dutton

Kareem and Lee Lee, captured just two weeks before her
accident. **Photo Credit: Kareem Rosser**

Kareem and Lee Lee celebrating her twenty-first birthday.

Photo Credit: Kareem Rosser

Lee Lee cherishing moments with her sisters at their home and family farm. **Photo Credit: Evie Dutton**

Kareem and Lee Lee having a great night out in Newark, Delaware.

Photo Credit: Kareem Rosser

Kareem and Lee Lee celebrating at her father's
wedding. **Photo Credit: Evie Dutton**

Lee Lee and Evie striking a pose before a family dinner. **Photo Credit: Evie Dutton**

Lee Lee with her brothers Harry, Barron, and Holcomb, and her stepmother, Ellet, at a family dinner.

A trip to NYC with Kareem and his mother, Lazette, to see Kareem and Gerb's Ralph Lauren ad campaign. **Photo Credit: Kareem Rosser**

A fun-filled family day at the barn with Kareem's nieces and nephews. **Photo Credit: Kareem Rosser**

Kareem and Lee Lee enjoying an afternoon lunch.

Photo Credit: Kareem Rosser

Chapter 16

ELLEN LEANED FORWARD IN HER CHAIR. Just the tiniest bit. And I smiled to myself because this was her tell. I knew she was about to hit me with another big question. I knew she was trying to lead me somewhere.

"What do you remember most about those days?" she asked. "Those first few days just after Lee Lee's accident?"

I stopped smiling. I hated thinking about those days.

I looked away. I let my eyes drift to the window.

Ellen tried again. "One memory, Kareem. Your clearest one."

I looked back at her. Took a deep breath.

"It was Christmas Eve," I finally said.

I WALKED INTO MY MOTHER'S PLACE. Not the place on Viola Street. She had moved away from there a few years earlier, to an even smaller, less expensive place on the other side of the Bottom.

Things were different in all sorts of ways. All the kids in our family had pretty much grown up. Washika was the only one still at home with our mom, and she was well into her teens. David and Bee were both still in prison. Kareema had just had her first child, a baby boy named Kash. She had converted to Islam, so she no longer celebrated Christmas, but she and her husband, Jala, and their son had come over that evening anyway. My mother's husband, Hank, was there. And David's daughter India. Gerb, too.

They all looked up when I came through the door. For a moment, I had to fight the impulse to turn around and leave again. It felt like too much.

Then Kareema handed Kash to her husband and ran across the room to me. My twin wrapped her arms around me and rocked us both back and forth. This was the first time she'd seen me since Lee Lee's accident.

"Inshallah," she said. "Inshallah, it's all going to be okay."

My mom was cooking in the kitchen, making the traditional Christmas Eve feast, and I'm sure the house smelled amazing, but my stomach felt sour and shriveled. Evie had tried to make me eat something at the hospital when I had been visiting Lee Lee earlier in the day, but even looking at food made my stomach twist.

"Go home, Kareem," said Evie after I turned down the sandwich she offered me. "Go home and celebrate Christmas with your family and then get some rest. We'll call if anything happens."

I hadn't wanted to leave the hospital. I felt lost when I wasn't at Lee Lee's bedside. But I was also sensitive to her family's need to have time and privacy with her. I didn't want to be in the way. So I said "Merry Christmas" to everyone, then leaned over to whisper it into Lee Lee's ear as well, and paused a moment, thinking maybe we'd get that Christmas miracle. Maybe Lee Lee would hear me and open her eyes and say "Merry Christmas, Kareem!" right back.

Instead, the ventilator hissed and beeped. Her eyes stayed shut. And her body continued to tremble and shake in the same way it had ever since I'd first seen her in that hospital bed.

"MERRY CHRISTMAS, BABY," said my mother as she walked out of the kitchen. She pulled me out of Kareema's embrace and into her own. She smelled like butter and sage. "How's our girl doing?"

"The same," I answered, as I gently disengaged myself from her arms. "She's stable for now. Nothing new to report."

I decided to change the subject. "Hey," I said to Kareema. "Can I hold my nephew or what?"

Kareema's husband brought Kash over and handed him to me. The baby yawned and stretched out his arms, clasping and unclasping his tiny fists. I looked at his little starfish hands waving in the air and immediately felt the tiniest bit better. I leaned down and smelled the top of his head. My nose grazed his fontanel, and I had to quell the urge to jerk back, remembering the way I had put my face to Lee Lee's head just a few nights before. Remembering the blood-spotted towel. The concave indentation in Lee Lee's skull.

I swallowed hard and hoped that no one noticed the way my hands were shaking as I handed the baby back to Kareema.

"Dinner's ready," my mom said. "We can all sit down now."

"We been waiting for you, bro," said Gerb. "If this food is cold, it's gonna be on you."

I tried to grin at his gentle teasing, but I'm sure my smile looked sickly. I felt shaky and weak.

"Come sit by me, Uncle Reem," said India.

I sat down by my niece and automatically accepted every dish that was passed my way. There was turkey and gravy and potatoes and yams. Corn bread dressing. There were slow-cooked greens and biscuits. Strawberry jam and whipped butter. Wine and beer. I took a little bit of everything and then sat and watched as it cooled and congealed on my plate. I loved my mother's cooking, but I couldn't force myself to eat even one bite.

I could feel their sideway glances and concern, but my family offered me the grace of pretending not to notice my lack of appetite and inability to participate in the conversation. They chattered around me instead, laughing and teasing one another. I let it all wash over me, not really listening. Not really seeing. Wishing that I could go back in time. That it was the year before. Or the year before that. Or before that. Or before that. Before I knew Lee Lee. Before I had done anything as terrifying as falling in love. Wishing I could be six years old again and getting ready to go climb into bed with Gerb and Bee and David while we waited for Christmas to officially start.

Abruptly, I stood up.

Everyone looked at me.

"Sorry," I said. "Sorry. But I need to— I— I'm gonna go back to my apartment."

Nobody argued.

"Let me fix you some food to take home with you," said my mother.

"No," I said. "I mean, thank you, but—" I was grabbing my coat. Hurrying to the door. "Merry Christmas, everyone."

"Go with him," I heard my mother command Gerb as I walked out the front door. My brother caught up with me before I hit the street.

"You don't have to come," I told him. "I'm okay."

He shook his head. "No, you are definitely not."

We walked silently side by side, heading for the car I was still borrowing from Joe.

We drove home in the same silence. Passing houses swathed in Christmas lights and seeing trees through people's windows, all lit up and decorated. It was my favorite time of year, and I couldn't feel anything.

Back in the apartment, Gerb sat down on my couch and looked up at me. "You want to talk about it?" he said.

I shook my head. "Nah. I'm beat. I'm just going to bed."

"You want me to sleep with you tonight?"

I almost said yes. I didn't really want to be alone in my bed. But then I shook my head again. I couldn't depend on my brother forever. "No. I'm good. Thank you."

He nodded, stretching out on the couch and pulling up the blanket over himself. "Well," he said, "I'm here if you need me."

"Thank you," I said again.

"It's one minute past midnight," he said, as I turned toward my room. "Merry Christmas, Reem."

I glanced back at him. "Merry Christmas, bro."

I walked into my room. Looked at the stack of half-wrapped presents I had piled in my closet. All those gifts for Lee Lee. I wondered if maybe I should finish wrapping them and then bring them to the hospital the next day. I imagined standing in her hospital room and unwrapping each gift for her. Telling her what was in all the boxes. Then I imagined myself with a lap full of gifts that she couldn't see or touch.

I shut my closet door.

I WOKE UP THE NEXT MORNING feeling like someone had kicked me in the stomach. There was no moment of ignorance or relief. I remembered absolutely everything before I even opened my eyes. My heart was racing, my breath was caught in my throat. I knew what had happened. I knew where I was. I knew where Lee Lee was. I knew that it was Christmas. And I knew things were not okay.

I IMAGINE THAT CHRISTMAS in any hospital is a weird experience. And Christiana was definitely no exception. The nurses and the doctors were all wearing Santa hats. There were Christmas carols piped into the waiting room. The front desk in the ICU was draped in red and green twinkling lights. Lee Lee's family had brought Christmas cookies and candy. There were big jugs of coffee and hot chocolate. Everyone greeted each other with hushed cries of "Merry Christmas!" and tried to be cheery and in the spirit.

But all I could see were the people sitting in the waiting room, slumped over and steeling themselves against bad news and loss. All I could see were the glimpses of patients in their beds as I walked the halls, their faces washed out and slack. All I could see was Lee Lee, lying on her back, storming under her silver shock blanket, pale and absent. She was somewhere else. Not with me at all.

I held her hand. I listened to the sound of the machines that were keeping her alive. I thought about telling her it was Christmas. But then I just bent my head to her shoulder and closed my eyes.

GERB WAS BACK AT MY APARTMENT when I got home that night. We'd all gone to Lezlie's to celebrate, but I had left before dinner so I could see Lee Lee before visiting hours were over.

"I brought you back some food," he said.

I shrugged. "Thanks, but I'm good."

He cocked his head. "Did you actually eat anything today?"

I shook my head. "Nah. But I'm not hungry."

He huffed out a breath of annoyance. Stood up and started opening all the Tupperware he'd left on my kitchen counter. "It's still warm," he said.

"I said I'm not—"

"Listen," he said, shoving a container of scalloped potatoes in my direction, "none of this will be over any time soon. This is going to be slow and hard, and you will need to pace yourself." He stuck a fork in the potatoes and pushed it even closer to me. "I know you're a mess, bro. I know you're hurting. I know you're sad. But you have to fucking eat. You have to eat, and you have to sleep, and you have to take care of yourself the best you can. Or you won't be able to take care of your girl. You feel me?"

I looked at him. Then I looked at the container of potatoes steaming in front of me. I looked at the bits of white melted cheese, the chunks of pink ham, the specks of parsley. I slowly pulled the dish closer to me. I picked up the fork. I took a bite.

It tasted like nothing. Like wet cardboard. Like sand in my mouth. I put the fork down, shaking my head.

Gerb picked the fork up and handed it back to me. "Nope," he said. "Try again."

I swallowed. Took another bite. This was slightly better.

"Again," said Gerb.

I considered my fork. Considered the potatoes. Had another bite.

Suddenly, it was like my mouth started working again. There was a creamy sauce. The potatoes were soft and velvety. The cheese was sharp. The ham was salty and tender. I realized that I was starving.

I took another bite. Another. I crammed my mouth. I didn't stop until the entire container was empty, and my stomach was full, and I was sitting there at my kitchen counter, panting a little like I had run a race or something.

Gerb raised an eyebrow at me. "Feel better?" he said.

I nodded. Washed with relief.

He pushed another container toward me. "Now eat this," he said.

I picked my fork back up. I ate.

Chapter 17

I HAD THIS IDEA that when Lee Lee finally woke up, it would be just like in the movies. The beautiful young heroine, who has been in a coma for months after a terrible accident, would finally hear or smell or feel the right thing: a song that played at her prom, the scent of her mother's apple pie, the weight of her true love's hand upon her own. I imagined that there was a certain item, a particular key, to bringing her back, and if I could just find that thing, Lee Lee would open her eyes, look into mine and say, "Kareem? Where am I? What happened? How long have I been gone?"

But that is not what happened. Lee Lee's return was not magical or instant or even all that easy to pinpoint. There was no one dramatic moment. There was, instead, a small series of tiny, almost insignificant changes that moved her closer to consciousness. And though I quickly learned to celebrate those tiny changes—because change, any kind of change, meant she was moving forward—it was hard not to wish for more.

Seven days after she was first admitted to the hospital, we were told that it was likely Lee Lee would live. Or, at least, we could stop worrying about her dying from the brain bleed itself. This, of course, was a huge relief. The most important thing. But it was also only the first step.

I was still at a point where I believed that the doctors would be able to accurately predict Lee Lee's future. I thought that the medical professionals should have been able to tell us if she would make a full recovery, when, exactly, that recovery would happen, and just about everything we could expect in between.

But the thing all the doctors kept telling us instead was *Every brain injury is different*. There was no one specific way that someone with a traumatic brain injury will recover. One person might just open her eyes one morning and have her entire vocabulary back. Another person might stay locked up and silent, stuck in bed, for their entire life. There was no real way to know what would happen. There was never a meeting with her doctors where they sat us all down and said, "Lee Lee won't ever be the same again." Nor did anyone say, "She'll be back to her old self within a month." What they did say was "Every brain injury is different. We have to be patient and see what she's capable of."

It took me a little while to accept this reality. Control—knowing what would come next, what could be expected—was a cornerstone of my fragile mental health in those days. Still heavily influenced by my time in military school, I believed in strict schedules and predictable outcomes. I did not like surprises or unknowns. Lee Lee's condition was torturous to me in more ways than the obvious.

So I did what I could to create something safe and predictable around the chaos of her injury. I fell into a pattern that ended up carrying me—in good and bad ways—through the years to come.

I started going to the office as early as possible every morning. I knew that I had to end my working day at 5:00 p.m. sharp if I wanted to make the hour-long drive to Christiana and still have any time left over to actually see Lee Lee. So, I was in the office by six o'clock every morning. Joe and my other colleagues were giving me a lot of latitude, but I didn't want to test their limits. When I was at the office, I tried to be at the office. I did my best to focus all my energy and attention on the job in front of me, to get things done in the most efficient, effective way I could think of.

Then, at exactly 5:00 p.m., no matter what was left undone, I shut everything down and left. Joe had essentially given me his car, allowing me to use it as needed. And so every night, I left work and then spent the next hour driving down 95 to Delaware.

That trip quickly became second nature. I knew every exit; where I could get gas or grab a quick snack. I learned the traffic patterns, when it was busy, when the roads would be clear. I started to pay attention to weird things. One day I was sitting in traffic, staring at the side of the road, and I decided to identify the tree I was staring at. I snapped a picture and then reversed imaged it on my phone.

Northern red oak.

I looked up another tree: *sugar maple.*

Then another: *eastern white pine.*

Pretty soon I didn't have to look them up. I'd just automatically name them as I zoomed past.

Redbud. Black gum. Redbud. Silver maple.

LEE LEE SPENT SEVEN AND A HALF WEEKS in the ICU. And almost every day she was there, I was there, too. Work. Drive. Lee Lee. Drive. Sleep. Work. Drive. Lee Lee. Drive. Sleep. WorkDrive-LeeLeeDriveSleep. That was my life. And that was enough. Almost more than I could handle, honestly.

Each day, I'd try to will some positive news into existence. It wasn't prayer, exactly. It was more like a very strong suggestion from me to the universe: *Today will be the day Lee Lee's storming will stop*, or *a doctor will actually say, "She's going to make a full recovery."*

I fell into a routine. I would spend thirty minutes in Lee Lee's room and then let somebody else step in while I took a walk around the hospital. Then I'd come back again and spend another thirty minutes with her. Our "conversations" were short. I'd tell her about work. I'd tell her about the trees along the highway. I'd remind her that I was there. That I loved her. We spent most of our time in silence. Just listening to the machines that were all around us. But the machines meant she was alive. And knowing that Lee Lee was alive was enough for me to keep hoping.

After that first night, I cried only on the way back home from visiting her. Or alone in my apartment. (I'd told Gerb that he didn't have to stay with me anymore, so it was just me and the cats.) I sometimes had to fight my tears when I was at the hospital; I sometimes wanted nothing so much as I wanted to climb into bed with Lee Lee and hold her while I cried. But that was impossible. It was impossible to hold her. Impossible to give in to my grief. I didn't know if she could hear me. And even if she did hear me, I didn't know if she could understand what I said to her. But I knew that I didn't want to be responsible for making her feel any worse. I promised myself that Lee Lee would never hear me cry.

I CAN'T REMEMBER when Lee Lee's eyes actually opened. Which seems ridiculous. All the daydreaming I'd done about that moment and how important it would be, and when it actually happened, it happened so incrementally that I have no memory of the first time that I looked at her and she looked back at me.

But maybe that's because she didn't actually look back at me. That's not the way it happened. Lee Lee's eyes opened, and they would move around in what seemed like an imitation of sight. As far as I could tell, she didn't recognize me or Evie or anybody else who came through. We certainly didn't lock our gaze and communicate without words like we used to. She didn't seem to follow sound or movement, either. Her eyes were open, but they seemed to roam the room without cause. I had no idea what she was seeing or not seeing. Or what interpretation of the world her still-healing brain was able to provide.

What I do remember about that time was that it was an unwelcome realization. A difficult reality check. I had been so certain that once Lee Lee's eyes were open, she would be there, intact and unchanged. But that wasn't true. She was there, but she wasn't with me. It was a reminder—the first of many—that her recovery was not on my timeline. That none of this was within my control. Lee Lee would meet my eyes and see me when she was healed enough to do so. There was no forcing the outcome. I couldn't magically will this into happening. My only job, I told myself, was simply to be with her, love her in every version of who she was, and to practice limitless, unselfish patience. It was the very least she deserved.

"KAREEM, this is Craig James and his mom, Janet."

"Hey, man," said Craig as he stuck out his hand to shake mine.

Evie had started to reach out to other families who had experienced traumatic brain injuries (TBIs). She was looking for information, she told me, for hope, for a sense of mutual understanding. Craig was a young white guy, probably close to my and Lee Lee's age. About my height, although a bit thinner. He had an open, winning smile and a strong grip. But the first thing I noticed was the scar on the side of his head.

"Lee Lee," Evie said, "Lee Lee, this is Craig and Janet. Craig had an accident while snowboarding about . . . eight"—she looked at Craig, and he nodded—"eight years ago, and he had a TBI just like you do now."

"Hey, Lee Lee," said Craig. He walked right up to her bed. "Really nice to meet you."

Sometimes when people came to visit Lee Lee, they would address me one way and then turn around and address her in a completely different way. People tended to either drop their voices into a whisper when talking to her or they would pitch their sound both higher and slower, like they were talking to a baby or a dog.

That wasn't true for Craig. His voice didn't change at all.

Lee Lee's eyes darted around the room, unfocused and wild, but Craig kept talking to her like they were sitting in a Starbucks, having a cup of coffee together.

"I heard you're an athlete," he said to her. "I'm one, too. But I can't do horses. Too big. Too smelly."

"Craig's TBI was very similar to Lee Lee's," his mother told me in a quiet voice. "He was in an almost identical state to what she is in now."

I looked at Craig with new interest. If you discounted the scar and a slight hesitation in his voice before he spoke, you would never know he'd had any injury at all.

"It sucks, right?" Craig was saying to Lee Lee. "I remember what it was like. Everyone's here, talking around you. You can hear them. You can understand them. But you can't talk back." He reached out and touched Lee Lee's wrist. "It will get better. I swear."

I felt a chill run down my spine. What Craig had just described was exactly what I had started to suspect was going on with Lee Lee. She was there. She could understand us. But she was trapped inside her own mind. She couldn't respond in kind.

I wanted to ask Craig a million questions. I wanted to pick through his experience and gather up all the information I could about what it had been like for him so that I could apply it to Lee Lee. But I couldn't bring myself to interrupt. If what he said was true, if Lee Lee could understand what was going on around her, then she needed this moment more than anyone else in the room. She needed to be seen and understood in a way that no one else had been able to do up until that point.

It was wonderful to have proof that Lee Lee was still here. That she hadn't been altered beyond recognition. And it was amazing to see Craig standing there, walking, talking, helping us like he was, knowing that he'd once been as challenged by his injury as Lee Lee currently was. But it was horrible to think about what she must have been feeling, how trapped. How angry. How frustrated. How helpless. That she had to tolerate all the people with their singsong voices, talking to her like she was an infant. That her eyes—which I had been imagining were practically useless to her—were actually taking in everything, but that she just couldn't show us what she knew and understood.

Craig and his mother stayed for a long time that day, talking to Lee Lee and Evie and me about Craig's recovery. When I drove home that night, even though I was still disturbed by the idea that Lee Lee was unable to communicate, and thinking about how desperately frustrating that must have felt for her, I also felt joy. I felt happy and calm in a way that I hadn't felt since before Lee Lee's accident.

Craig had shown Evie and me videos from the time he'd been in the ICU. He'd looked just like Lee Lee, covered in tubes and wires, a trach in his throat, unable to move or speak. And yet, eight years later, there he was, standing in the room with us, laughing and talking and helping us, giving us the kind of hope that no doctor or medical professional had dared to offer.

After they left, Evie had put her arm around my shoulder.

"That will be Lee Lee," she said. Her voice was strong and sure. "She's going to get through this, sweetie. I just know it."

I nodded.

If Craig could recover, so would Lee Lee.

He was proof of her future.

Chapter 18

THE BARN WAS THE SAME as it ever was. Shabby and welcoming. Quirky horses and hand-me-down saddles. Air heavy with hay and horse manure. Jackets and boots and riding gear that were passed from kid to kid to kid until they were so thin and patched even Work to Ride folk couldn't keep wearing them.

Lezlie had called me earlier in the week and asked me to stop by. She said that the kids missed me. That my pony missed me. And she didn't say it, but I could tell that she probably missed me, too.

It was the first time I had returned to the barn since Lee Lee's accident.

I had my reasons for staying away, of course. If I had even one extra moment, there was an ever-growing list of things that I should be taking care of. Things I had shoved aside in favor of my need to spend time with Lee Lee—things like my family. My friends. My job. My apartment. Riding certainly didn't feel like anything I could justify spending time on.

I knew that some people in my life wondered if I wasn't taking the time to ride because I felt differently about horses since the accident. If I was angry, or afraid to get back in the literal saddle. But that honestly never even crossed my mind.

I remember being in Wellington one summer, wondering how a family I worked for could stand to play the game after losing a son to a polo accident, but now I understood. It didn't matter to me that Lee Lee's accident happened while she was on a horse. It didn't alter my feelings about riding. Or my essential need for the release it still gave me. Everyone who spends any real time around horses knows how dangerous, and even deadly, they could be. But Lee Lee's accident had been so random. So arbitrary. Barely a trot. A divot in the ground. A green horse.

Me never riding again was like expecting me to stay out of the rain because someone I loved had been struck by lightning.

So after spending some time with Lez helping out around the barn, I saddled up my pony to go hack in the park. I had come dressed to ride. I was wearing my boots and my breeches and my gloves. But before I left the barn, I realized that one thing about riding had actually changed for me. Before Lee Lee's accident, I had never been particularly careful about wearing a helmet. Of course, I always wore one when I was playing polo, but if I was just going to hack, or mess around with a horse in the ring, I'd more often than not go bareheaded. Now I knew that I'd never get on a horse without wearing a helmet again. And I would refuse to ride with anyone who didn't want to wear a helmet, either.

And while I knew it was a change for the better—a sensible shift—it tasted a little bittersweet. Like something very small but somehow very symbolic had been taken away from me. As I swung up in the saddle and steered my pony into the woods, I wasn't afraid to ride. I still needed it. I still wanted it. I still craved it. But there was a difference. I suppose I had to admit that, along with the thousands of other things that had changed with Lee Lee's injury, here was one more alteration made.

AFTER TWO MONTHS and several more operations, Lee Lee was finally stable enough to leave the ICU in Delaware and be transferred to a rehab facility in Pennsylvania. We were now allowed to feel the relief that she would live but knew almost nothing else about how she would recover. She was still completely nonverbal and bedridden, in a catatonic state. She had lost more than thirty pounds and was still being fed through a tube. She was all sunken cheeks and huge, unfocused eyes. Her bones showed through her skin, her hands were twisted into a permanent gripping position. Her left foot bent inward and looked like it would never bear weight again. She had no control over her head, which was always to one side, held up either by pillows or one of her own shoulders.

And she was still storming, an electric current of fear and panic that held her body in its unforgiving grip.

I had been at the hospital almost every day for the past two months. When she was moved to the rehab center, I didn't see a reason why I would do things any differently.

People continued to make allowances for me. My boss never said anything about my hours. My colleagues never asked me to work late. My friends and family accepted that they would rarely see me. My world had shrunk to a small, regimented schedule, and my time with Lee Lee was at the heart of it.

The Bryn Mawr facility was one of the best in the country. The campus was beautiful, and Lee Lee had a big, airy room all to herself on what was called "the Oak Floor." I remember being grateful that Lee Lee's family had good insurance and could afford that kind of care. I remember thinking about what it might have been like if they couldn't.

At first the room felt impersonal. Better than the ICU but still empty and sterile. Then people started bringing in things. Fresh flowers. Pictures from home. A quilt for her bed. Posters and throw pillows. Within a week or so, it felt less like a hospital room and more like a dorm room or a teenage hideout.

Evie set up a rotating schedule that allowed someone to be there with Lee Lee during the morning and afternoon, and I volunteered to be there in the evenings. Lee Lee's family would generally leave just before dinner, so I knew that any time I didn't come, Lee Lee might be on her own for hours until the next morning. And I couldn't stand that thought.

I continued the ritual of our time together. I would walk into her room every night, pull up a chair, maybe turn on the TV to fill a little bit of the silence. I'd reach for her clenched fist, gently unbending her twisted fingers, careful not to hurt her, so we could hold hands. Then I would start talking to her about anything I could think of. Sometimes it was a lot. Things I had been mulling over. Memories we had together. Plans for our future once she was better. Sometimes it was random, stuff about what was going on in my old neighborhood, a funny story about our cats, or maybe what I'd done at work that morning. Sometimes I would simply repeat the same things I had told her the day before because my life had become so small that nothing new had actually happened in the last twenty-four hours.

She never answered, of course. She couldn't even meet my eyes yet. But her voice was still strong enough in my head for me to fill in her end of the conversation. I could still remember what her laugh sounded like. I could close my eyes and see her smile. I knew what kind of joke would make her giggle. So I'd tell her those jokes and then settled for hearing her laugh in my memory.

Occasionally a visitor would come while I was there, and I always enjoyed that. It changed the mood in the room. It took a little of the pressure off me.

But mostly, it was just me and Lee Lee.

Sometimes I would run out of words and let things go silent. Sit there with her, holding her hand, listening to her breathe. And

I would fantasize about the day that she would finally be able to respond to me again.

But sometimes I went beyond imagining a simple conversation between us. Sometimes I indulged in wild happy endings in my head. I'd fantasize that Lee Lee's recovery would be like one of those inspirational sports stories I had consumed like candy when I was a kid. Top-notch athlete suffers an almost fatal accident, then spends years working to get back in the game. I fantasized about Lee Lee competing in the Olympics and the introductory package that they would play on TV before her ride. How the announcer would describe the accident, her heroic struggle to recover, and her eventual, triumphant return to being an elite athlete and champion. I saw gold medals in her future. Blue ribbons. The winner's circle made sweeter by just how hard she'd had to fight to step back inside it.

After her accident, the doctors had all commented on how fit Lee Lee was. They said the fact that she was such a strong athlete gave her the ability to fight.

Sometimes I would think about that. The fact that her being a horse girl had saved her life.

But I also thought about the fact that her being a horse girl had been the genesis of all that came after as well.

HERE ARE SOME OF THE THINGS that got better in the first six months:

After her parents insisted on switching the quality of food that she was given through her feeding tube, Lee Lee gained some weight. Her face filled out a little. She didn't look so gaunt. After another month, she finally stopped storming. This was the sweetest relief. It also meant she could have her tracheotomy tube removed so she could relearn to swallow. Which meant the nurses could take out her feeding tube and start giving her pureed solid food by mouth.

The doctors would come in and say, "Lee Lee, do you understand what I'm saying? Blink if you do." And sometimes she would blink.

There was more controlled movement in her hands and eyes. Sometimes she would look at me. Meet my eyes and hold her gaze to mine for a few seconds. She didn't yet give me any sign that she knew who I was, but she could look at me in the same brief way a stranger might glance at me as we passed on the street. Connection without recognition.

She couldn't speak. She couldn't cry. Her voice box had atrophied with lack of use. But because the trach was out, she started to make random guttural sounds. Groans and grunts and squeaks.

Lee Lee started participating in all sorts of therapy. At first, her exercises would happen in bed, with nurses just moving her arms and legs around for her, turning her head right and then left. Trying to loosen up her sore and underused muscles.

After a bit, they lifted her into a wheelchair. She had to be strapped in at first, and her head had to be propped, but it felt like a small bit of freedom to wheel her out of the room and to be able to roam the halls, and even the campus outside, together.

Then the physical therapists started working with her in a designated room, encouraging the small amount of movement in her hands and fingers. Building strength back wherever they could.

She held her head up. It was only for thirty seconds or so, but it felt like a turning point. It felt deliberate. A moment of control.

ONE DAY, I joined her on the bed, lying by her side and holding her hand. I was chattering away like I always did.

"And then my mom said that she needed me to drive over because she forgot to buy a chicken, which was the whole damned reason she'd made me drive her to the store in the first place, so I said—"

Suddenly Lee Lee rotated her head away from me. Turned in the other direction and faced the wall.

I stopped talking mid-sentence and blinked.

"Lee Lee?" I asked carefully.

She didn't answer.

I mean, of course she didn't answer.

"Lee Lee?" I said again. "Are you done talking?"

She kept her face turned away from mine.

Reem. I'm done, I could practically hear her saying. *I have been more than patient, and I am so done listening to your long, boring story.*

I laughed. Thrilled to have such clear communication. "Okay, then," I said.

I took her hand and kissed her palm. She wiggled her fingers against mine. And we stayed there together on the bed, side by side, silent and content.

After a little while she turned her head back toward me. Met my eyes.

"Ready to talk more?" I asked.

She couldn't respond. But I knew. I knew what she was telling me.

EVER IN SEARCH OF more order, I added arbitrary rules for myself. I had to visit Lee Lee at least five days a week. Six was better. If Evie called and asked if I could visit outside of my normal time, I always dropped whatever else I had planned and made it happen. I tried my best to come early every weekend so I could be there for Lee Lee's physical therapy appointments. If I missed them, I would ask Evie to record them for me and send me the video.

I continued to stick to my rule that I could never cry in front of Lee Lee. No matter what. I walked into that room every day with a smile on my face and kept it there until I walked back out. I might look at the woman I loved and see her in obvious pain, twisted up and uncomfortable, propped on pillows, and with a look of either absence or anger in her eyes, but I made sure I never showed her how that made me feel. I was convinced that the last thing Lee Lee needed was to see my unhappiness. I didn't want to add to her burdens. I told myself that my job was to stay strong, be there for her, and save my pain for when I was alone.

I also made it a ritual to call or see Evie every day. I still felt the need to know every little detail of Lee Lee's life even when I wasn't there with her. And Evie was more than happy to oblige. Those informational phone calls quickly became something much more intimate and encompassing, a lifeline for us both. There were times that I thought only Evie could understand what I was going through. Sometimes Evie would invite me to a family dinner at the farm, or we would meet up at the rehab, and then, at the end of the evening, she'd walk me out to my car, and we'd stand there for a minute, or ten minutes, or an hour, tears in our eyes, talking about Lee Lee.

"I think she almost smiled today," Evie said. "I swear it just about happened."

We were at the farm. Sitting on the hood of my car. I had been invited back for dinner after spending my usual time with Lee Lee.

Evie wasn't looking at me. She was looking up at the sky. I followed her gaze. There were no streetlights, no moon that night. The stars were sharp; hard and bright and fixed.

I shivered. It was early October and starting to get cold again.

I wanted to believe Evie. But I hadn't seen anything close to a smile from Lee Lee since the accident.

"Really?" I said. "That's great. That's amazing."

I sounded doubtful. I could hear it as soon as the words left my mouth.

Evie turned her head and looked at me. She had a rueful twist to her mouth. "Maybe not," she said. "Maybe I'm just wishing."

I shrugged. "It's okay to wish for stuff."

She sighed and patted my hand. Looked back up at the sky. "I miss her so much. Sometimes I look at her, all crumpled up like that, and I think, *Where is she? Where the hell is my girl?* I mean, she has to be somewhere, right? She must be somewhere in there."

I cleared my throat, pushing against the ache. "Yeah. She's there. We just have to wait. Be patient. She's coming back. I can feel it."

It was starting to sound like a platitude, or maybe our mantra.

Evie squeezed my hand again and then let it go. "It's getting cold," she said. "You should get home, sweetie."

Nobody, I thought, as I drove home through the darkness, *nobody knows and loves Lee Lee like Evie and I know and love Lee Lee.*

I had always liked Lee Lee's mother. Evie had always been kind to me. But our relationship turned into something much more primal and all-consuming over those years—it seemed like she was the only person who got it. Our mutual grief bound us inextricably together.

THE ONLY REAL CONTACT I allowed myself with my family and friends was on the way to the rehab center each night. Every day, as soon as I got into the car, I would call a friend, or my brother, or my mother, or Lezlie, to keep me company as I made my way there.

I had never quite been able to shake the feeling I'd first had when I'd forced myself to enter Lee Lee's hospital room in the ICU. There was always a part of me that felt like I was ripping open a wound every time I saw Lee Lee again. There was anxiety and dread and worry. What if she hadn't gotten any better? What if she was worse? What if things never changed? So I allowed myself the luxury of those phone calls in order to mute that panic.

"HOW'S SHE DOING, KIDDO?" said Lezlie in her rough, alto voice. "Anything new?"

"She's good," I said in return. "She's eating a little more solid food."

"Well, that's great," said Lezlie. "And how about you? How are you doing?"

"I'm fine. Totally fine. Hey, how's that new pony doing? I heard he's a biter."

"REEM, BABY, I'm so glad you called," said my mother. "How's our girl doing?"

"She's great, Mom. She's holding up her head a little now. The doctor said that's a good sign."

"Well, that's a blessing for sure. I bet she'll be up and walking in no time."

"Yeah, I hope so."

"And how about you, baby? How you doing?"

"I'm fine, Mom. Hey, did you talk to David? How's the new job?"

"HEY, BRO," said Gerb. "You driving again?"

"Yup."

"Anything new with Lee Lee?"

"Nothin' too much. I think they're going to try a new wheelchair."

"That's tough, man."

"Naw, it's all good. It's progress."

"Yeah? Well, that's cool, then, I guess. How about you? You still a fuckin' mess?"

I laughed. "Naw, bro, I'm good. I'm gettin' by."

He hesitated for a moment. "I mean, if you say so. Because sometimes I wonder—"

I interrupted him. "Hey what about that date you went on last week? How'd that end up, anyway?"

THE DRIVE BACK HOME was the only time I allowed myself to really feel anything. I couldn't think about Lee Lee while I was at work. I had to concentrate on the tasks at hand. And I couldn't allow myself to think too much on my drive out to see Lee Lee, either, because if I did that, I was pretty sure there was a chance I would turn the car around and just never stop driving.

I allowed myself the indulgence of feeling anything only when I was driving home, usually in the dark, crying and listening to music and thinking the kind of thoughts that left me gasping for breath. I would play and replay different scenarios in my head. Sometimes I would imagine a miracle. Waking up and getting Lee Lee back entirely as she had been before. Our life together just picking up where it had been left off. Sometimes I would think about certain couples I'd seen at the rehab center—where one person was sick or disabled and the other was seemingly healthy—and I would play this game of chicken. Of *What if . . . ? What if Lee Lee never got out of her wheelchair? What if she always had speech and communication issues? What if she had debilitating, chronic headaches?* Those things would be fine. I could manage those things. We could still have a perfectly happy life together.

But then I'd go darker. *What if . . .* , my mind would hiss. *What if she never speaks again? What if she has absolutely no mobility? What if we can't ever be sexually intimate again? What if she never recognizes me? What if she is trapped, stuck in her head, for the rest of her life? What if? What if? What if?*

We'll work it out, I promised myself. *I'll stay loyal no matter what. I told her I would. There's no version of this story where I leave.*

I didn't party anymore. I rarely drank. Before Lee Lee had her accident, I had been living a young man's life, enjoying my freedom in the city, going to bars and clubs and sporting events. All those things were pretty much off the table now. I had to stick to my strict schedule. I had to be in bed by ten so I could have enough energy for Lee Lee the next day. I was hypervigilant. Always ready to spring into action. I lived in a constant state of readiness.

In my darkest hours, late at night, alone in my bed, I sometimes wondered if losing Lee Lee this way was punishment for my previous infidelity. Some kind of karma or retribution for my sins. I flagellated myself, thinking about how I had been so stupid and selfish. How I had hurt her before. How I had wasted time and happiness for us both, made her suffer when she was still healthy and strong. Of course, I knew that it was both ridiculous and incredibly self-absorbed to imagine that Lee Lee would somehow be punished for something I did, and I rationally knew that I couldn't have actually caused the accident, but on those sleepless nights, there was an ugly, rusty corner of my brain that liked to whisper, *But maybe? Maybe you did.*

I LIVED BY THOSE RULES, that schedule, in that hypervigilant state, consumed by magical thinking and motivated by guilt, for another year.

By the time Lee Lee was ready to leave rehab, she was able to sit up in a wheelchair. She could hold up her head on her own. She'd had surgery on her left ankle and recovered some mobility there. She was eating solid food.

And she could speak again.

She could say, "You bitch. You fucking bitch."

First in the tiniest little whisper. Like a baby voice. The muscles in her throat and tongue were still underdeveloped and she had no ability to project.

But then she said it louder. "YOU FUCKING BITCH." And she said it all the time. She said this to the nurses. And to her mother. And sometimes to me. Sometimes it wasn't directed at anyone in particular but just seemed like a commentary upon her general state of being.

"You fucking bitch!" she'd yelp as she was moved from her bed to the wheelchair.

"You fucking bitch!" she'd sneer when she was done eating and someone tried to get her to take one more bite.

"YOUFUCKINGBITCHYOUFUCKINGBITCHYOU-
FUCKINGBITCH!"

It was actually amazing just how perfectly that particular exclamation fit into almost any situation.

When Lee Lee first started emerging out of her catatonic state, she was visibly upset. When she finally started having some consciousness about other people in the room, I could tell that she had strong opinions about them being there. Usually negative. When it became clear that Lee Lee had an awareness about just how much she had lost, I could see just how intensely it must have hurt. Both physically—her muscles were sore and twisted, she was too thin, too weak. Her skin was fragile and easily irritated. She developed bedsores and rashes—and mentally, I was convinced that Lee Lee was all too aware of her situation.

It was honestly no wonder to me that the only words she could spit out were hard-core profanity.

I'm sure I would have felt the same way.

The funny thing was, before the accident, Lee Lee never, ever swore. I used to tease her about it, she was always so buttoned up. So sweet and calm. Nothing seemed to shake her. And even when she was really mad, she might yell or cry, but she never resorted to profanity. I had never even heard her say the word *damn*.

Sometimes I wondered if it might have been something of a relief for her. She had kept herself so constrained before she had the accident. She had never allowed herself the satisfaction of really cursing someone out. Even when they truly deserved it. (I knew, for instance, that there were quite a few times when I had deserved an absolute shower of profanity from her.) Now she truly didn't give a fuck. She didn't care. And if these were some of her only words, she sure as hell was going to wield them.

The fact that the first language she mastered was *you fucking bitch* proved to me that she *knew.* Even if she couldn't express it beyond calling people names. She knew what had happened. She knew what she had lost. She remembered who she was before the accident. She noticed that the friends she'd had before didn't visit her now. That she didn't live at home. That she had lost her independence and ability to communicate. And she was angry and frustrated because even if she understood what had happened, she couldn't express what she wanted or how it made her feel, or anything beyond spitting out the f-word and glaring at everyone in the room.

I didn't mind. I didn't care that her only words were so angry. I was never hurt or angry when she yelled at me. In fact, I mainly felt a thrill of visceral joy. *Here was my girl.* She might not be exactly as she was before. But, then again, neither was I.

Let her say whatever she wanted to say. Let her rage and scream and fight. Someday we'd look back at this period of our lives and laugh.

And in the meantime, I would stay by her side and take whatever she offered up.

I would wait for her.

Because I was certain that Lee Lee would have waited for me.

Chapter 19

GETTING LEE LEE BACK HOME had been the focus for almost two long years. Evie and I talked about it all the time.

"I can't wait to get her out of this place," said Evie.

We were standing in the parking lot at the rehab center. Evie had been there when I'd visited that evening, and we'd walked out together.

She ran her fingers through her hair. "I mean, they've been great. They're great. But she's gone as far as she can go here. She needs to come home."

"I bet she has a huge reaction when she sees Kipper again," I said.

Evie smiled to herself. "That horse. He misses her. He's been a total devil since she's been gone. But yes, I bet he'll help. And the dogs. And her cat. Oh, and the twins, of course. They'll certainly give her plenty of stimulation whenever they're around."

I laughed. "I'm sure just about everything will change once she's home again."

Evie frowned. She was quiet for a moment.

"I hope so," she finally said. "It has to. Because there was the hospital, and then there was rehab, and now there is home. And . . ." She looked at me then. And quickly smiled. "It will make all the difference," she said. "I'm sure of it."

I nodded my head. "It will," I said. "I know it will."

I THINK WE ALL WANTED Lee Lee to come home more than Lee Lee herself did. Aside from the idea of getting her back into her home environment, we were all horse people. And horse people have a deep belief in the healing power of equine therapy. We'd all seen horses work miracles. Or in my case, experienced those miracles firsthand. We all expected that—even if Lee Lee couldn't ride right away—once she was back in the barn, once she could touch and smell and be with her horses again, it would invoke some of that pony magic that would bring back the carefree horse girl we had all once known.

"YOU OKAY?" I asked Evie.

We were sitting in the kitchen after Lee Lee had finally gone to sleep one night. It had been a rough couple of hours. Lee Lee had obviously been both uncomfortable and unhappy, twisting and moaning in her bed. Refusing food. Refusing to make eye contact with me or her mom.

Evie sighed. "I'm fine, sweetie. Just tired. Thank you for asking."

I looked at the dark circles under Evie's eyes, and I wanted to say more. But I sipped at the glass of wine that Evie had handed me instead.

Lee Lee's homecoming had not been what anyone expected.

There had been so much preparation. Both Evie and Phillip, and Lee Lee's dad, Richie, had done major renovations on their houses to make sure that Lee Lee's physical needs could be accommodated. There had been an extensive search trying to find the right at-home caregivers. We had all enthusiastically counted down as Lee Lee slowly met her milestones: made gains in her speech, her strength, her ability to eat and drink, getting the hang of her wheelchair. There had been a couple of times when we thought she was ready to be released, but there had been last-minute setbacks, and we'd all had to recalibrate our expectations once again.

But now Lee Lee was home, and it was so much harder than anyone expected. There had been no miraculous change as soon as Lee Lee had been wheeled into the barn. Instead, Lee Lee seemed to have almost regressed. Her sleep was disturbed, and eating became more difficult. Her vocabulary was still confined mainly to profanity. The family had to be responsible for her meds and figuring out a new daily routine. She was still going to Bryn Mawr a few times a week for outpatient therapy, but now she had to be transported from her home to the campus.

Lee Lee seemed angry. Angry and uncomfortable all the time. Instead of blossoming in a familiar home environment, she seemed to be undone by the change. And it was hard to track any small wins in her healing when the basic necessities of her being comfortable and relatively at peace seemed so out of reach for her.

I had some theories about what was happening. One was that Lee Lee's memory had, actually, been jogged by returning home. And that she didn't like what she was remembering. Perhaps it was hard for her to be in a place where she had once been so free and independent. Perhaps her limitations felt more acute and frustrating when everything around her was a reminder of her life before the accident.

Or perhaps she didn't actually remember her home. And so, coming back to it felt less like a return and more like an alien landscape. At Bryn Mawr, she had been surrounded by competent, kind, and highly trained medical professionals who were there 24-7 to attend to her needs. Now she was relying on her family's loving but inexpert care. There was a steep learning curve for everyone involved.

I wished, more than anything, that Lee Lee could tell me what she was experiencing. I wished I was fluent in her language so I could help more.

I worried about her, of course. As happy as I was to have her back in her home, there had been a layer of insulating protection at Bryn Mawr because it was still a medical facility. If anything happened—if Lee Lee started to seize, or choke, or got ill—she had been in the safest place she could possibly be. Now that she was home, I worried about her physical fragility. I worried about a medical emergency and the time it would take to get her help.

And I worried about Evie and the rest of Lee Lee's family, too. I worried about them being stretched too thin. I worried about how tired they all looked. I worried that they weren't getting enough sleep. That they weren't taking time for themselves. I worried that they didn't have enough help.

And so I felt like it was even more important that I show up every day that I could. That I was there predictably and consistently. That I was willing to take on whatever responsibility the family would let me. To help lighten the caretaking load. And despite the fact that I had started to occasionally hide in the bathroom at work and cry, it never occurred to me that maybe I should have been alert for the possibility of my own burnout.

It was funny, though, because whenever her family was all together, you'd never met such a positive group of people. We talked about Lee Lee all the time. Our lives circulated around her. But our conversations were always conducted in the most optimistic of terms. We applauded every gain and downplayed every setback. We only talked in terms of "when" she'd have her full recovery. Never "if." We discussed every new therapy, dietary change, and doctor's opinion as if they were the holy grail. Of course, I don't know how anyone was feeling privately. I couldn't hear their thoughts after they turned out the lights every night. But their certainty in her full recovery never publicly flagged. And honestly, I wouldn't have wanted to be around them if it had.

I'd always been a relentlessly optimistic person. And I'd always thought of that quality as my greatest strength. Despite the difficulties I'd faced growing up, I'd always been determined to believe that things would turn out okay. Better than okay.

Though her healing was taking longer than I had initially expected, I still looked forward to the day when Lee Lee was walking and talking and riding again. I still believed that would happen. And I believed that I just needed to be patient and supportive and keep on loving her until it did.

We all believed it.

SLOWLY BUT STEADILY, things started to get better for Lee Lee.

The most important thing that happened was Lee Lee's pain management was sorted out. We knew her medication was working when she stopped calling everyone a fucking bitch and her vocabulary started to be a bit more neutral. She still made it very clear when she didn't like or want something, but she now was more likely to simply say no, rather than cuss us out. She was trying new things like aqua therapy, and she started to learn how to move her legs with assistance from a machine. In theory, Lee Lee was perfectly capable of walking, running, even riding a horse again. As far as her bones and muscles and tendons went, her body had pretty much healed completely. But her brain didn't seem to know that. There was a disconnect between her brain and her legs. Her brain and her arms. Her brain and her tongue. The messages that needed to travel between her brain and her body simply weren't being delivered. But aqua therapy seemed to be helping that communication a bit.

With the help of some specially designed cutlery, she was starting to eat on her own. She was drinking both with a straw and out of a cup directly. Her hair was growing back. She was gaining much-needed weight.

She was making eye contact. She was smiling. Laughing. She started to recognize people and say their names.

She visited the barn and closed her eyes in utter joy when her horse lowered his muzzle and gently laid it against her cheek.

Of course, none of this happened overnight. These improvements happened very slowly over months. Years. But, in so many ways, Lee Lee was healing.

And in so many other ways, I was not.

I STARTED TO FORGET what it felt like to hold Lee Lee.

It had been three years since her accident, since the last time we had wrapped our arms around each other and breathed the same air.

Lee Lee had started to smile when I came to visit. She seemed to know who I was. Though whether that was because she remembered me as Kareem, her boyfriend, or just Kareem, the guy who showed up almost every day and held her hand while he told her silly stories about his cats, I was never quite sure.

"She gets so excited whenever I tell her you're coming," said Evie.

And then, because her short-term memory was still compromised,

Lee Lee would quickly forget about my imminent visit, and be even more excited when I walked in the door.

It was beautiful to see her so happy. Her big smile. The way she would lift her head toward me, demanding my kiss on her cheek in greeting. I thought this was one of the few pleasures of memory loss, the way that good things could feel like a never-ending surprise party. Her genuine shock and delight when I reappeared, seemingly out of nowhere. The sheer magic of my return.

Lee Lee had necessarily given up her old basement bedroom. Evie and Phillip had created a bright, welcoming, wheelchair accessible space for her on the main floor. The room was covered in photographs of Lee Lee at all stages of her life, beaming and radiant. With her sisters, with her brothers, with her horses, her friends, her parents, her grandparents, and with me.

Sometimes I would take pictures down off the wall and show them to her. "Do you remember this?" I'd ask. "The time we went camping? The debutante ball? The beach in Wellington?"

And Lee Lee would smile and nod but then crease her eyebrows in a way that made me wonder whether her memory was fractured, or that maybe she didn't actually remember at all. Maybe she was just humoring me.

I was learning to read her in a new way. The noises she made. Her body language, the way any emotion she was feeling was so plain on her face. But there were still so many things I couldn't yet interpret. I still sometimes thought that she was exactly the same woman inside her head that she had always been, only trapped.

And sometimes, I thought she was someone new. Someone who was relearning the most basic of life skills. Someone who was growing into an entirely different person with every ability she remastered.

I wanted to hold her. I wanted to climb into bed with her and snuggle up beside her. But her bed was too small. I would have crushed her trying to fit myself in next to her. It hurt, not being able to hold her. It felt like a phantom limb, a thing that no longer existed but still ached.

So I held her hand as always, and one day, feeling desperate to have more contact with her, I asked if I could lay my head against her chest.

Lee Lee smiled and nodded at me. "Yes," she whispered. When she spoke, she often whispered rather than using her full voice.

I scooted up as close as I could get to her and the bed, and I gently put one arm under her back and one arm around her shoulders, and I lay my cheek against her chest, just under her chin, that soft, warm space where I could hear her heartbeat.

It wasn't exactly comfortable for me. I was twisted and a little awkward. But it didn't matter. The moment my cheek touched Lee Lee's skin, fierce, buried feelings flew back into the light. That need, that reverence, the satisfying warmth that I used to feel with this woman. The closeness I just took for granted every single day I knew her. The way I could casually fit my body to hers and be comforted and sweetened. The way I used to rest against her. The physical manifestation of our love.

Of course, it wasn't the same. Lee Lee couldn't put her arms around me. She couldn't return the embrace. But she was quiet, and her heart beat slowly, and even if I wasn't sure that she was feeling just what I was feeling, I was certain that she was, at least, content.

After a bit of time, not wanting to overstay my welcome, I lifted my head again and kissed her forehead before I let go.

I wanted to kiss her lips. I hadn't since the accident. I had often wanted to, but it didn't feel right when she couldn't fully consent or kiss me back.

And I didn't know if that was something Lee Lee would ever want from me again.

"ARE YOU OKAY, sweetie?"

This time it was Evie worrying about me. She had walked me out to my car after another visit. I had turned to say good night to her, and apparently my mask had slipped.

I pushed my mouth into a smile that felt absurdly fake. "I'm fine," I insisted. "A little tired. A lot on my plate. Just work stuff."

Evie nodded. "It's a long drive."

I blinked at the non sequitur. "Nah, the drive is fine," I said.

Evie raised her eyebrows. "One of the best things about finally getting Lee Lee back home was that I didn't have to make that daily drive to Bryn Mawr anymore." She put her hand on my arm. "But you're still doing the commute."

"I don't mind," I insisted.

Evie met my eyes for a moment. I could see the concern all over her face. "You know, sweetie, no one expects you to—"

"Oh gosh," I said, digging my phone out of my pocket. "It's later than I thought! I should really get home."

Evie stopped talking. She cocked her head. Just looked at me.

"My cats," I explained weakly.

Finally, she nodded and then hugged me good night. "Okay. Have a safe trip home, sweetie."

"Thanks. Thank you!" I practically dived through my car door, slamming it behind me. "Good night!" I called through the window. "See you tomorrow!"

Evie slowly raised her hand and wiggled her fingers goodbye as I willed myself not to peel out of the driveway.

As I drove home that night, I played music. Loud. I was desperate to drown out the memory of Evie's unfinished words. I knew exactly what she had been going to say to me. I knew exactly where that conversation had been heading. And I was not ready to hear it.

Chapter 20

ABOUT THREE YEARS AFTER Lee Lee's accident, I finally went to see a therapist because I was convinced that I had attention deficit disorder.

Lee Lee was getting better, but I couldn't concentrate at work. I was crying all the time. I could barely sleep. Completing even the simplest tasks felt herculean. I was bouncing from panic attack to panic attack. And so, instead of facing up to the trauma and grief I was going through on a daily basis, instead of considering the idea that I might have any kind of caretaker burnout, I took an online quiz and believed the result. I told myself, *Oh, so this is what's wrong! Here is proof that I have ADD. Now I just need to convince some doctor to give me a pill to make this all go away.*

And so I did. I searched online and found a psychiatrist who took my insurance. I made an appointment. But I didn't tell anyone in my family I was going to therapy.

People from the Bottom don't go to therapists. When you're hustling for your daily subsistence, when you feel like you've had a pretty good day if you managed three meals and didn't get shot, when there's a makeshift memorial on every corner, and every other friend you have is in prison, it's pretty hard to imagine using any of your hard-earned dollars to sit in some clueless doctor's office and whine about your childhood. Plus, admitting that you needed help meant admitting that you were having mental issues to begin with, and there wasn't any tolerance for that. You were allowed to be sick if you had AIDS or cancer or diabetes. You were in trouble if you had a crack addiction. You might have a problem if you got shot. But you were never supposed to say that you had depression or anxiety. Those were bougie bullshit complaints. Admitting you had a mental health issue was just making it clear that you were a weak-ass pussy.

That's what I believed growing up, anyway. And that's what a lot of my family and friends still believed. But, as an adult, away from the Bottom, the idea of therapy was starting to become a bit more normalized for me. At work, and even back when I was in college, I heard people talking about their psychologists, or how they had to go to their therapy appointment, as casually as they talked about going to the dentist. At first it shocked me. Like people were putting their dirty laundry, their deepest shame, out there to flap in the wind. But after years of therapy being part of casual conversation, the idea lost its power to surprise me. I sometimes even caught myself wondering if it was something I could benefit from myself.

What I didn't yet understand, though, was that therapy was a process. Not a magic pill. I had always imagined that it worked the same way a visit to my GP worked. One and done.

I thought that if I sucked it up and saw a therapist, the results would essentially be instant. And painless. And I would be cured.

Now, if I had been going to any decent kind of therapist, that would have been laughable. That therapist would have asked me about my past, my family, the important moments in my life. They certainly would have heard all about Lee Lee. That therapist would have realized fairly quickly that if I had trouble concentrating, it might have had just a little something to do with the ongoing, violent trauma and loss I had experienced over and over again in my lifetime and was still working through day after day.

But the first psychiatrist I saw was not the right one for me. He was young and white, mild-mannered and soothing. And he seemed nice enough. He had an office on the sixteenth floor in Center City, and a soft, caring voice. He greeted me and introduced himself, and then asked me to sit in his waiting room and fill out some forms. Once I was done with those, he called me into his office and sat behind his big mahogany desk while he talked to me in a voice that reminded me of all the years that Lezlie made me listen to NPR in the car while we drove to polo games. He talked to me for exactly thirty minutes.

He asked me why I was there to see him.

I told him I was feeling distracted at work. I told him that I had graduated from college a few years before and had moved back to the city and that I sometimes struggled with my work-life balance. That I had a hard time concentrating.

He didn't probe any further than that. He didn't ask me about my childhood. He didn't ask me about my family. He didn't ask me where I grew up or if anything specifically difficult had ever happened to me. He certainly didn't ask if the woman I loved was recovering from a TBI. To be fair, I didn't volunteer any information about Lee Lee, either.

I'm not sure why. I guess I was embarrassed. As soon as I walked into the office, I started to feel like I had made a mistake. I didn't really *want* to talk to this guy. I didn't think he would get it. And even if he did, how was that going to change anything? I felt resistant and foolish. Like I was participating in bougie nonsense.

Also, I think I just really wanted to believe that whatever was wrong with me had absolutely nothing to do with Lee Lee. I didn't want to compare my pain to hers in any way. After all, I wasn't the one who'd been in an accident. I wasn't the one struggling with a TBI. How could I imagine that this situation was somehow hard on me, when Lee Lee was still learning how to pick up a spoon and feed herself?

And even if I could admit that this had anything to do with Lee Lee, what was the possible cure? A pill wasn't going to change how short my days were or just long that drive was. A pill couldn't push away my grief. A pill couldn't make her get better any faster.

So I told my psychiatrist I had taken an online test and I thought I had ADD. Because I knew that ADD was something a pill could help.

And just before our thirty minutes was up, he agreed. And gave me a prescription for Vyvanse.

NOW, I ABSOLUTELY BELIEVE that something like Vyvanse could help someone who truly has ADD. But for me? Someone who was actually struggling with what I now know to be anxiety and depression? Who had countless unresolved and unexamined childhood traumas? Who suffered from regular panic attacks? It was speed. It was speed that made me feel great for about two to three hours—like I could solve any problem at work, like I could drive all night without stopping, like I didn't need to sleep or eat—until it drained out of my system and left me crashed and miserable.

I knew this pretty much right away. I could tell that it wasn't a stabilizing drug as much as it was a bright red, not very effective bandage over what was really wrong. And on my second appointment a couple of weeks later, I mentioned this to my psychiatrist, that I thought maybe the pills weren't so great for me. And instead of questioning whether I actually needed it or not, he just adjusted the dosage. When I went back to him again a few weeks after that, complaining about more of the same, he switched me to Ritalin.

Though I try to fight it, I know I have an addictive personality. If I taste a new food that I really love, I will eat it every day for weeks. I don't allow myself to travel to Las Vegas or any kind of casino because I know that I will gamble away every penny that I have. Anything that will produce endorphins or get me super excited or make me do stupid, dangerous things, I try to avoid. Because I have a genetic predisposition. On both sides. My father is an alcoholic and my mother is an addict. My grandparents were alcoholics and addicts. And I'm fairly certain their parents were, too. So I am careful. I don't do recreational drugs, and I'm thoughtful about the amount I drink, and I do my best to keep my more compulsive pleasure-seeking appetites under control.

But Vyvanse was a prescription. Given to me by a doctor. And weren't all those people who had been casually talking about their therapists taking the same stuff? And it did give me energy. When I was riding its high, I was chatty and smiley and warm and fuzzy with everyone I met. And it did give me confidence. I felt like I was crushing it at work. And it did make me cry a little less. I floated around in a happy haze. And it did—at least for a few hours every day—make me stop thinking about the unthinkable. It gave me a place to go where everything was bright and shiny and bad things never happened.

So I started taking the pills closer and closer together. I timed them so they would kick in just before I had a big meeting at work. I'd pop one before a conversation that I felt unprepared to handle. Or before that long, long drive that I took every night.

It was a recipe for disaster. I absolutely knew it. But I kept taking those pills for months and months more. I kept taking them and then promising myself I would cut back. I kept taking them and then thinking about flushing the whole bottleful down the toilet (but never following through). I kept taking them because even though they made me feel shaky and empty and like absolute crap when they faded out of my system, they still felt better than my reality. They were still easier than facing up to what was really wrong.

"GOOD MORNING, BABY! What are you up to today?"

It was a Tuesday morning at the office. My mother had called just like she did every morning. It was a ritual: she would call, I would answer, we'd chat for a few moments, usually about not much, and then I'd go on with my day.

I felt a sharp bolt of annoyance.

"Work," I snapped. "I'm trying to get some work done like I do every Tuesday morning, Mom."

I could hear how mean and begrudging I sounded, but I didn't care.

"Oh," she said. "Well, of course. I won't keep you, then."

"Good," I said before I could stop myself. "I'll talk to you later."

And then I hung up before she could answer and went back to the report I was outlining on my computer screen.

Another thirty minutes passed, and my phone rang again. I glanced down and saw that it was my mother.

For a moment, I contemplated not answering.

She does this all the time, I thought to myself. *Calls me whenever she feels like it. She never respects my work schedule. She never respects my time. She knows I have better things to do than deal with her shit.*

The phone kept ringing.

I shook my head. I always answered if my mother called. Because

I loved her. Because I cared about her. But also because, in the back of my mind, I was always expecting disaster. Emergencies and tragedies were nonstop in West Philly.

"Hello?" I said.

"Baby?" she said.

"Hi, Mom."

"Hey, I just wanted to check in to make sure that you're still coming to help me move the couch this weekend."

Oh God. Fuck this shit.

"Why can't Hank help you move the couch?"

She was quiet for a beat. "He hasn't been around the last couple of days." Her voice sounded small.

I snorted. *Then maybe you should have picked a better fucking husband.*

"What about Washika?"

"Washika isn't any help, either. You know that girl. Always out with her friends. Hardly ever even seen her these days."

Can you blame her?

I closed my eyes and bit my tongue because I wanted to scream at my mother. I wanted to scream at her so she would stop talking. I wanted to scream at her so she'd stop bugging me. I wanted to scream at her so she would hang up the phone and never call me again.

"It's just that I can't really lift it by myself, and I think it would look better on the other side of the room."

I took a deep breath. In. Out. I gritted my teeth so hard they hurt. My hands curled into fists.

"Mom?" I finally said. "I gotta go."

"But are you still coming or—"

"Don't call me again."

And then I hung up on her before she finished talking. Before I said or did something much, much worse than hanging up the phone.

I uncurled my hands. They were shaking.

I got up from my desk, went into the bathroom, flipped the lid shut on the toilet and sank down with my head between my legs.

I can't believe I just talked to my mother that way.

This was not me. I had never hung up on my mother before, never mind twice in one morning. I never talked to her with this kind of anger or disrespect. I *loved* my mother. I didn't mind helping her out. I *liked* that I could be there for her when she needed me.

But now I sounded like Hank. I sounded like Marcus. I sounded like all the men in her life who made her feel like shit. Who barely tolerated her.

This is not me.

The feeling of losing myself was absolutely terrifying.

This is how it all started. This is how it started for my mother and father and grandmother and grandfather. This is how they became addicts. This is how they started choosing drugs over everything else.

This is not me.

THAT NIGHT, I dumped the rest of my pills down the toilet.

The next few days were tough. I felt groggy and sick and like I would never get out of bed again. Then it was a tough couple of weeks after that when I missed all the superpowers I felt the drug had given me.

Before I quit, I had seen my psychiatrist only often enough to get refills on my scrip. Thirty minutes, in and out, every couple of months or so.

"How are you doing? Are you eating well? Are you getting rest? Do you feel okay?"

"Yes, Yes, Yes," I'd say.

Then he'd dial in my prescription, and I was good to go.

Once I quit, I didn't bother to call to tell him our relationship was over. And he didn't call me to find out where I had gone.

Well, I thought. *I guess that was therapy.*

And therapy obviously did not work for me.

In some ways, I felt better. My head was clearer. I wasn't so prone to losing my temper. My appetite came back.

But in other ways, I felt myself sinking back down into my unhappiness. There it all was again. The endless commute. The hard thoughts about what I would do if Lee Lee never fully recovered. The possibility that this was *it* for me. That the rest of my life would be me barely hanging on at work, crying on my lunch break, driving back and forth through the dark, and ending my day sitting by the bedside of the woman I still loved, wishing I could hold her. Wondering if she would ever love me back in the same way again. Feeling the numbness inside of me grow and grow.

Chapter 21

I SPENT A LOT OF TIME thinking about Lee Lee's right hand.

From the day she had her accident, that hand was stuck in the same position: curled up into a loose fist. She couldn't straighten her fingers. Whenever I wanted to hold that hand, I would gently push her fingers open, fit my palm to hers, and then allow her fingers to spring back and tighten once again.

I wasn't the only one who was focused on it. Her team of physical therapists spent a lot of time working with her on that right hand. They were always doing small-motor exercises, trying to strengthen and stretch her fingers. Heaping on the praise when she'd manage to scoop something up.

I had always seen Lee Lee's right hand as a symbol, a predictor of her recovery. *When Lee Lee uncurls her fingers and can pick up a pen or a fork . . . When Lee Lee's hand gets better and she can wave and high-five and flip me off again . . . When Lee Lee's hand opens up and her fingers stretch, and she can grab my hand in hers instead of vice versa . . .*

That will mean that Lee Lee will recover.

It was silly, really. With all the progress she had made, I was still standing around, acting like her fisted fingers were somehow going to tell me my future.

WHAT IF HER HAND NEVER CHANGES?

I was driving back from visiting her. Playing the what-if game.

What if this is the way her hand will always just be?

I let myself sit with this thought for a moment as I squinted at the highway. The car behind me flashed their brights and then pulled into the left lane to pass me.

It wouldn't matter, I finally decided. *Of course it wouldn't matter. Lee Lee is still the same person whether she can fully open her hand or not.*

It's just her hand.

I leaned back in my seat, thinking harder. I listened to the hum and whoosh of the highway traffic. I saw the shadowy outline of a tree on the side of the road.

River birch.

I reached for the car stereo and turned it on, skipped a song I was tired of listening to.

And what if things never change for me?

I took my exit into Philly, heading back home in the dark.

What if this is the way it will always be?

IT HAD BEEN ALMOST four years, and despite all her advances, it became clear that Lee Lee had plateaued in certain ways.

It seemed more than likely that she would need 24-7 care for the rest of her life. There was almost no chance she would ever live independently. And though she could follow most simple conversations, her vocabulary was still limited, and she often struggled to express more than the most basic of her wants and needs. Although we couldn't really measure just how much of her long-term memory was intact, her short-term memory remained compromised, and she tended to live almost exclusively in the moment.

"Water," she would demand.

"Tired," when she was done with having company.

"No," she said, pushing away something she didn't want around anymore.

IT WAS BECOMING CLEAR to me that we would never go back to what we once had. Maybe Lee Lee would walk again someday. Maybe her vocabulary would continue to improve. Maybe she would even get back on a horse.

But Lee Lee would never be my wife. Or the mother of my children. Or my partner.

That part of who we were was in the past.

I loathed myself for even thinking it, but I began to suspect that, though I loved Lee Lee desperately, the romantic love I had felt for the person I had known before the accident was of an entirely different nature than the love I felt for her now.

I didn't know what to do with these realizations. I had promised to be there. I had promised to stay. I owed it to Evie and Phillip and Richie.

And, of course, I had promised it to Lee Lee.

I was convinced that I would be the worst kind of person if I didn't follow through.

I was exhausted and depressed and overwhelmed, but I continued to get into that car every night and make my pilgrimage to her bedside. There didn't seem to be any other choice I could make and still be the man I thought I should be.

I was hurtling backward, getting worse. The lack of focus returned. The crying jags. The panic attacks seemed nonstop. I further isolated myself from my friends and family. I was living with constant feelings of guilt and regret and dread. I had no world outside of Lee Lee. And I could barely breathe on that particular planet.

"HEY, KAREEM, can you come into my office, please?"

I stood up from my desk and immediately felt like I was going to throw up. Or maybe black out.

This was it. Joe was going to fire me.

I deserve this, I thought as I followed him into his office. He had been incredibly supportive and patient, and, in return, I had turned into an epically horrible employee. I was distracted. I was slow. I was exhausted. I practically ran out of the building every night at the stroke of five. I was pretty sure someone had heard me crying in the bathroom earlier that afternoon.

"Take a seat," said Joe.

I sat. I closed my eyes. For a moment I considered yelling, "I quit!" before he could say "You're fired."

"I'm not going to beat around the bush," said Joe.

I opened my eyes. Steeled myself.

"I'm worried about you."

I blinked. Not what I'd expected.

"I've noticed that you seem distracted."

I couldn't help it. I laughed. Then I snapped my mouth shut, horrified.

He smiled grimly. "I mean, I know you're distracted. Of course you're distracted. But it seems to be worse than usual."

"I'm sorry," I said. "It's just been kind of a crazy week. I haven't been sleeping much. But it should be better soon. I'll be fine."

I cringed inwardly. I knew I sounded dumb and desperate. Making excuses.

He shook his head. "It's been longer than a week, Kareem. A lot longer."

I sucked in my breath. Opened my mouth. Then I closed it. He was right. And I was too exhausted to argue.

Just get it over with, I silently begged him.

"You know," he said. "I went through a pretty rough patch myself a few years back. We don't need to get into the details or anything, but there were some days when I didn't even know how to get out of bed."

I almost laughed again. That was me *every* day.

"Finally I found a really good psychiatrist. I got some help."

I nodded slowly. Thinking about the Vyvanse.

He frowned. "There's nothing wrong with getting help when you need it, man," he said.

"Sure. I know," I said automatically.

He slid a piece of paper across the desk at me. "Her name is Dr. Ellen Berman. She's pretty well known in the Philly community. She's got a reputation for helping some difficult cases. I don't think it's an exaggeration to say that she saved my life."

I looked at the paper. Looked at it without really looking at it.

"I'll pay for the first six months," he said.

I raised my eyebrows. "So I'm not getting fired?"

Joe laughed. A shocked little wheeze. "Uh. No. That wasn't my plan for today, anyway." He shoved the paper closer to me. "Seriously, Kareem. Please. Fucking call this doctor."

I picked up the piece of paper.

Ellen, I thought.

THE TRUTH WAS, I had needed therapy for years, and I kind of knew that. I'd gone through the kind of violent, day-to-day trauma that left me with serious mental health issues. I suffered from anxiety and depression. The panic attacks. I fully expected to lose pretty much everyone I loved one way or the other. I was an expert in denial and compartmentalization and magical thinking and all sorts of half-assed coping mechanisms. But those things just weren't helping me anymore, and I finally came to the point where I didn't fucking care if someone in the hood might think I was less of a man if I got myself help.

I finally got to a point where I was willing to risk another prescription—more pills—if that's what it took.

I couldn't cope any longer. I knew that if I didn't do something, I was going to lose my job. I wouldn't be able to help Lee Lee.

I honestly felt like there was every chance that I might actually lose my mind.

That's when I called Ellen.

I WAS INCREDIBLY NERVOUS the first time I went to see her. Her office was in her home, in a detached garage, on the Main Line, out in the suburbs. I remember walking through her door and looking around, seeing a couple of comfortable-looking chairs and a kettle to make tea, and then coming face-to-face with this little old white lady and thinking, *No way. Not her. Maybe I'll just lie.*

I still didn't understand therapy. I still thought that it was like having a headache and taking a Tylenol. That there was some sort of magical instant cure. And I thought even if Ellen didn't want to prescribe me anything, surely one conversation ought to be enough to fix whatever was going on with me.

Ellen introduced herself and offered me a cup of tea. I waved her off, but she made a cup for herself before she sat down across from me.

"Let's talk about the elephant in the room." She sipped her tea. "I am an old, white Jewish lady."

I blinked. Wondering how I was supposed to respond to that.

She put down her cup. "And because of the fact that I'm an old, white Jewish lady, I might not be right for you. You might feel more comfortable talking to a Black therapist. Perhaps even a Black male therapist. And if that's the case, that's totally fine. I will help you find him. There are many good Black male therapists in our fine city."

I swallowed.

"But since you made the trip out, I am more than happy to talk to you today and see where we end up." She settled back with her yellow legal pad, obviously ready to take notes, and said, "Now, tell me, why are you here?"

I looked at her for a minute, trying to read her. And I could see that she was trying to read me right back. And I was in so much pain. I was filled with shame and embarrassment and desperation. And I thought about the last time I tried therapy. How he asked me nothing. How I told him nothing. And how nothing had helped me.

I looked at Ellen again. She met my eyes and smiled. And there was something encouraging in the way she looked at me.

Something safe.

Maybe I should just start talking.

And that's when I opened my mouth and started telling on myself.

"I first heard about Lee Lee Jones at the barn where I ride . . ."

AFTER I FINISHED TALKING, Ellen settled back in her chair and looked at me.

I tried to keep eye contact but it was too intense. I looked away.

"Kareem, have you ever heard the term *ambiguous loss?*" she asked.

"No. I don't think so," I said.

"*Ambiguous loss* is a clinical term for living in the in-between. It's losing something while still clinging to the slight chance that you might get it back exactly as it was before."

I shifted in my chair, uneasy.

"It's not as definite as death," she went on. "It doesn't allow for the clear rituals that might lead to closure. It leaves you constantly suspended between despair and hope. Because circumstances aren't entirely concrete or clear, it doesn't allow you to accept the idea that things will most likely never be the same. Does that make sense?"

I shrugged. "Sure. I guess."

She nodded. "A parent whose child was kidnapped suffers from one kind of ambiguous loss. A wife whose soldier husband is missing in action does, too. When you lose someone physically, but they still have a psychological hold in your life, and you know there is a small chance that they might one day return, that is a kind of ambiguous loss."

Ellen leaned forward and caught my eye again.

"Then there is another kind of ambiguous loss. When someone is still there physically but they have drastically changed. It's when you still have that person in your life but they have transformed so much, there is little to nothing left that is recognizable as who they were before. Someone who has a loved one with Alzheimer's, or drug addiction, or severe depression—or yes, a traumatic brain injury—knows this kind of loss in the most intimate of ways."

I leaned away from her. Shrunk into the back of my chair. I knew this loss. I recognized it as soon as Ellen described it. And I thought that maybe I could apply it to my brothers' incarcerations. And I knew that I could definitely apply it to my mother and her addictions. But I didn't like the fact that Ellen was bringing Lee Lee into things. I didn't want to face the idea that I had to accept and apply this concept to Lee Lee, and then, I assumed, find a way to move on with my life.

There can be a relief in naming your pain. There is some level of hope when you find out that other people share your issues and that there are tools and ways to cope with them that you might not have tried just yet.

But putting a name to what's wrong with you doesn't entirely cure the problem, either. How could something so personal, so intimate, so devastating, be encapsulated by one simple psychological term? And in the case of Lee Lee, naming what I felt—admitting that other people might be going through it, too—felt like I was betraying her and the very specific and particular pain and loss that we had gone through both together and separately.

Like lots of people who have experienced ambiguous loss, I was frozen in the very first stage of grief—deep, deep in denial. But I got lucky, because Ellen was tenacious and caring and smart enough to figure out a way to lead me through and out.

There would be conditioning. And talk therapy. And tons of work on my part. Ellen made it very clear that I would have to put in time and thought and sweat and emotion. That she couldn't just instantly "fix" me.

"SO I'LL SEE YOU NEXT WEEK?" asked Ellen as I stood up after our first session. "Same time?"

I nodded slowly, still not sure that I would actually come back. I had told Ellen a lot. Certainly more than I'd told my first psychiatrist and in some ways, more than I'd told anyone for years. Maybe ever.

She had asked about Lee Lee. Which made sense to me. But she had also asked about my family. My mother. My neighborhood. My history. I wasn't sure how I felt about that.

And I still didn't know how I felt about shrinking the complicated, tender feelings I had about Lee Lee down to a single clinical term. That felt almost too easy—too simple—for something that had shrouded my life for so long.

ONCE I WAS OUT OF the office and walking down the street, I tested myself, poking at my own mood and emotions.

Do I feel any better?

Still tired. Still sad. Still need to go see Lee Lee tonight.

So. No. Not really.

Still, the next week, I found myself back in Ellen's office.

"SOMETIMES," I hesitated. "Sometimes I get this feeling like, I can't breathe. Like my heart goes really fast. Like"—I laughed an uncomfortable little laugh—"like I might die, actually. But then . . . I don't."

Ellen nodded. "So. A panic attack."

I snapped my head up and looked at her. "That's what a panic attack is?"

She nodded. "I mean, assuming you have cleared all other medical reasons. Sure sounds like one to me."

"And so, other people get these? It's not just me. And I'm not crazy?"

Ellen was quiet for a moment. Then she said, in a very gentle voice, "No, you're not crazy, Kareem. And no, you're certainly not the only one who has this issue."

LATER THAT NIGHT I lay in bed, taking deep breaths, thinking, *I'm not the only one. I'm not the only one.*

"SO YOU ARE THE ONE your mom calls when she's fighting with her husband?"

"Well, sometimes one of my sisters calls me."

Ellen nodded. "And how long has that been the situation?"

I shrugged. "Since I moved out, I guess."

"So, college."

"No." I shook my head. "Since I went away to military school. When I was fourteen."

Ellen's eyebrows shot up.

"Someone's got to do it," I explained. "My mom was really young when she had us. She struggles with a dependence on drugs. I barely know my dad. My grandparents are gone. My brothers are incarcerated. Someone has to step up."

Ellen cocked her head. "Step up to do what?"

I shrugged. "Manage the chaos. Keep everyone safe. Make sure we survive as a family."

Ellen narrowed her eyes. "And you think you can do all that?"

I lifted my chin. "I can try."

WEEK AFTER WEEK, I kept coming back. And Ellen kept asking me questions. Kept helping me connect the dots. She made me realize that though Lee Lee's accident had been a triggering event for me, my problems ran so much deeper. They went all the way back.

All the way down. My history, my past traumas, Mecca, had set the stage for all the ways I'd acted, all the decisions I had made, since Lee Lee had first been hurt.

I was the caretaker in my family. It was my role to worry. To pay attention. To make sure everyone was okay. The best way I knew how to express love was to desperately work my ass off to make sure that everyone around me was safe and secure.

"DO YOU THINK that the care Lee Lee gets when you're not around is different from the care she gets when you're there?"

I shook my head. "No. They take great care of her."

"Do you think that Evie expects you to care for Lee Lee?"

I shook my head. "No. No way."

"How about Phillip or Richie?"

"Of course not."

"So, then, why do you feel obligated to take care of Lee Lee?"

I blinked. "Because . . . because I promised Lee Lee that I would."

"Did she ask you to do that?"

That stopped me for a moment. "Well, no. No, she didn't. But she couldn't."

Ellen was quiet. Just looking at me. Then she said, "You know, Kareem, no one wants to see you run yourself ragged. No one wants you depressed and exhausted. No one expects you to single-handedly take on Lee Lee's burdens."

I looked back at Ellen. "But I told her that I would."

She nodded. "You are not Lee Lee's husband."

I frowned. "I know that."

"You never made that kind of commitment to her."

"But I would have. I would have married her."

Ellen looked at me for a moment and waited. She was always doing that. Waiting for me to catch up.

Finally, I said what I knew she was waiting for me to say. "But I didn't." My voice was barely audible. "I know that. I know she's not my wife."

Ellen nodded. "And Lee Lee is not alone. She has her parents. She has her family. She has her caretakers. She has a whole community of people around her. And actually, it sounds like Lee Lee is capable of shouldering many of her challenges herself."

I nodded in return. That was true. Lee Lee was incredibly strong.

"You are twenty-six years old." Ellen's voice was gentle. "You have a whole lifetime ahead of you. Is this what you want it to look like? Work and driving and Lee Lee and nothing else?"

I shook my head. I couldn't say it out loud.

Ellen leaned toward me. "Then I'd like you to consider the idea, that maybe, just maybe, you won't be a terrible, awful person if you do what you have to do to survive. If you found other ways, instead of running yourself into the ground, to show Lee Lee how much you care."

THE HARDEST PART OF LEAVING Lee Lee behind every night had always been the way I couldn't help imagining her in her bed, alone, the lights off, the door closed, and the fact that, if she was sad or lonely, she couldn't pick up a phone and call anybody. She couldn't turn on her TV to distract herself. She couldn't read a book or listen to music. She could only lie there in the dark, with her cat and her thoughts for company, and wait for morning.

ELLEN STARED AT ME. Waiting.

"What?" I finally said.

"Didn't you tell me just last week that you usually leave after Lee Lee goes to sleep?"

I shrugged my shoulders. "I guess so."

"And haven't you told me many times that she gets tired very easily? That she often naps and goes to bed quite early? That she needs a lot of sleep?"

I shifted uncomfortably in my seat. "Yeah."

"So?" said Ellen.

"So what?" I said in return.

Even though I knew.

"So, who does this actually sound like? Who hates the dark and lies in his bed and gets lonely and sad and only has his cats for company every night?"

"But I can pick up my phone," I protested. "I can turn on the TV. I can turn the light back on. I can get out of my bed."

Ellen stared at me. Waited some more.

I stared right back. Making her wait this time.

She finally smiled at me and shook her head. "Okay, sure," she said. "But this thing, this thing that you imagine being so hard for Lee Lee, that you torture yourself thinking about, is that her nightmare, or is it yours?"

"I don't know," I admitted.

"Well, was Lee Lee afraid of the dark before her accident?"

"No."

"Did she have trouble sleeping?"

I smiled at the thought. "She always fell asleep before I did."

Ellen waited.

"But it's different now," I said. "And we don't know what she's feeling. She can't really tell us anymore."

Ellen nodded. "Exactly," she said. "And I'm not saying that Lee Lee doesn't get scared or lonely or sad or depressed. I'm not saying that this isn't all very hard for her. Because I'm sure, in lots of ways, it truly is. I'm just saying, you don't know. She isn't telling you. The only person who you absolutely know is unhappy is . . . ?"

"Me," I mumbled.

Ellen folded her arms over her chest. Leaned back in her chair. She smiled at me.

"You," she said. "The only thing you have any control over in this world is you."

Chapter 22

MY MOTHER PROBABLY TRIED to quit drugs a dozen times in her life.

"I haven't touched a thing in three days," she'd tell us. So proud of herself for keeping clean.

But then another few days would pass and we'd see that hazy look in her eyes. We'd hear that slur in her voice. And we'd know.

It wasn't that she was lying to us, or that she didn't want to quit. But things were hard in her life. Sometimes so hard that she needed the thing that made it easier—even if it was only a temporary fix—more than she wanted to be sober.

So in the summer of 2019, when my mother told me that she had quit again, I was barely listening.

I was at work. We were having one of our early morning check-in calls. My mom was at Kareema's house because she had left her husband, Hank, about seven or eight months before, and he'd refused to move out of their shared home.

We were all relieved when she'd finally left him. None of us liked the way he talked to her. The way he tried to control every aspect of her life. The way he tried to come between her and us. He'd always been threatened by our loyalty to our mother. He didn't want anyone to be on her side. And they were both addicts who not only enabled each other's addictions but also centered their entire relationship upon drugs, like they were throwing gasoline on the fire of their dependence.

"I haven't taken a thing for six months," my mom said to me.

"What?" I said, thinking I had misheard. "How long?"

"Six months," she said. "It's been six months."

For a moment, I wondered if she was telling the truth. But why would she lie about something like this? She knew that we accepted and loved her whether she was using or not.

"Wow, Mom," I said. "That's great."

"I just got tired of being so tired," she said. "So I stopped."

I smiled and shook my head, glad that she couldn't see me over the phone. She was talking like it had been this easy all along. Like she hadn't quit a dozen times before and then taken it right back up again.

"Why didn't you tell me sooner?"

"I wanted to wait." She sounded almost shy. "I wanted to see if I could do it."

Don't get too excited yet, I reminded myself. She had stopped and then slipped so many times before.

But still, six months was a long time.

"I'm really proud of you," I kept my voice measured and calm. Like it was no big deal. Like it really was an easy thing she could just continue doing. "If you need any help, let me know."

"BUT WHAT WOULD HAPPEN if you left Lee Lee just twenty minutes early?" asked Ellen.

My response was instant. "I couldn't do that."

Her gaze was steady. "But what would happen if you did?"

"I can't do that," I said.

"Okay, then," Ellen said. "What about fifteen minutes early?"

"No," I said.

Ellen picked up her teacup and then put it back down without taking a drink. She met my eyes. "Is this it? Is this what you want the rest of your life to be?"

I looked away from her. I swallowed, trying to push down the burning lump of tears in my throat. "No," I finally whispered. "No."

"Ten minutes, then," she said. "Just ten minutes."

WHEN I HAD FIRST DECIDED to see Ellen, it was not with the intention that she would somehow help me decrease my time with Lee Lee. The idea that I would change my schedule was not something that was under consideration. What I thought she would do (if she didn't just give me a magic pill that would fix everything) was help me figure out how to better endure the situation. I thought she would help me find a way to continue doing exactly what I was doing, except that I'd now be happy while doing it.

But she soon made it very clear that she did not consider this a tenable plan. She soon made it very clear that what I had to learn from therapy was not how to tolerate the status quo but to identify what needed to change and then figure out how to make that change happen.

"SO, DID YOU DO IT?" Ellen asked at our next appointment. "Did you leave early?"

I nodded. "I did. Yes."

"And how did that feel?"

"Not great," I said.

She nodded, waiting.

"Her friends barely visit anymore," I said. "I don't want to do that to her."

Ellen nodded again. "How do you feel when you're visiting Lee Lee these days?"

I frowned. "What do you mean?"

"I mean, do you feel like you're happy when you visit? Do you feel like you're bringing her good, productive energy?"

"I mean, I try to."

"But do you? Are you your best self when you are with her?"

"I mean, I pretend to—"

She lifted her hand. "Gonna stop you right there. That word, *pretend*. From what you have told me, Lee Lee is very sensitive. Don't you think she knows when you're pretending? Don't you think she deserves to have you at your best?"

I was quiet for a moment, staring at my hands.

Finally I looked up at Ellen. "How long this week?"

She smiled. "Let's try fifteen minutes early."

SOMETIMES I WISH I could point to a villain in this story. I wish I could tell you all about the asshole who wanted me to move on too soon. Who thought I was an idiot for hanging around and waiting for so long. Or maybe it would be the person who told me that I would be the worst kind of shit if I ever even considered leaving. But there was no one like that. All my friends, my family, my boss, Lezlie—they all understood. They were all patient and kind with me. They didn't complain when I ghosted them. They always answered my calls. They showed up in those rare moments when I had time to see them. They listened. They asked about Lee Lee. They asked after me. They cared. They loved me. I was supported.

And Lee Lee's family was equally great. Phillip and Richie were both kind and generous. Her little siblings made me laugh. And Evie was my lifeline. She was a friend and a confidant and fellow sufferer. She had all these little bits and pieces that reminded me of her daughter, so being with her was almost like having certain parts of Lee Lee back again. And she only wanted what was best for me.

And, of course, Lee Lee herself never asked me for anything.

I mean, actually, that wasn't true. She asked for lots of things. She had moved beyond *Fuck you, bitch* at this point, but she had not returned to the preaccident, sweet, easy Lee Lee, either. She would beam at me when I first walked into the room, but that joy was usually fleeting. She never really lost her edge or gained much of a filter. "Water!" she demanded. "Hungry!" "Bed!" "Yes!" "No!" "Quiet!"

But Lee Lee never asked me to wait. She never, ever asked me to wait.

So, unsurprisingly, the only person I was battling was myself.

I was battling my tendency to push my own needs so far down that I could barely feel them anymore. I was battling my resistance to telling anyone that I was not okay. I was ignoring the fact that I was lonely. That I was physically and emotionally depleted. That I missed having someone to really talk to. That I missed being touched. I missed sex. I missed riding horses. I missed having more to my life than work, the drive, my visit with Lee Lee, the drive back, and then off to bed, where I may or may not sleep.

I missed looking forward to things. I missed thinking about my future with any kind of hope.

I hated waking up every morning and thinking I was a piece of shit because I didn't want to make the drive that day. I hated myself. I hated my life. And I hated the fact that I constantly stood in my own way.

"AND HOW WAS IT this week?"

"Better," I admitted. "Easier. But I really don't like telling you that."

Ellen laughed.

FIFTEEN MINUTES became half an hour became an hour. Five days a week became four. I started to tell Evie I had plans when I actually had plans. I started telling people how I honestly was doing when they asked. I set some very soft boundaries. And then some more concrete ones. I cried even more. But mostly in therapy.

"HOW ABOUT THIS WEEK? How'd it go?"

"It was good. I left thirty minutes early. And I didn't go on Friday."

Ellen smiled. "That's great! That's a big step."

I looked away from Ellen. Bit the inside of my cheek.

"Okay, that was a lie. I went every night, and I didn't leave early at all."

IT WAS A GRADUAL, excruciating process. And there were plenty of days I slipped backward. Sometimes I would go to sleep, telling myself that I would take the next day off from seeing Lee Lee, and wake up panicked and filled with self-loathing. How could I possibly even think about skipping a day? She *needed* me. I would go to visit and then tell Ellen that I hadn't, feeling ridiculous that I was so worried about what my therapist thought that I felt the need to lie to her about when and if I saw Lee Lee.

———————

ONE DAY I DID TELL EVIE that I wouldn't be coming the next evening. And I didn't even have an excuse, except that I really wanted a day off. She was, of course, entirely understanding. Evie never pressured me or made me feel guilty about Lee Lee.

Still, I felt less than great about myself as I drove home that night.

But the next morning, I woke up in my own bed and watched the morning light slowly move across my bedroom ceiling and thought about the fact that I had a whole day stretching in front of me with absolutely no commitments.

My cats had snuggled up on either side of me, and I imagined that they were purring because, for once, I was lingering in bed instead of jumping straight up in a panic to get everything done.

Maybe I would go out to the Bottom. Visit my family. Check in with my friends.

Maybe I would go to the barn and ride.

Maybe I would take a walk around my neighborhood. Get some breakfast at a restaurant I hadn't tried before.

Or maybe I would just stay home and do nothing at all.

"WHAT ABOUT THIS WEEK?" said Ellen.

"I only saw Lee Lee three times."

She nodded. "That's great. And how was that?"

I thought for a moment. "You know what? It was really good. I wasn't tired. I was happy to be there. We joked around and laughed a lot. One of those days, we went down to the barn and visited her horse. Evie and I had a glass of wine after Lee Lee went to sleep."

"And how was the drive back to Philly?"

I smiled at Ellen. "I didn't cry at all."

COMPLETELY LETTING GO was never an option. Even as I progressed, even with all the hard work that Ellen and I did together, there was never any chance of me turning my back and walking away completely. I loved Lee Lee too much for that.

But you are allowed to change, Ellen told me. *It is okay to change things that are untenable.*

I started to believe that. And eventually I started to tell myself the same thing.

"YOU KNOW," said Ellen. "I think we can probably start seeing less of each other as well."

I looked up, surprised. "What do you mean?"

Ellen sipped her tea. "I mean, you're doing great. You've made huge progress. I think we can switch over to a schedule that reflects more maintenance than active therapy."

For a moment, I felt panic. Was she crazy? How was I supposed to get through this without Ellen?

I opened my mouth to argue.

"You're ready, Kareem. You've got this. Trust me. Trust yourself."

I shut my mouth.

Then I felt a glow. A warmth. A flush of pride.

Ellen was right.

That part of myself—that scared kid, that traumatized teen, that sad, lonely man who had just been groping his way through life—that part of myself had become someone else.

Someone new.

Someone who was strong and whole enough to do this on his own.

AFTER THAT SESSION, I walked out into the afternoon heat of a Philly summer, and I stopped a moment to check myself like I always checked myself. Searching myself to see how I felt.

I felt good.

I felt light.

I felt the way I used to feel before the accident, like I had great things to look forward to.

"I'm happy." I said this out loud.

A woman passing me gave me a funny look.

I didn't care.

"I'm really fucking happy."

"YOU KNOW, sweetie," said Evie. "It would be okay with me—it would even be good—if you started dating again."

I turned and looked at her, aghast. We were sitting on the hood of my car; it was warm and muggy. Fireflies were blinking all around us. I could just make out Evie's face by the light coming from the kitchen window. She looked earnest but a little sad.

How many glasses of wine did she have? I thought.

"I don't want to date anyone," I finally said.

She sighed but she didn't look away. "Listen," she said. "Listen. You have done so much. You have done more than anyone ever expected you to do. You have been by her side from the beginning. You have gone above and beyond."

"But I still love her," I said.

"I know, sweetie," she said. "And we so appreciate you for that. You are family now, and you will always, always be part of our family. But you can love her, and you can also move on." She took a shaky breath. "You should move on."

"I don't want—" I said. "I don't think—"

She kept looking at me. Staring. Finally she dropped her eyes.

"When you're ready," she said.

"I don't think I'll ever—"

I stopped myself, and just looked at Evie's face. The face that looked so much like her daughter's.

And I knew. I knew this was more than her telling me to date. This was more than her letting me go. This was her admitting that maybe this version of Lee Lee, the one we knew now, the one we both loved so much but who was so different from the Lee Lee we had known before, was going to be the Lee Lee we would always know.

And that was okay.

She met my eyes again. She smiled at me.

Lee Lee's smile.

"When you're ready," she repeated.

Part III

Chapter 23

I DON'T ACTUALLY REMEMBER what the first date after Lee Lee's accident was like. I don't remember the woman's name. I don't remember what she looked like. I don't remember where we went or what we talked about. I just remember thinking, *This is not Lee Lee.* And deciding that I probably would not be getting serious with any women anytime soon.

It was not that I felt like I was cheating on Lee Lee, exactly. My conversation with Evie had helped negate that feeling a bit. But Evie was not Lee Lee. Evie was not my girlfriend. I still hadn't talked to Lee Lee about any of this.

I didn't even know how I would begin to broach the subject with her. I was pretty convinced that, whether Lee Lee remembered our relationship from before the accident or not, she still thought of me as her boyfriend. It was the way that people always referred to me in her family, "Oh, this is Lee Lee's boyfriend, Kareem."

It was the way I still referred to myself.

But I also didn't know what, exactly, Lee Lee thought me being her boyfriend meant. And it wasn't something she was really capable of explaining to me. And I didn't know how to say, "Lee Lee, I still love you and I always will, but I'm going to see other women now," or "Lee Lee, I will always be in your life, but we need to break up," without risking the chance of really hurting her in a way that I wasn't entirely sure was necessary.

Because I didn't know if she would understand what I was telling her. And if she did understand, I didn't want to cause her that kind of pain. It seemed both unnecessary and cruel. After all, even if I was going to start talking to other women, I wasn't really looking for anything serious. I didn't think I would ever meet anyone I could love like I loved Lee Lee.

FOR A LITTLE WHILE after that first date, I didn't go out again.

But I was lonely. I was spending more time with my friends and family, but friends and family couldn't be everything to me. So I tried again. And this time, I worked very hard on not comparing the women I was talking to with Lee Lee. I didn't expect to find anyone I would connect to like I had connected with her. And I knew it wasn't a fair comparison for anyone involved.

I tortured myself, imagining that even if I did find someone I liked, I'd have to keep telling them I was *going to see my friend* every time I went to see Lee Lee, and then one day they would ask, *But who is this friend anyway?* And I'd blurt out, *My soul mate. My other half. The woman I love.*

So then I decided to pretty much start every date by telling them about Lee Lee. The whole story. Getting it all out in the open. And I thought that, surely, telling that story would end most dates, right there and then.

And often, it did. There were plenty of women who I could see visibly detach the moment I told them that there was a woman I was still tied up with and always would be, even if it was no longer in a strictly romantic, monogamous way. A lot of women listened patiently when I told them my story, then sat through the rest of our drinks or dinner, made a polite excuse, and hurried on home.

And then there were other women who actually seemed moved by the story. But maybe moved a little *too* much.

"Oh my God. That is so, so sad." Her eyes were actually welling up with tears.

"Naw, I don't think of it that way," I said. "I mean—"

She grabbed my hand. "But you are so brave!"

"Well, I just—"

She pressed my hand to her chest. Looked up at me from under her lashes. "Such a good, good man," she murmured. "Such a *sad* good man!"

It turned out being overly praised and pitied was almost as uncomfortable as being immediately written off.

But honestly, I didn't blame any of them. I knew I was carrying a lot of baggage and complications. The situation wasn't easy.

SOMETIMES I LIKE TO THINK of this time I spent dating again as my movie montage. The kind of scene in a film where you see a guy sitting at a table in a bar and having a conversation with a woman but it's kind of the same conversation over and over as the light changes, and time passes, and the woman keeps morphing into other women. And some of these women are nice, and some of these women are interesting, some are even horse girls. And some of these women say stupid or rude or problematic things, and some believe in ridiculous conspiracy theories, and some have trust issues, and some are just looking for one night of a good time.

And all of these women don't want to date a guy who still loves someone else.

And then finally the montage ends, and the guy walks home alone.

But honestly, I didn't really mind. I liked dating. I enjoyed meeting new people. I spent some real time with a few women, and I actually made a few new friends. It felt good to simply be back out in the world again. And the main thing was, I didn't have to worry about anything getting so serious that I'd actually have to break the news to Lee Lee.

I'D ONLY BEEN ON A dating app for a week when I got a message from someone called "YolandaS."

I liked her main picture. She was a brown-skinned woman with big, dark eyes; long, straight black hair; and a wide, bright smile. But it was her introductory message that caught my attention. It was a little different than the usual dating app chat.

"Hello. Nice pictures on your profile. I am wondering what kind of camera you used."

I smiled when I read her message. I noted that her compliment could initially be viewed as a compliment about me, personally, but if you thought about it for a moment, it was really just a compliment to the photographer. At first, I thought that maybe it was just an ice-breaker. A way to get into a conversation, but later I realized, no, this woman really just wanted to know what kind of camera I was using.

This was lesson number one about Yolanda. She never played games.

I returned her message, and we chatted back and forth for a few days. I laughed out loud pretty much every time she sent me a message. She was charming and funny. Smart. Didn't take any shit. And it quickly became clear that we had a lot more in common than almost any other person I'd dated since Lee Lee.

In fact, in some important ways, Yolanda and I had more in common than Lee Lee and I ever did.

I REMEMBER ALMOST EVERYTHING about that first date. I remember that there was a miscommunication about the pub we were meeting at. (I thought we were meeting outside the pub and then going somewhere else; Yolanda assumed we were eating there and got a table before I arrived. We stayed.) I remember that she was wearing a white turtleneck sweater, jeans, and a pair of little white Converse. That she had glasses and her long hair was down. I remember her smile, which was stunning. I remember how tiny she was. I hadn't realized how tiny—she barely topped five feet.

I messed up my order. It was a German restaurant, and I didn't know that brats were just sausages, and so I somehow managed to order almost every brat they had on the menu. A flight of brats. And nothing else. Which I could tell that Yolanda thought was a bit weird. But I decided that admitting that I hadn't known what I was ordering was worse than having to eat all those sausages, so I choked them down and acted like I loved them.

Yolanda and I had texted long enough for me to know her basic bio. She lived with her parents in New Jersey. She was an ophthalmic assistant. She was a couple of years older than me. Her family nickname was Yogi. She was a Pacific Islander. And she was the middle child in a group of seven siblings.

I knew that we had our big families in common, and I liked that. But it wasn't until that first date, when I got a chance to hear her talk about them in person, that I felt how deep our connection actually went.

As Yolanda happily talked about how close she was to her mom and stepdad, how her family spent their holidays, the music they listened to, the food they ate, the way her parents had disciplined their kids, it was like she was talking in a language that only the two of us could understand. She hadn't grown up in the hood, exactly. Her family was more blue-collar, working-class. But her family definitely had to scramble up some pennies from time to time. Her stepfather, who had pretty much raised Yolanda and her siblings, was also a recovering addict, and he had come from a rough part of Bridgeport, Connecticut, in a primarily Black and Puerto Rican neighborhood. So nothing in my past was particularly new or shocking to Yolanda.

But even more than all these cultural references we had in common, it was the *way* that she talked about her family that really attracted me to her. Her family seemed like it could be as chaotic as mine. Her stepfather basically sounded like the male version of my mother—emotional and funny and deeply involved in his kids' lives. They all obviously leaned on Yolanda for stability. But she *loved* them. She talked about them with nothing but humor and understanding and affection. She was different from them in some ways. She had more of an education. She was a professional. She was making a life for herself outside of the one she had grown up in. But she didn't think that made her better than them. She respected them. She adored them. And she certainly would never want to be without them.

Her family was everything to her.

And when I spoke about my family—my mother, my siblings, my cousins—I saw the same gleam of recognition in her eyes when she looked back at me.

"I'M NOT INTERESTED in dating just to date," she said as she dipped a fry in ketchup. "I want to get married. I want to have children. I am looking to build a family. And I'm real tired of messing around with men who are still acting like little boys." She popped the fry into her mouth and then neatly dabbed at her lips with her napkin. "So"—she met my eyes—"if you're not interested in pursuing the same thing, let's not waste our time."

And it was funny, because had someone asked me if I was looking for something serious even a week or two before, I would have said hell no. I would have said that I was happy being a bachelor. That I liked casual dating. That I had absolutely no desire to tie myself down or get serious with anyone. That the responsibilities I already had were big enough, thank you very much.

But when Yolanda talked about her desire for family, stability, a home—when she raised her chin and looked me in the eyes and told me that if I wasn't looking for the same thing, I might as well go kick rocks—I could only smile and nod. I felt calm. I felt hopeful. I felt like she was *right*.

"Well, I know I want a second date, at least," I said. "Should we start there?"

She rolled her eyes and shook her head. For a moment, I could see her holding back her smile, but that didn't last long.

And then, I took a deep breath. Because I knew that I had finally got to the point in the conversation where I needed to let Yolanda know that there was another woman. Someone I would always love and who would be part of my life. And I felt a little pang, because I also knew that no matter how much I liked Yolanda, this would probably cut things off before they could really begin.

"Listen," I said. "There's a woman. Her name is Lee Lee Jones."

Yogi was quiet. She took it all in with a serious look on her face. She listened and nodded but didn't say a word until I was finished with my story.

My chest felt a little constricted. I wondered if this was the end of what had felt like such a promising beginning. I waited for her response.

And then she leaned across the table, looked up into my eyes, and said, "Well, Lee Lee is family to you. So of course. Of course, you take care of your family."

I INVITED YOGI up to my apartment that night, but she turned me down. She said she was going to get on the train and go home. And even though I was extremely attracted to her, I liked her consistency. She had already told me what she was looking for, and it didn't look anything like a one-night stand. I walked her to the train, and we hugged goodbye, and I watched her walk into the station, her long black hair swinging behind her and catching the streetlight as she slipped through the entrance doors. And I already had my phone out and was texting her, trying to pin down the next time I could see her again.

SHE WAS BACK in three days. Marching into my apartment with her arms full of groceries, wearing a sweat suit, with her hair pulled back into a bandana. Not a stitch of makeup on her face.

I felt my heart squeeze in my chest. She was frigging adorable.

"I'm going to make you dinner," she announced as she handed me a paring knife. "Here. You can devein the shrimp."

Chapter 24

WHEN I'D FIRST TAKEN Lee Lee to meet my family, I had so many worries. Would she like my family? Would she be comfortable in the Bottom? Would she feel out of place? Would my mother be sober?

But with Yolanda, I already knew the answers to those questions. Yogi would like my family because they were good people, and she would see that. She would be at home in the Bottom because to her, it was just another neighborhood where families were trying to get by. She'd feel comfortable there because my people would make her feel comfortable. And my mother would be sober because it had been almost a year since she'd last been high.

In the past year, my relationship with my mom had changed. It was both deeper and sweeter. It was more respectful because I honored all the work she put into her sobriety. And, as she became more independent and self-sufficient, my mother started respecting my boundaries a bit more. My sober mother no longer chose men who abused her, so there were less frantic midnight calls. My sober mother didn't spend her money on drugs, so her finances were in better shape. My sober mother was present and involved with her family. My mother was only forty-eight years old. And with David and Bee, her two oldest boys, finally home from prison, and her youngest child, Washika, about to graduate from high school, she had all her children safe around her again—and they were all grown up. So she had the possibility of finally living a new life.

She once told me that she was thinking about leaving the Bottom.

She thought maybe she'd move to a little house in Jersey with a decent-size backyard. She wanted a garden and a table big enough for the whole family to gather around.

My mother had dreams.

My mother was making plans.

WHEN YOGI FINALLY met my mom, I wasn't worried at all. I sat with them both for a little while, and then excused myself to use the restroom. I took my own sweet time returning to the table, watching them from across the room.

My mother was smiling at Yogi. Yolanda was throwing her hands around like she was telling a story. Then they were both laughing.

By the time I sat back down, my mother was calling Yolanda "Baby."

YOLANDA *WAS* NERVOUS about me meeting her family. She rarely, if ever, brought men home. The first time I picked her up for a date in New Jersey, she made me park a block away from her house so that her stepdad, Ray, wouldn't come out and interrogate me.

"This is so silly," I said after she climbed into my car. "Why can't I just meet your family?"

She shot me a side-eye. "You don't bring just anyone home," she scolded. "You bring people who you love. You bring people who are safe for your family to meet. You bring home people who matter."

"Don't I matter?" I said.

She patted my hand. "We'll see."

YOGI STARTED COMING INTO PHILLY most nights. Sometimes we'd stay in, and sometimes we would go out, but we always ended up back at my apartment in the end. We'd talk and cuddle on the couch. We'd watch movies or listen to music. Sometimes we would dance. Yogi would cook for me, and that was always an incredible meal. She was a spectacular cook. We'd laugh and tease. And then we'd look at the clock and it would be past midnight, sometimes one or two in the morning, and I would say, "Don't you want to just stay the night?"

And Yogi would blush and shake her head and say her parents were expecting her home. Or she needed to let her dog out. And then she'd go.

I didn't realize, until much later in our relationship, that she was going home, sleeping for maybe two or three hours, and then getting right back up and going to work. I didn't realize what an effort she was making.

But I would have done the same if our situation had been reversed. If I was living at home, and it had been Yogi who had her own place, I would have traveled for her. I would have gone without sleep. I would have stayed, lingering into the night, so we could talk and eat and laugh and dance. I would have moved mountains to have a little more time with that woman.

I CAMPAIGNED RELENTLESSLY to meet Yolanda's family. I'm sure that part of my desire was just wanting to prove that I "mattered," but also, I just loved the way that Yogi talked about them all. I loved the warmth in her voice whenever she told me a story about what they had for dinner. Or about a stupid fight she'd had with her sister. Or how much she missed her mother, who was in the military and often abroad. I loved her funny details and childhood memories. And I wanted to see where she came from. I wanted to know her better.

When she finally invited me out, I felt like I had won a hard-played polo game. I celebrated like someone had just handed me a trophy.

"Okay, okay," said Yogi, smiling and shaking her head. "Calm your silly ass down before I change my mind."

EVERYTHING WAS GOOD about meeting Yolanda's family. They were warm and welcoming and curious about me. They teased each other and joked around just like my own family did. We sat around the kitchen table and ate and talked and laughed. I could tell that Yogi was relieved to see how quickly I fit in.

And at one point, near the end of the evening, Yolanda's mom, Merle, took me aside and said, "You know, Yogi told me about your Lee Lee."

"She did?" I wasn't entirely surprised. It seemed like something too important to keep from her family, but I did feel a little worried about what her mom would say next.

Her mom nodded. "Yes, she did. And I just want to tell you, I respect what you're doing. I am so glad that you are staying in her life."

I cleared my throat. "Thank you," I said. "I appreciate that. Lee Lee is a great person. I love her a lot."

Merle reached out and patted my arm. "And that's a good thing. That's the right thing. That tells me something important about you." She smiled at me. "Would you like another glass of wine?"

"YOLANDA, HUH?" said Ellen. "So what's Yolanda—"

"Actually," I interrupted, "I call her Yogi."

Ellen's eyebrows skyrocketed. "Hmm," she said. "Okay, then. What's *Yogi* like?"

I thought for a moment. "You mean, compared to Lee Lee?"

Ellen's eyebrows went up even higher. "I did not ask that," she said.

"Right, right," I said. "You did not. But actually, she's nothing like Lee Lee."

Ellen managed to keep her eyebrows under control this time. "Oh?"

"Well, she's Hawaiian, Puerto Rican, and Japanese, for one," I said. "And, you know, Lee Lee is white."

"Uh-huh," said Ellen.

"And she grew up pretty poor. Maybe not as poor as me, but not like Lee Lee, either."

"Right," said Ellen.

"And she's short," I said. "And Lee Lee is tall."

"Okay."

"And you know, Lee Lee always liked to say she was shy, but actually she was super outgoing, and Yogi is—"

Ellen put up her hand. "All right," she said. "Let's stop there. Why don't you try telling me about Yogi without saying Lee Lee's name."

"Right," I said. "Yes. I can do that."

She waited a moment. "So?" she said.

"So," I finally said. "So." I took a deep breath. "The other day Yogi was at my apartment. And it was the first time she—or any girl, really—had spent consecutive days at my apartment since . . . you know . . ."

Ellen laughed, exasperated. "Just say it."

"Okay, yeah, since Lee Lee." I shifted in my seat and looked out the window. "And it was just pillow talk, really. I was sitting on the floor on the side of the bed, and Yogi was still on the mattress, and she was leaning over, with her arms wrapped around my neck, and she was kind of murmuring into my ear and kissing me on the cheek. And look, I know that it's early, and we're still in our honeymoon phase, or whatever you want to call it, but these kisses just felt . . . different."

Ellen tipped her head. "How so?"

"Well, you know, this might sound corny, but there were butter-flies. I felt butterflies. And it wasn't . . . it wasn't just lust. It was love. Pure love. And every time she kissed me I just felt closer and closer to her. And I wanted her, but not just in a sexual way. It was a bigger, soul-to-soul kind of way. It was just me and Yogi and no one else in the room. Not even . . ."

I hesitated.

Ellen waved her hand. "You don't have to say it. I understand."

We were both quiet for a moment.

"I didn't think I'd ever get to feel anything like that ever again," I said.

And Ellen looked at me and smiled. "I'm so happy for you, Ka-reem," she said. Her voice was soft.

I looked out the window again. "I think I might be all in with this girl," I said. Then I looked back at Ellen. "I'm all in."

Ellen nodded. "So, then, when are you going to tell—"

I closed my eyes. "I know," I said. "I will."

I WAS TAKING LEE LEE out for ice cream. This was a big deal. It felt kind of like an actual date. We were going off the farm for the

first time, just the two of us. Evie told me that she and Lee Lee had
been talking about it all week. That Lee Lee just lit up whenever her
mother reminded her about it.

There had been a time, after Lee Lee became verbal again, and
after she had stopped telling everyone *Fuck you, bitch*, when Lee Lee
just didn't really care to be around anyone. Even me. She would
often get furious if anyone touched her. She would go into an absolute rage if she was picked up. And you could never predict when it
would happen. Some days she was peaceful, smiling and making eye
contact. But most days she was flailing and crying and screaming
incoherently.

I think part of this was Lee Lee trying to come to grips with
how she had changed. Hating the dependence and helplessness she
so obviously felt. But I also think that part of this was that even the
people who knew her best didn't really know how to communicate
with her just yet.

I remembered early on, how Evie and I had watched Lee Lee
sleep, and Evie asked me where I thought Lee Lee had gone, as if
Lee Lee had left her body like a hermit crab leaves its shell. And, of
course, I understood what she meant. And in that moment, it did
seem that the Lee Lee we both knew was absent and might not ever
come back.

But now, I could look Lee Lee in the eyes and see her there. Not
exactly the same as she had been before, but then, none of us were.
We had all certainly changed within the crucible of her accident.
Lee Lee could understand almost anything you told her if you were
slow and patient with your explanations. She could make most of
her urgent needs known. She could participate in a conversation in
two- or three-word sentences.

And sometimes I wondered whether it was less that Lee Lee had changed so much, as much as the fact that I had finally learned to read her better. I had learned to recognize almost all her new facial expressions. To parse out her words, even when they weren't entirely clear. I could recognize her cues. I knew when she was angry or upset or just bored. I knew her body language, the way she rolled her eyes in exasperation, the way she huffed and puffed when she was frustrated. And I recognized her unmistakable joy as well.

When I walked through that door for our ice cream date, Lee Lee looked like she was just about to explode with happiness.

"Reem!" she yelled, and started edging her wheelchair toward me.

"Hey there!" I stopped to give Evie a kiss on the cheek hello, since I was walking past her.

"No!" said Lee Lee as she attempted to wedge her wheelchair between us. "Me!" she said.

I laughed. She never liked it if she didn't get the first kiss when I came to visit. I leaned down and embraced her. "You want to go get some ice cream?"

She grinned at me, her eyes bright with joy. And there she was. Lighting up the room like always. That was my Lee Lee.

I HAD DECLARED MYSELF to Yolanda. Told her I loved her. We had started talking about a future together. And I had learned my lesson. I wasn't going to waste any of our time playing games or wondering whether I should be honest about my feelings. I knew I wanted Yogi in my life in a permanent way. And I also knew all too well how everything could change in a split second.

Even now that we were getting serious, Yogi wasn't jealous or resentful of the time I spent with Lee Lee. She approved of the way I prioritized her. She was fine with my visits. She would always ask me how Lee Lee was when I came back from the farm, and then really listen to my answers. She made it all extraordinarily easy for me. And I did my best to make sure that she understood that she was my priority as well. That I loved her and needed her and appreciated the miracle of her being in my life.

But still, I hadn't been able to bring myself to tell Evie and Lee Lee.

On the drive over, I'd thought maybe that day would be the day. I thought after we got the ice cream, maybe after we returned home and if Lee Lee still seemed like she was in a good mood and not too tired. It would be the time.

But now that I saw how happy she was. How excited. How much this day meant to her, I changed my mind. I knew I couldn't do it. How could I possibly spoil this one good day for her?

"You ready to go?" I asked.

"Yeah!" Lee Lee practically shouted. "Go!"

And so I stepped aside, and watched her wheel herself out the door. Her happiness was still ephemeral enough that it didn't matter what I was feeling or thought I needed. I was happy to see her happy, and for the moment, I decided that was enough.

Chapter 25

IT WAS THE END OF WINTER, 2020, and I was alone in my apartment, taking an afternoon nap. The cats were curled up behind my knees. Yogi had stayed late the night before, and I was catching up on sleep before I went back to work.

The sound of my phone ringing jerked me awake. I squinted in the afternoon light that poured through my window as I fumbled to pick up.

It was my mom wanting to FaceTime.

"Hey, Mom." I sat up in bed, yawning. "What's up?"

"Kareem! Oh God! Kareem!" she wailed. Her face was twisted with agony. "Your brother! Your brother! David's been shot! Your brother's been shot in the head!"

THERE ARE SOME SUPERPOWERS to having anxiety. Because anxiety leaves you in a constant state of arousal and fear—always expecting the worst—and so, when the worst does happen, in a weird way, I am prepared. Sometimes a crisis can feel more normal to me than good news ever does.

I had been both dreading and expecting this call ever since I left the Bottom at fourteen. I didn't know which person in my family would be hurt, but I knew—I absolutely knew—that this call would come. I had spent countless sleepless nights obsessing over this call.

Thinking about what I would do, how I would react, the list of things that would need to be taken care of.

And who it would be.

And now I know. It's David.

That was the first thing I thought after I turned off my phone and stumbled around, getting dressed so I could get to the hospital.

But it could have been any of us. It could have been one of my sisters. Or Bee or Gerb. It could have been my mother. A niece or a nephew. For a long time, I expected it to be me.

Nobody is safe in the Bottom. Nobody. And just because I had made it out, that didn't mean that I could avoid the loss that I always knew was coming for us.

DAVID WAS TAKEN to the same hospital my mother had gone to when she'd had her breakdown: Penn Presbyterian Medical Center, in the Bottom, a few blocks from where he had been shot. In a weird twist of fate, it also happened to be the hospital that Yolanda was working in as an ophthalmic assistant that day.

I called her from the Uber on the way over.

"My brother's been shot," I said.

I could hear her sudden intake of breath. "Oh no. Oh God, Kareem. Which—"

"David. I don't have all the details yet. He's at Penn Pres."

"Oh!" she said. She sounded stunned. "That's where I am right now."

I nodded. "My mom was out of her mind when she called me. She said he was shot in the head, but I'm hoping she was wrong."

"Oh, Kareem. I'm sorry. I'm so, so sorry."

"Yeah. Thank you. I'm heading over to the hospital right now."

"I'll find you," she said. "If you or your family needs anything—"

"Thank you," I said again. "I'm almost there. I'll be there soon."

IT WAS THE FIRST TIME I'd been back in a hospital since Lee Lee, and as soon as I smelled that horrible, familiar, sterile smell, it was like I was walking two parallel paths. One path was present, and one was past. On the present path, the waiting room was filled with my family and friends. The hospital was so close to our hood, everyone had just hurried over as soon as word got out.

In the past, I was seeing Evie, Phillip, Richie, and the twins.

In the present, we waited while David was in surgery.

In the past, we waited for Lee Lee to get through hers.

In the past, the surgeon told us that Lee Lee had made it through. That things were still dire, but there was some small hope.

In the present, the surgeon told us that the surgery was over, but it had been unsuccessful. There was no chance of David surviving.

We were taken in to see David.

And there it was: that white towel, spread over the wound on his head. Blood seeping through.

Past. Present. All the same.

MY MOTHER COLLAPSED, crying and screaming when she saw her eldest child. Bee and I stood on either side of her, holding her up until the nurse brought in a wheelchair she could sink down into. Kareema's face was covered with her scarf, but her niqab was soaked with tears. Bee was crying, too. The first time I'd seen him cry since we were little kids. Washika was bent double, wracked with guttural sobs.

But I knew I was not allowed to cry. I knew I had to maintain myself. Someone had to be composed. Someone had to be able to talk and respond and answer questions. Someone had to speak with the doctors and the nurses. There were a couple of policemen haunting the door to the hospital room; and they needed my attention as well. David was a gunshot victim, so there was a whole protocol with security that had kicked in.

When Lee Lee had her accident, I fell into my mother's arms. I crumbled. I sobbed over Lee Lee while she lay in her hospital bed. I made promises and bargains. I kissed her face and hands. I begged her to stay.

With David, I stood in that hospital room, dry-eyed, as my family fell apart around me.

It was horrible. It was a horrible scene. But I knew that I couldn't lose my shit. That was not allowed.

YOLANDA WAS STANDING in the waiting room when we finally made it out of the ICU. She was surrounded by all of our extended family and friends, but she didn't know any of them yet. She had met only my mother and Gerb (who was still driving down from Massachusetts, where he'd been working). She was standing a little apart from everyone. Alone. Tiny and fierce. A deep worry line between her brows. Her hands stuffed into her pockets.

Her eyes widened when she saw me, and she stepped forward, opening her arms toward me.

I allowed myself one moment. One moment of comfort in her arms. One moment to smell her hair, and let her hold me. And then I felt a knot of tears forcing its way up my throat, so I stepped away. Pushed it all back down. Made myself take a deep breath.

"How is he?" she whispered. "How are you?"

"I'm okay," I said. "But he's not going to make it. They said that once he's off the machines, it won't be long."

She looked up at me. Her big dark eyes were swimming with tears. "I'm so sorry. What can I do? I can leave work. Whatever you need."

I shook my head. "We're going back to my mom's house now. I'll be back at the apartment later tonight, probably."

She touched my face. "I'll be there, then. I'll wait."

THAT NIGHT WAS A BLUR. My mother's house was full of people. The hospital had asked if we wanted to donate David's organs, and we had agreed, so they were running tests before they removed him from life support to see what was still viable and undamaged.

Once he was taken off the machines, the doctors said they would keep him comfortable and that it would be quick. And then they would rush to harvest his organs so that other people could have a second chance.

I thought about staying at my mom's that night. I thought about sleeping on the living room floor like old times. But there were so many other people there. Her cousins and my siblings and various other friends and extended family. And most of them were staying. There was literally no room. So late that night, I decided to go back to my place.

My apartment was quiet when I walked in. So different from all the chaotic noise and grief and emotion at my mother's house. My apartment was clean and still and dark, except for a dim light shining out of my bedroom.

I stood in the doorway for a moment. Sort of leaning against the wall, thinking about taking off my jacket and boots. Feeling like I could barely move my arms or legs.

Then Yolanda stepped out of the bedroom, wearing one of my T-shirts, which came down to her knees.

Without saying anything, she walked over and helped me ease my jacket off. She sat me down on the couch and took off my boots. Then she went into the kitchen and heated up some soup that she must have made earlier. She watched me eat. Then she gathered me up, led me to bed, and curled herself around me.

"Just breathe," she whispered.

And she matched her breath to mine, long and slow, a steady, soothing rhythm, until I let go and fell asleep first.

After that night, she stayed. And she never left again.

MY BROTHER PASSED AWAY the next morning at 8:03 a.m.

I COULDN'T COUNT the number of funerals I had been to in my life. I had attended them multiple times a year, every year that I could remember. But I'd never had to plan one before. And I certainly had never planned a funeral while the world was shutting down around me.

I remember sitting in the funeral home with Bee and my mother. We were perusing what looked like nothing so much as a cheap dinner menu—lamination and all—filled with caskets and flowers and burial packages. I knew that I would be paying for everything out of pocket, so I was trying to figure out the most economical way to properly see David off.

"The church won't be able to hold the viewing," the funeral

director told us. He shrugged. "This virus thing. Philly is shutting down all indoor gatherings. It will have to be a graveside service."

AFTER WE GOT BACK from the funeral home, I called the family in for a meeting. I had seen what deaths like these could do to other families. I had seen the arguments and the infighting. The perceived slights and long-suffering silences. I had seen families fall apart around a death. And I was determined that would not happen to us.

So we all sat down in my mother's living room, and I told them, "Look, we're all going to do this together. And we don't need any financial help from outside our family. And we don't need any input from anyone but us. We'll do what we need to do. We'll honor David. And we'll stay strong as a family." I looked around, checking in with each of my siblings and then my mother. "Agreed?" I asked.

One by one, they nodded. And I felt this swell of love for them. My family. We were all grieving. We were all in shock. But we were fucking strong. And we were going to get through this together.

I THOUGHT A LOT about the last time I had talked to David. I had been visiting my mom when he called her, and she had put him on speakerphone while she cooked, so I listened to him asking my mother for advice about the two women he was involved with. He had separated from his wife and now had a new girlfriend, but they were not getting along, and he wanted my mother to intercede.

I remember that I rolled my eyes at this. This grown man wanting his mom to solve his romantic issues. But at the same time, I was just happy to hear from him. Happy to have him home. He'd been out of prison for a few years at that point, and he had really turned his life around. He was concentrating on his kids and his family. He was working as a handyman. He had given up the street life. He was making music, trying to find the time to do some recording. I touched base with him as often as I could. We'd talk on the phone or have lunch or a beer together. He had grown up. He was done with the life. And I was proud of him.

"Hey, David," I said, "if you're done talking to Mom about how to fix your love life, want to make a plan to get lunch sometime soon?"

He laughed. "Sure, bro," he said. "Let's make a plan."

I ALSO THOUGHT a lot about what would have happened had David survived. A shot to the head is no small thing. Not many people walked away from that kind of injury. You either died, or your life was changed forever.

What if David had ended up with a severe TBI? He didn't have insurance. He didn't have any money. We didn't have the resources that he would have needed for any kind of decent quality of life. What would happen to someone like David if they were hurt like that? Who would have taken care of him?

In some ways, I was glad that he had died rather than gone on to live with that kind of injury. David had already spent his life struggling to survive. Anyone who grew up in the Bottom knew how that was. But the idea of him getting through almost ten years of prison, finally making it back, and then being gunned down in the street and left without the kind of care he would need—without the resources to get any better—that almost felt worse than an early death.

THE GRAVESIDE SERVICE was on a rainy, gray day. And even though the city was shutting down because of Covid, hundreds of people from the neighborhood showed up. The funeral home had hired a pastor, someone who didn't know David but kind of kept things on track. He said some nice, generic things about my brother. He talked about death in general. About the afterlife that awaited us all. He read a little from the Bible. And then he asked if anyone had anything they wanted to say.

A couple of girls from the neighborhood spoke up. One talked about how David had fixed a broken light in her home free of charge. Another said that David always made sure the local kids had something to eat when they needed it.

And then there was a beat. An awkward silence. And I realized that I needed to basically give the eulogy. But I hadn't prepared anything.

So I started talking off the cuff. Improvising. I decided that I should lighten things up. Make people laugh a little, because that's what our family did, even in the worst of times.

For a second, I hesitated. I was afraid that this was the moment when I would finally break down and cry. But then I looked up and I saw Yolanda standing in the very back of the crowd. And she met my eyes in this steady, comforting way and kind of nodded at me.

And that was enough to get me through.

I talked about how David always saw me as a pesky little brother. How I spent most of my childhood tagging after him because I thought he was so cool. And how he wanted nothing to do with me.

How he was always trying to get out the door without having to take me along with him anywhere.

People laughed when I mentioned what a little tattletale I had been. Always ratting David out to my mom so she'd make him take me out with him.

"I used to think that David just didn't want me to come along with him because I was a pest," I said. "And you know, I'm sure that I was. But now, I also think that David was trying to protect me a little. I think that David was trying to keep me out of the streets for as long as he could."

I also talked about how David and Bee had stumbled upon Work to Ride one day when they were biking through the park. How they had brought me, and later Gerb, along to meet Lezlie. I remembered that David had been the first person to ever lift me onto a horse.

It started to rain as I finished up, talking about how much we were going to miss him. How much we loved him. How I hoped that my brother was happy now, wherever he might be.

And then the pastor gave the final benediction, and we all stood in the rain together, murmuring *Amen, Amen, Amen* before the crowd broke up and slowly moved away, leaving my brother to his rest.

THE REPAST FELT more like a neighborhood barbecue than a sober, formal event. It had stopped raining. The sun had come out. And we all gathered at my mother's place, and spilled out into the streets. It was nice to see my aunts and uncles, my cousins and friends, all hanging out, drinking and smoking. People came and went, bringing food and drinks. Neighbors stopped by straight after the funeral, and then went back to their houses to change their clothes and grab a covered dish to help feed the crowd. There was music and laughter. Some people got drunk. Some people cried. Everyone gathered around my mother, holding her up and giving her their strength.

I had been watching my mother carefully over the last week, worried that the loss and depression would drive her back to using. But so far, though she was absolutely, incoherently grief-stricken, she hadn't shown any signs of backsliding. In this one way, she was holding strong. And I was so glad that she had all the support and love around her to stay sober.

After the repast, Yogi and I went home together. It was late, already dark, and I was relieved but exhausted. I had been working nonstop over the past week or so, planning the funeral, dealing with all the aftercare, making sure all the little details and necessities that my mother couldn't handle were taken off her plate.

And now, it was finally over. And not only was my brother buried and gone, but all the rules around Covid were coming into play. Work was shutting down for me and Yogi. People were staying home, masking up, taking care. Getting scared.

When Lee Lee had been hurt, after my initial breakdown, I had made the mistake of pushing away everyone's concern. I didn't want anyone's help, or pity, or consolation. I thought that my job was to be strong, be patient, keep my shit together, and see it all through. And that's exactly what I had done for years. Until I simply couldn't do that anymore.

By the time David died, though, I had learned a few things. Ellen had taught me that it wasn't weak to ask for help when I needed it. That grief was natural, and finding a way to process that grief was necessary. That there was a community of people around me that I could depend upon. I still felt responsibility for my loved ones—my mother, having just lost her firstborn child, was especially broken and consumed—but I knew that I needed to let other people help me shoulder the burden.

I knew that I had better tools, I knew what I was supposed to do, but when Yolanda and I got back to the apartment—before we walked through that door and shut the world away behind us—just for a moment, I hesitated. I lost my breath. I lost my footing. The sky seemed to flicker, like it would go dark all over again.

But Yolanda saw me. She saw what was happening. And even if she had never experienced the kind of loss that I had, even if she had never lived with the kind of violence that had been part of my day-to-day life, she never once flinched. She never turned away. And she didn't let me turn away, either.

She led me through the door, and through the next months—almost a year—it was just her and me. The two of us, in our own little Covid pod. And she held me. And she talked me through it. She listened. She cooked for me, and we ate together. And we binge-watched *Martin*. And danced to Stevie Wonder. And we got to know each other in a way that I had never known any woman before.

And sometimes I was sad. And sometimes I panicked. And never, not even once, did she make me feel like I was a burden or a drag. She gave me adult, mature, steady, and unconditional love. And after spending a lifetime taking care of everyone else, her tenderness and loyalty felt like nothing so much as the lifting of a great, crushing weight that I had carried through my life since before I could even remember.

Sometimes I played the what-if game when I was thinking about Yolanda. *What if I hadn't gone to see Ellen? What if David hadn't died? What if the world hadn't shut down? What if Yogi hadn't agreed to move in with me? What if I'd decided it was too risky to love again when I knew so much about loss?*

But, I reminded myself, *those things did happen. And I lived through them. I accepted them. I even embraced them.*

And there, in my bed, curled up next to me, her long black hair thrown across my pillow, her breath soft and even, her warmth pulling me ever closer, was my beloved reward.

Chapter 26

"BUT WE STILL HAVE TO open our stockings," said Yolanda.

I froze. "Wait, you put stuff in my stocking?"

She looked at me, shaking her head. "You didn't put anything in mine?"

It was 2020, the first Christmas that Yogi and I had spent together, and apparently, I had just screwed it up.

It had been good up until then. We had a tree and had decorated the apartment. I had piled up presents for Yogi under the tree, and she had piled up hers for me. We had slept in a little late and then had our coffee while we exchanged gifts.

After we finished up with our private celebration, we were going to my mother's to have dinner and see my family.

But there I was, apparently too ignorant to know that a stocking was more than a decoration.

"We didn't do stockings at my house growing up," I said. "This is a new concept for me."

Yogi shook her head but smiled. "Fine. So open your stocking, then, at least."

I shook my head in return. "But now I feel bad that I didn't get you anything."

Yogi reached over, unhooked the bulging stocking, and handed it to me. "You got me plenty. Go ahead."

"Okay, then," I said, plunging my hand into the thing. I groped around and pulled out a tube of lip balm. "ChapStick?" I said doubtfully.

Yogi laughed. "That's the kind of stuff you're supposed to put in there!"

I lifted my eyebrows. "If you say so."

"Just keep going."

Some facial scrub. An Eagles mug. A candy cane. A pair of novelty socks with cats wearing Santa hats on them. (I put those right on. My feet were cold.) A small box of artisanal chocolates. A pack of Altoids. An airplane-size bottle of whiskey. A clementine.

And then, shoved into the deepest part of the toe, I grasped a cylindrical something that I thought maybe was a pen but once I got it out and looked at it, I almost dropped it to the floor in shock.

It was a pregnancy test.

I squinted at it.

A positive pregnancy test.

At first, I thought it was a joke. I thought that Yogi was doing her best to give me a scare. But then I looked up at her, and I saw the expectant smile, the soft focus in her eyes, and I knew that it was no prank.

"You're pregnant?" I asked.

"I'm pregnant," she said.

"You're pregnant."

"I'm pregnant."

And then, I was crying. Just one tear. I felt it slide down my face right before I gathered Yogi up in my arms and held her to me.

"I'm in shock," I whispered.

"I know," she whispered back. "But are you happy?"

I sat with myself for a second. Poked around until I could name how I was feeling. "Yes," I finally said. "I am scared. I am in shock. But I am very happy."

But there was something else. Another feeling. Something I didn't say out loud.

And that was, *Oh God, what will I tell Lee Lee?*

WE REWRAPPED THE pregnancy test—this time in a little box with a bow, to give to my mother that evening.

"Here, here," I said, shoving the gift at my mom once she had finished opening all her other gifts. "You're going to love this one. You're going to be so surprised. Just wait until—"

"Ka-reem!" Yogi dug me in the ribs with her elbow. "Just let her open the thing." She dropped her voice. "My God, you have absolutely no gift game."

Something to know about my mother: she makes the same noise when she is really happy, really upset, or really surprised. It's like this scream that is so sharp, so loud, that it pierces through your body.

This time, it was a scream of joy.

"My baby!" she hollered, waving the test in the air. "My baby is having a baby! My babies!" She spread her arms out wide, tears pouring down her face. "Oh, come here, all you babies!"

My mom's hugs are larger than life and can encompass several people at a time. She held me and Yogi. And then all of my siblings joined in until we were all in one big group hug, laughing and crying, celebrating the fact that our family was getting bigger again. That even after such a painful loss, our family still persisted. Our family was growing.

I LOVED THAT YOGI was pregnant. I couldn't wait for her stomach to pop. I wanted her to wear form-fitting clothes all the time so I could see her belly. I downloaded an app that gave us weekly updates on how big the baby was, what had developed, what we could expect, and it was all I could do not to rush ahead and look at every iteration of our child-to-be.

But at the same time, I was terrified. What if something went wrong? There was now so much to lose. Yolanda could get hurt. The baby might not make it. Both Yolanda and the baby might be in danger. So many things could go so bad, so fast. And our little family was suddenly so vulnerable to the possibility of tragedy.

But Yogi didn't share my fears. She was perfectly confident that everything would be just fine. She had almost no symptoms. No morning sickness. Hardly any fatigue. She gained weight, but she was so small to begin with, she could just put on a baggy shirt and no one would know the difference.

We told almost everyone we cared about. Family first, of course. And then friends. And everyone was delighted for us. They were so excited that our little family was about to grow by one.

Still, there were people who we didn't tell. Yogi hid her pregnancy at work for almost her entire nine months. She was deeply private, and she didn't love some of the people she was working with. She wanted to avoid them nosing into her business.

And I? I hadn't even told Evie or Lee Lee that I had a girlfriend yet.

"BUT WHY?" asked Ellen. "Why haven't you told them?"

We were having our appointment over Zoom. I didn't mind so much. It was better than not being able to see her. But sometimes I missed Ellen's little office. All that tea.

I shrugged. "It just hasn't come up."

Ellen shook her head. "Kareem," she said. "Come on."

I sighed. "Look, I haven't been able to see them as much. You know, because of lockdown. And now that things have loosened up a little, when I do see them, there are usually other people around. And if Evie and I ever get a chance to talk, it's always catching up on Lee Lee stuff. And honestly, Evie just hasn't asked. She hasn't said a word about me dating or asked anything about my private life since we had that original conversation."

"That was ages ago," said Ellen. "And I would like to note that you don't seem to have volunteered any information, either."

"What would I say?" I protested. "It's not like they need to know about my failed experiments in online dating."

"Failed?" said Ellen. "I'd say that the experiment was quite successful."

"Well, now it is," I said. "But when I first started dating, I didn't think I was ever going to meet anyone I'd want to introduce to them. I thought I was going to stay a bachelor and have the occasional good time. I figured I could keep things permanently separate."

"But then you met Yolanda," said Ellen. "And now you *live* with Yolanda. And you're having a baby with her. You're going to be a dad."

I threw up my hands. "I know. Obviously, it's time that I tell them."

Ellen leaned forward. "Did you ever consider," she said. "Did you ever consider the idea that maybe you haven't told them because you don't really believe that Yogi will stay?"

I frowned. "What is that supposed to mean?"

Ellen gave me a little shrug. "Well, you've lost a lot of people in your life, Kareem."

"So?"

"And so, do you think that maybe losing those people had some sort of effect upon you?"

I lifted my hands, confused. "Sure. Of course."

She waited.

I sighed. "I don't know what we're talking about here. Avoidance? Attachment issues?"

She laughed. "I guess you have the jargon down now. How about plain old fear?"

"Sure. Yes. That's always lurking somewhere."

"Fear of . . . ?"

"Fear of loss. Fear that everyone I love is in danger. Fear that nothing good can stay."

Ellen nodded. "Yes."

"But Yogi isn't going anywhere," I said. "I know that. I know that she is absolutely ride-or-die. It's one of the things I love best about her."

Ellen cocked an eyebrow. Waited.

I shook my head, trying to clear it out. "Okay. I get your point. But new subject, kind of."

Ellen extended her palm. "Be my guest."

"You know what's awful? I don't want to hurt Lee Lee. Of course, I don't want to hurt Lee Lee. But there is a tiny part of me that kind of wants her to get really mad when I tell her. There is a part of me that hopes she frigging throws hands, she's so pissed off." I looked at Ellen. "Is that terrible?"

Ellen's face softened. "Before the accident, Lee Lee would have been mad."

"Absolutely," I said. "Of course."

"And so if she gets mad now, you think it will prove that that part of her hasn't changed?"

"Yeah," I said. "I know. I understand why I'm being fucking terrible. But I'm still being fucking terrible."

Ellen nodded. "Self-awareness is a hell of a thing."

"Yup," I agreed.

"But, Kareem?"

"Yes?"

"You still have to tell them."

I TOLD EVIE FIRST. It was after a dinner party at the farm. Lee Lee had gone to bed earlier, and we had all been drinking, maybe a little too much wine, but I knew it was time. There could be no more excuses.

I waited for all the other guests to go home. I helped Phillip and Evie clean up. I waited until my head was clear, when I knew I was sober again, and then, as was our ritual, Evie walked me out to my car.

"This was a good night for Lee Lee," Evie said. "She seemed really happy."

I nodded. Willing myself to speak.

"Did you notice when Phillip was talking about his horse, Lee Lee—"

"Evie," I said. "I'm going to be a father."

Evie looked at me, her eyes wide and mouth slightly open. She blinked. "What?"

"I—well, me and my girlfriend, Yolanda—we're having a baby."

She blinked again. "You have a girlfriend?"

I nodded.

"For—for how long?"

"About a year."

Evie made this little huffing sound as she sat down on the hood of the car. "A year," she said faintly. "But——"

"I didn't want to tell you or Lee Lee at first," I said. I could hear the desperation in my voice. "You know, when I first started seeing other girls? I thought, I thought, what was the point, right? And then, I met Yolanda, and, you know, it got serious pretty fast. But then David was killed, and the pandemic happened and you know, there are always people around when I was here, so it never felt like the right time and——"

She held up her hands. "Stop. Kareem. Stop."

I stopped.

She let her hands fall with a sharp slap onto her thighs. "You don't have to explain. I get it. And I should have asked you about this a long time ago. I feel so bad that I didn't check in. And, I don't know, maybe I kind of didn't want to know that you were dating again. And certainly Lee Lee . . ."

For a moment she looked stricken.

"Oh. Lee Lee," she breathed.

"Evie," I said. "I——"

She shook herself. "No," she said. "No. Lee Lee will be okay. This is all good news." She smiled at me. A big, sort of watery smile. "You're going to have a baby. You're going to be a father! This is amazing! A new baby in the family!" She was still smiling at me but she reached up to angrily wipe the tears from her eyes. "I'm sorry," she said. "I don't know why I'm crying. I just——"

"It's okay," I said. "I know it's a lot."

"No. It's wonderful! It's such good news! It's only that——"

I finished for her. "Lee Lee."

"Yeah," she kind of half sobbed. "Yeah. Lee Lee."

I swallowed. "How do you think she'll take it when I tell her?"

Evie shook her head. She raised her hands and let them fall again. Helpless. "I—I have no idea. I mean, I think, in her mind, you and she are still together. She thinks you still love her."

"I do," I said quickly. "I do still love her."

Evie laughed. A wet little gurgle. "I know. I mean, I know you do and you probably always will, but—you know what I mean. You've got someone else. You're going to have a baby. Your life is about to change in this huge way. Things will have to be different."

"I'm not going anywhere, Evie," I promised. "I'll still see you guys all the time. I'll still be there for her."

Evie nodded. And then she looked at me with her big, teary eyes and she took both my hands in hers. "Congratulations, sweetie," she whispered. "You're going to make the most wonderful, wonderful father."

"HOW DID IT GO?" asked Yogi when I got back home that night.

She was sitting on the couch with both cats hanging off her lap.

"Good," I said. "I mean, not bad, at least. But I only told Evie. Not Lee Lee yet."

Yolanda nodded. "And how did Evie take it?"

I sat down beside her, leaned my cheek down to the top of her head. "How are you?" I asked. "Everything good? Do you feel okay?"

Yogi waved her hand. "I'm fine. How did Evie take it?"

I sighed. "She was great. She's always great. Surprised, but totally supportive."

"But?" said Yogi.

"But," I agreed. "But I can't help wondering if when she heard that I was going to be a dad—that you and I were having a baby together—I can't help wondering if she was thinking about the fact that it could have been me and Lee Lee. It could have been our baby. Her grandchild, you know? And how that will never happen now."

Yogi was quiet for a minute. "I mean," she finally said. "I'm sure she *was* thinking about that. How could she not?"

"Yeah," I said.

"And how about you? Were you thinking about that, too?"

I looked at her.

"Of course you were," she said, answering her own question. "How could you not?"

"I'm sorry," I said. "I know that's not fair."

Yogi shook her head. Snuggled up closer to me. "It's not about fair or not fair. It just is." She put her hand on her belly. "But you know, Evie and Lee Lee, they're your family. And that means that this little girl will be their baby, too."

I smiled. "What did the app say this week? Grapefruit size?"

She laughed. "Don't get ahead of yourself. She's barely a lemon."

THE NEXT NIGHT, I returned to the farm. It was a little late, and Lee Lee had already gone to bed, but Evie told me she was still awake. That I could go and see her.

Lee Lee was lying back in bed, wearing a soft white T-shirt and pajama bottoms. Her eyes gleamed with warmth when I came into the room. I carefully sat down next to her.

"Reem," she breathed. She smiled at me. Her sweet, sweet smile.

"Hi," I said as I reached down to kiss her cheek. "Hey. You got a minute, Lee Lee?"

"Yes," she said. Still smiling.

I took her hand. My heart was hammering. I couldn't feel my legs. I reached up with my other hand and pushed a lock of hair off her cheek. "First of all," I said. "You know how much I love you, right? You know that I always will love you?"

Her smile got bigger and she nodded firmly. "Yes," she said.

I nodded and smiled back. "Good. Good. Because I gotta tell you something, and I hope this will be okay but I've—I've been seeing someone. A girl."

I held my breath as I watched Lee Lee's face, waiting for anger. Tears. Anything. But she just wrinkled her nose and looked a little puzzled.

I tried again. "Do you understand what I'm saying, Lee Lee? I've met someone. And we've been dating."

She bit her lip. "Okay," she said.

"I mean, do you get what I'm saying? There's a woman—"

"Yes," she said. "Yes."

"All right," I said, still not certain that she was taking it all in. "And also, this woman and I—her name is Yolanda—are going to have a baby together. Yolanda is pregnant."

"A baby," said Lee Lee. And she smiled again. The softest smile. Lee Lee loved children. She always had.

"Right." I nodded. "Yolanda. My—the woman I'm with? She's having my baby. Mine. Do you understand?"

She nodded. The smile still there. "Yes."

I needed to make sure she really knew what I was saying. "I'm telling you that I am going to be a daddy."

She nodded again. More firmly this time. "Yes."

"So you understand? I'm having a baby."

Her eyes got big and she huffed with frustration. "Yes!" she said. "Yes! Yes! Baby! Baby! Baby!" And then her voice kind of dropped into this tender croon, and she patted at my face and smiled at me again. "Reem," she said. "Baby."

And I smiled at her, and she just kept smiling back.

Lee Lee wasn't mad. She wasn't going to stand up and fight. This wouldn't be the moment where she was shocked back into being some version of her old self.

But that didn't mean she didn't understand. She had made it very clear she understood me. And, I realized, even if Lee Lee had never been in the accident, even if that entire part of her life had never happened, I was wishing for the impossible. Because she still wouldn't be the same twenty-two-year-old girl who I had known back then.

During all this time that Lee Lee was healing, she had also been growing up. That transformation had not ended, TBI or not. Lee Lee had grown up just like I had grown up. We had matured. And we were both different people than the kids we'd been back in the day.

"Baby," Lee Lee breathed.

I laughed, but I also got a little choked up. "That's right." I took her hand again. "Baby." I leaned my head against her shoulder. "I love you, Lee Lee. You know that, right?"

She didn't answer. But she knew.

She knew.

Chapter 27

EVEN THOUGH THINGS continued to get easier for me, I still spent part of every day automatically pushing down fears, both realistic and not, and managing my anxiety. Like a person who puts Post-it notes up on their mirror—positive affirmations—I spent a lot of time telling myself everything would be okay. And, to some degree, it worked. It worked well enough for me to get out of bed every morning, and get on with my day. To feel joy and take chances and not be frozen in one spot, waiting for disaster.

But deep down? There was still a tiny part of me that was curled up into a little ball, frozen and waiting. And that part was always prepared for the worst.

So when Yogi woke me up in the middle of the night frantically scratching herself, saying that there was no rash, but it felt like she was covered in mosquito bites, that old friend inside me—the one who feels most comfortable with fear and chaos—oozed right up into my head and hissed, *I told you so.*

WE STARTED WITH URGENT CARE. And I was already certain that Yolanda and the baby would not get the medical attention they needed. Because I knew that Black and brown people were rarely taken seriously in the emergency room. And I knew that Black and brown women were especially endangered when they were pregnant.

"I'll tell you exactly what they're going to do," I said as we walked to urgent care (we lived only two blocks away). "They're going to say that you're having an allergic reaction."

"Maybe," said Yogi, unperturbed.

"And they're going to give you a Benadryl."

"I can give myself a Benadryl," she said.

"And then they're going to send you home."

"Welp," she said, as we turned into the entrance of the building, "I guess we'll find out."

And then, two hours later, we walked out with a bottle of Benadryl and the assurance that absolutely nothing was wrong.

"Something's wrong," I insisted as soon as we left the urgent care.

"Maybe not," said Yogi. "Probably not." She scratched furiously at her arm.

I shook my head. "Let's call Kareema."

At this point, Kareema had four kids of her own, and she had been through it all.

"Uh-uh," she said, when we told her what had happened at urgent care. "Nope. Go to the PER at the hospital. That's the Pregnancy ER. They'll figure it out there, inshallah."

"IT WILL TAKE A FEW DAYS to get the test back, but I'm fairly certain you have cholestasis," said the doctor.

I felt my heart squeeze. *Of course*, I thought, even though I didn't yet know what cholestasis was. *So the baby is in danger. Maybe Yogi is in danger. Maybe they will both—*

"We checked all your levels, and you're fine right now. But you will need to come in for daily monitoring, and if the amniotic fluid starts to decrease around the baby, we will need to induce right away."

"And what happens if we don't induce?" I asked.

The doctor looked at me. "She will have a stillbirth."

"REEM," said Yogi as we walked back to our apartment. "Reem, take a breath. I'll be fine. The baby will be fine. I'm already at thirty-five weeks. If they have to induce tomorrow, she'd still be totally fine."

"I just think I'd feel better if you stayed in the hospital."

Yogi shook her head. "That wasn't even an option. You gotta relax. I'm not worried. You shouldn't be worried, either."

I stopped on the sidewalk. She didn't notice for a moment, but then stopped, too, and turned around. I could hardly look at her; it was almost too much to bear. Too much to lose.

She stepped back toward me. Took my hand. "Maybe you should call Ellen?"

I shook my head. "I'm going to walk you home. I'm going to make sure you're good. Then I think I'm going to go visit my mom."

"HERE, BABY." My mom handed me a plate of rice and beans and a glass of juice. "You eat this and you'll feel better."

I looked at the plate. "I'm not really hungry," I said.

My mother shrugged. "Eat anyway. You look skinny."

I pushed the plate away.

Mom cocked her head. "Okay, now. I know you're worried, but there's no need to be rude."

I sighed and pulled the plate back toward me. Dutifully took a bite. "I'm sorry," I said. I took another bite. "It's good. Thank you."

She watched me eat for a moment. "Yogi and that baby are gonna be just fine. You know that, right?"

"I know," I said.

And I guess I did know that. The doctor had assured us that, as long as she was monitored, Yogi's condition was manageable. He had said that all her levels were great, and that if anything changed, they would take care of things right away. But I still felt like I was going to jump out of my skin.

"Mom," I said. "Do you remember when Tyree died? How I had to take you to the hospital."

She bit her lip. "That was a bad time."

"I think you had a panic attack."

She nodded. "Yes. That's what the doctor at the hospital told me."

I reached out to touch her arm. "I have those, too," I said. "A lot. Ever since I was little."

Her eyes met mine. She looked sad. "I'm sorry," she said. "I've had a few more since we lost David, too. It's not easy."

I thought about this for a moment. About our mutual, inherited pain and challenges.

"I don't think I've had one day since Yogi told me that she was pregnant where I wasn't scared," I admitted.

My mother laughed softly. "Well, you always were my sensitive one."

I looked at her. "How did you do it? How did you have six kids and not go out of your head with worry?"

She laughed again. "Who said I didn't?" She pulled my plate over toward herself, took a little bite, and then shoved it back toward me. "Needs salt," she said, getting up and going into the kitchen.

She handed me the saltshaker and sat back down. "You know,"

she said. "I think one of the biggest reasons I used was because I was so scared that something bad would happen to one of you kids."

I started to say something, but she held up her hand. "I know. I know that doesn't make any sense. I know that me being messed up like that made it even more likely that something could happen to one of you. But"—she tapped her fingers on the table—"sometimes the worry was so big that I just needed to check out, you know?"

"Yeah," I said. "I guess I can see that."

"But then, of course, it was only after I got sober that the worst actually happened. That my worry came true."

I nodded.

"So, what then?" I asked. "What if something happens? What if I can't keep her safe? You have panic attacks, and I have panic attacks. What if my daughter has them, too?"

She shook her head. "You're already keeping her safe. You picked a good mother for her. And you got your ass out of the hood. And you're bringing home decent money. And you're sticking around. You're gonna be a real daddy to her."

"What do I know about being a dad? What if I'm terrible at it?"

She met my eyes. "You are going to be a great dad, baby. That I know for sure."

I nodded doubtfully.

She reached over and put her hand on top of mine. "Listen to me, Reem. If your daughter has panic attacks, it will be okay. Because you will know what is happening to her. You will recognize it. And you will get her the help she needs."

I took a deep breath. "That's true."

She smiled at me. "Listen. Even with all that worry. Even with all that fear. Even with the worst kind of loss. Having kids was the best thing I ever did. You guys are my greatest accomplishment. I wouldn't change anything about any of you. And you know what? I'm going to be around to help you and Yogi raise up that little girl. I will be there to give you all the help you need."

I met her eyes, surprised by just how much that idea made me feel better. Surprised and grateful that I now actually had a mother who I could wholeheartedly trust to care for my child.

"Thank you," I said. I took another bite of the rice and beans. "Seriously. This is really good, Mom."

FIVE DAYS LATER, Yogi got a call from the doctor as she was walking to work.

"We don't like the levels that we're seeing," he said. "There's no rush, but you should go home, pack your bag, and then head on over to the hospital for your induction. It's time to meet your baby."

YOLANDA WAS AMAZING. I had only ever seen anyone give birth on TV or in the movies. So I expected her to be yelling and screaming and swearing at me. I thought she'd be breaking my hand in her grip. But from the moment we got to the hospital, she was calm and curious. Joking and laughing with the nurses. Waiting patiently on her doctors.

"I'm going to take a nap," she said, after they started the Pitocin. "And I guess if the pain is bad enough to wake me up, I'll know that I'm ready for the epidural."

"Okay," I said. I was pacing a little bit. I was so excited about finally meeting my daughter, but I also hated being back in the hospital again. I knew how quickly things could turn. "That sounds like a plan."

There was so much more waiting around than I had expected. The nurse told us that birthing rooms were all full up. They were timing Yogi's induction based on when there was a room available for her to give birth.

So we waited on that. And then, once they started the medication to bring on her labor, we waited on that to take effect. And now I was waiting for Yogi to wake up and say that she was ready for her epidural.

I sat by her bed and watched her sleep. And she was beautiful. And I knew everything was fine. But I couldn't help thinking about all the other times I had sat by a hospital bed and waited for the woman I loved to open her eyes.

I couldn't help it. I reached over and took Yogi's hand.

Her eyes blinked open. She looked at me and smiled. "Hi," she said.

That is a miracle, I thought. *It is a miracle that the woman I love is in a hospital bed and she just opened her eyes and looked right at me and smiled.*

"Sorry," I said. "I didn't mean to wake you up."

She shook her head. "That's okay. I think I'm starting to feel some cramps. Let's get that epidural going."

YOGI PUSHED FOR EXACTLY four minutes, and she laughed almost the whole time.

And then, there she was, Zara Makanalani Rosser.

She was so small, only six pounds, because she was four weeks premature. She had dark brown skin and a headful of thick, black curly hair, and she was utterly beautiful.

I could see Yogi in her. I could see my mother. I could see myself.

They placed her on Yolanda's chest for a moment, and Yogi

touched her and looked at her and just smiled and smiled. And then they handed her to me and it felt like I was dreaming. I couldn't believe this was my child. My daughter. My baby. Right there in my arms.

Then they whisked her away to the NICU because she was a preemie and her blood sugar was low.

But it was funny, because from the moment I saw her, I let go of the fear. From the moment I had my daughter in my sight, I knew she was going to be okay.

I WAS LYING in a hospital bed next to Yogi's. My shirt was off, and I was waiting for the nurse to unwrap Zara and hand her to me so I could hold her.

"Skin-to-skin therapy" they called it. All babies need it, but preemies need it even more than most.

The nurse lay Zara across my chest so that her face was turned toward mine. I put one hand on the back of her head, and tucked the other under the curve of her behind. Her tiny legs were splayed out like a frog. Her mouth was in a sweet little pout. She opened up her eyes and stared at me.

"Hi," I whispered. "Hi, baby. Hi, Zara."

Her nose twitched. She worked her mouth like she was trying to suck on something. I bent down and smelled her head, and I swear, there was nothing sweeter on this earth.

I looked over Zara's head at Yogi, who was watching us from her bed. Yolanda's cheeks were flushed, and she was smiling.

"Pretty spectacular, right?" she said.

I smiled back at her. Dipped my nose into Zara's curls again.

I'd thought I understood love. I thought that the love that I felt for my mom, my siblings, my grandma, Lezlie, Lee Lee, Evie, Yolanda . . . I thought all that love covered pretty much every color in the emotional spectrum. And that I was lucky to have it in my life.

But this feeling? This feeling that I had for this tiny, silly, sweet thing? This wide-eyed child? This soft little mystery that I held in my arms?

It was singular. It was incomparable. It was bigger than anything I'd ever felt. And I knew, right then and there, that I would spend my lifetime trying to be a good enough father to my daughter. I knew that there would never be anything more important or more valuable in my life.

Zara squirmed in my arms. Made a little mewling sound.

I laughed. "She sounds like Nolan."

Yogi reached out her arms. "Here, give her to me. Maybe she's hungry."

And so I carefully carried our girl over to her mother. And Yolanda scooched over so that I could sit beside them as she nursed. And I sat back in the bed, sometimes looking over and admiring how pretty they both were. And sometimes just looking out the window at the sky outside.

Chapter 28

IT WAS CHRISTMAS EVE AGAIN. 2022. And I was standing outside, in the dark, on the coldest night of the year.

Everyone else was inside Yolanda's family house. Including my own family, who had come out to New Jersey to celebrate.

I could see people passing by the windows, holding drinks and plates of food and wrapped packages. Laughing and talking. I could see the Christmas decorations, the glowing lights and candles and tinsel.

I shivered. I was freezing. But I knew I couldn't go back inside.

Not yet at least.

"BUT WHAT IS IT you're afraid of?" asked Ellen. "What do think is holding you back?"

I shook my head. "I don't know. I want to be with Yogi. She's the mother of my child. She stood by me through some really awful times. She's funny and sweet and smart. I love pretty much everything about her. But sometimes . . ."

Ellen waited. Like Ellen always did.

I sighed. "Does love ever really stay?"

Ellen shrugged. "Well. I suppose not all love. You know that from experience. But think about how you feel about Lee Lee. About your mother. How you feel about Zara. Do you think that love is going anywhere?"

I shook my head. "No. That love will never leave."

"And the way you feel about Yogi?"

I nodded. "I love her just as much as I love them."

Ellen knit her brows. "So if your feelings for her aren't going to change, what is it you fear?"

I was quiet for a moment. I swallowed hard. "I suppose I'm afraid that she'll leave. Or be taken away from me."

My voice was small.

Ellen leaned forward. "Let's try a little thought experiment," she said. "I want you to imagine that you never met Lee Lee. That you never had that shared experience of first love. But that, also, you didn't have to go through her accident. None of that happened. No love. No pain. If you could, would you erase all that from your life?"

I shook my head. "No. Everything that happened between us made me who I am today."

"And would you change anything between you and Yogi? Would you take anything back?"

"No. Not for anything."

"So, knowing that sometimes love can end or drastically change, that sometimes you can even lose a person permanently? Do you think it would be better not to know them or never to have loved them at all?"

I blew out a long breath. "I see what you're getting at."

"Nothing is guaranteed, Kareem. But if you move through life avoiding anything that leaves you vulnerable, if you won't take chances on something good because it might eventually turn bad, what kind of life would that ever be?"

I shrugged. "I dunno. Maybe a safe one?"

Ellen shook her head. "No. It would be a dissatisfying one. A disconnected one. A very, very lonely life." She smiled at me. "Take a chance, Kareem. Don't self-sabotage. Don't let fear make you turn away from something so good. Leave yourself open to love."

IN NEW JERSEY, someone tripped a switch, and the backyard suddenly went from dark to dazzling. There was a huge tree that had more Christmas lights on it than the tree inside. There were strings of tiny white bulbs that had been draped over every possible surface and were now in a frenzy of twinkling.

Between the frozen snow on the ground, the ice in the trees, and the dancing lights, the night was lit up like a star.

My heart sped up and I shifted from foot to foot, trying to keep my toes from going numb.

The back door crashed open, and a warm yellow glow spilled out of the house. One by one, our families—our mothers and brothers and sisters and nieces and nephews, Lezlie, and Yolanda's stepfather, Ray, who was carrying Zara—came pouring out the door. And then, finally, blindfolded, and kind of being pushed along as she laughed and protested, came Yolanda herself.

My mother led her right up to me.

"Okay," I said. "Go ahead and take it off."

My mother reached over and pulled the blindfold from Yolanda's eyes, and Yogi stood there blinking and looking confused.

"Kareem?" she said, spotting me. "What in the—"

But then she gasped when I dropped to one knee in the snow.

It was silent for a second. Silent in the way that only a frozen northeastern winter night can be.

I pulled out the ring box and flipped it open.

"Oh," whispered Yogi. And she started to blink away her tears.

"Yolanda," I said. "When I was growing up, I didn't think that love could really last. I never really believed that love could be a forever thing. And that's because I didn't think that the people I loved would ever be able to stay.

"But then"—I smiled at her, and she smiled right back at me, tremulous and happy. "Then I met you. And you showed me that there was another kind of love. A real love. A true and deep and rooted thing that might change and grow over time but would never completely disappear. You gave me a safe space to heal. You saw me through some of my darkest times, and you brought me so much light." I looked at Zara. "We created this amazing daughter together. And all I want is to spend the rest of my life with you both."

I reached up and took her hand. I looked into her eyes.

"I love you so much, Yogi. Will you marry me?"

And then she gasped yes, and I slid the ring onto her finger, and everyone clapped and cheered, and Zara fussed as we held each other, so Yolanda plucked her away from her stepfather and brought her into our embrace.

And I kissed Yogi as she cried, and I could feel my tears mingling with hers, and Zara laughing and wiggling in between us. And on that icy cold Christmas Eve, I was happy and warm. Sweet, and safe, and loving and loved, as we three stood with our arms wrapped around each other, and all looked up at the twinkling lights on the tree.

Afterword

AS I CAREFULLY PUT Zara into Lee Lee's arms, I couldn't help but think about the fact that, once upon a time, I had believed that any child I handed to Lee Lee with this much love and reverence would be a child we had created together.

ONCE, I had imagined that Lee Lee and I would have a very specific life together. One filled with horses and parties and travel and fox-hunts on Thanksgiving morning, and tuxes and long silver dresses, and kisses on the warm, white sand on New Year's Eve. Lee Lee would be beautiful and I would be dashing, and people would never get tired of telling us how perfect we looked together.

I thought that our life would be intimate, and passionate, and sometimes a little stormy. I thought that we would live a lot of it in the public eye. I thought that our children would be extraordinarily attractive and gifted. I thought that we would be so safe, so protected, so privileged, that the scared, broken kid inside of me would never dare show his face again.

I ADJUSTED LEE LEE'S arms so that she could cradle Zara. I watched the way that Lee Lee lit up as my daughter's sweet, dark eyes met hers.

"Baby," Lee Lee crooned.

THAT LIFE WITH LEE LEE was a beautiful dream. One that I sometimes can still feel in the very tips of my fingers. One that I can still see when I close my eyes.

ZARA'S HEAD BOBBLED. She was just learning to hold it up. And Yolanda reached over to steady them both, earning a smile from Lee Lee that was almost as brilliant as the one she gave Zara.

THAT OLD LIFE is gone now. Burned away to ashes. But there is something bigger and better and truer in its stead. There is Yolanda, my life partner and love. There is Zara, my blood, heart, and soul.

ZARA SHIFTED in Lee Lee's lap and laughed. Her giggle rising deep from her little tummy, joyful and delighted. After a second, Lee Lee joined her, and their mismatched duet of laughter filled the air.

AND THERE IS STILL LEE LEE.

For me, there will always be Lee Lee.

She is different now. But she is just as beautiful in her new form. She survived. She got stronger. She fought like hell. She continues to grow. She is still here.

ZARA STARTED TO SQUIRM too much, and Lee Lee's mouth creased into a frown. I could tell that she was worried that she would drop the baby. But before I could act, Yolanda gently took our wiggling daughter from Lee Lee's arms.

I MAY HAVE CREATED more space between us, but I will never leave Lee Lee behind. I will never permanently step away. I think she still sees me as her soul mate and other half. And honestly, so do I. Our relationship necessarily changed, but it did not end. There was no closure.

Instead, there was a metamorphosis. For both of us.

"BABY," crooned Lee Lee as she smiled and watched Zara settle into Yolanda's arms.

The three of them sat together, and I couldn't help but think, *Yolanda was right. Zara is Lee Lee's child, too. We are a family. And I am so lucky to be so well loved by all three of these people who I love so much in return.*

LEE LEE changed me.

Yolanda changed me.

Zara changed me.

Love changed me.

Because true love is never static; it renews and transfigures, it morphs and grows and fills the silence and the empty, broken places. It takes on whatever shape we need it to become.

And I have been so lucky. So lucky to have been offered so much love. And so lucky that I was taught to have the patience it took to recognize it, and that I was healed enough to not only be able to accept that love, but to have the ability to return it over and over again.

IT WAS GETTING DARK. Well past Zara's bedtime. She was yawning big, wide baby yawns and starting to fuss a little. And I could see that Lee Lee was lagging a bit, too. We gathered up our things. Evie and Phillip came out onto the porch to say good night. Yolanda hugged Lee Lee, and then held Zara up so that Lee Lee could kiss her goodbye. I hugged Evie and Phillip. We made plans for the next time I would come out to visit. Evie and Phillip led Yolanda and Zara into the house so Yolanda could change Zara's diaper one more time before we got on the road.

I looked at Lee Lee, who was sitting in her wheelchair, watching me.

And her eyes met mine, and Lee Lee smiled. Lighting up the room like she always does.

Like she always will.

And I bent down to kiss her good night, and for a brief moment, she leaned her forehead to mine.

And she whispered, "Reem."

And with that one word, I could hear all the other things that she wanted to say.

"I know," I whispered back. "I love you, too."

AND YOLANDA AND ZARA and I got into our car, and Evie and Phillip and Lee Lee waved us off.

And as we drove, Zara fell asleep.

And then Yogi fell asleep.

And I was, once again, driving that dark, familiar road.

But this time, I was not alone.

Acknowledgments

I extend my deepest gratitude to the exceptional doctors, therapists, and dedicated staff at Bryn Mawr Rehab Hospital. Their commitment to providing extraordinary care to Lee Lee has left an indelible mark on my heart.

A special thank-you to the remarkable surgery team and the attentive ICU staff who played pivotal roles in saving Lee Lee's life. Your skill and compassion during a critical time is truly commendable.

My sincere appreciation goes to my editor, Ronnie Alvarado, whose expertise and support were instrumental in bringing this story to life.

Heartfelt gratitude to the Jones and Dutton families—Evie, Phillip, Richie, and Ashley. Your enduring strength and resilience over the years are an inspiration. Your steadfast commitment to Lee Lee is a shining example, and I am deeply grateful for the privilege of joining you on this journey.

I am thankful to Joe Manheim for his belief in me during one of the most challenging periods of my life.

A warm and appreciative thank-you to all my friends who have been a constant source of support and exhibited incredible patience during moments when I may not have been at my best.

Mom, I am immensely proud of you and grateful for all you have sacrificed for your children. Your strength is my inspiration.

To my siblings, your love and friendship make me feel invincible.

Thank you for being there through thick and thin; I cherish each one of you.

Maia Rossini, you are incredibly gifted, and I am truly fortunate to have you on my team. Thank you for helping me share something so profoundly important with the world.

A heartfelt acknowledgment to my agent, Emma Parry, for her continued guidance and unwavering support.

A sincere thank-you to all the friends and family of the Jones and Dutton families who have continued to support Lee Lee and her family throughout her journey. The unwavering, unconditional love you provide is felt every day.

To the Lauriano, Serrano, and Kapule families, my deepest thanks for graciously welcoming me into your lives. Your support has been a beacon of strength throughout the years, providing solace and encouragement during some of my most challenging moments. I am grateful for the genuine warmth and kindness you have consistently extended to me.

Dr. Berman, I am forever indebted to you. When I first walked into your office, I was a lost young man desperately searching for answers and hope. Throughout our time together, you have been my guiding light through some of the darkest moments of my life. I will always be grateful to have you as my therapist. Your unwavering support and expertise have allowed me to grow into a better friend, son, and father. Thank you, from the bottom of my heart!

And to Yolanda, I am so grateful to have you in my life. From the very beginning, you have been an extraordinary life partner. I deeply appreciate your loyalty and commitment to being a wonderful mother. Zara and I consider ourselves incredibly fortunate to spend every day with you.

About the Author

KAREEM ROSSER is from Philadelphia, Pennsylvania. He received a BA in economics from Colorado State University (CSU). While at CSU, he led his collegiate polo team to a national championship. At the same time, he was honored as the Intercollegiate Polo Player of the Year. After graduation, Kareem pursued a career in finance and took on the role of executive vice president of Work to Ride. He lives with his family in Philadelphia.